TECHNIQUES IN HOME WINEMAKING

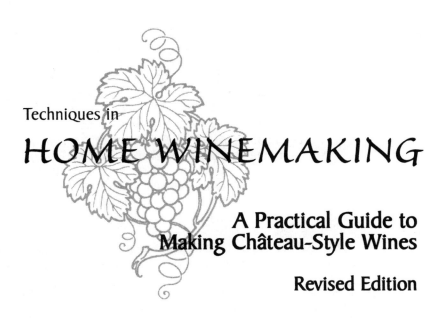

Techniques in
HOME WINEMAKING

A Practical Guide to Making Château-Style Wines

Revised Edition

Daniel Pambianchi

Véhicule Press

Cover design by J.W. Stewart
Cover imaging by André Jacob
Typeset by Pathology Images Inc.
Printed by AGMV-Marquis Inc.
Technical Editing by Thomas Bachelder

Published with the assistance of the
Book Publishing Industry Development Program
of the Department of Canadian Heritage

CANADIAN CATALOGUING IN PUBLICATION DATA

Pambianchi, Daniel
Techniques in home winemaking:
a practical guide to making château-style wines
Revised and expanded edition
Includes index
ISBN 1-55065-157-9

I. Wine and wine making—Amateur's manuals. I. Title.

TP548.2.P346 2002   641.8′72   C2001-903439-3

Published by Véhicule Press
P.O.B. 125, Place du Parc Station
Montreal, Quebec H2W 2M9

http://www.vehiculepress.com

Distributed by General Distribution Services in Canada.
Distributed by LPC Group in the United States.

Printed in Canada on alkaline paper

DISCLAIMER

All chemical products referenced in this book have applications in wine-making. These can be safely used in home winemaking although many of these are not recommended or approved in commercial winemaking in certain countries. Commercial winemaking regulations may prohibit the use of specific chemicals as they may be deemed as unnatural and against traditional winemaking methods. More important, these chemicals may also pose a health hazard if not used in the recommended concentrations or if used by unskilled winemakers. For home winemaking use, chemicals approved for œnological applications should be used with care, and rec-ommended concentrations should be strictly followed. Generic substitutes for œnological chemicals should not be used.

Neither the author, editors, or the publisher assumes any responsibility for the use or misuse of information contained in this book.

References to winemaking supplies from various sources are included to illustrate typical use of these supplies from companies whose products are the most prevalent in the home winemaking market. The use of these references and all trademarks and copyrighted material from cited manu-facturers, suppliers, wholesalers, retailers, distributors or other constitute neither sponsorship nor affiliation of these companies with the author, editors and publisher, or with this book. Companies have not paid any promotional fees to have their names and/or products listed here.

TABLE OF CONTENTS

ACKNOWLEDGMENTS

I wish to express my sincere thanks to Simon Dardick, Nancy Marrelli, and Vicki Marcok of Véhicule Press, and Irving Dardick (Pathology Images Inc.) for helping me publish this book, and to the following individuals and companies who have helped tremendously in this project. They all demonstrated great support by reviewing sections of the manuscript, providing technical data and equipment for photo sessions, and granting permission to use their material. This project would not have been possible without their help.

Specifically, I wish to acknowledge the following people and companies: Russ Nicol (Vinothèque), Gordon Specht (Lallemand Inc.), Peter Tudisco (Buon Vino Manufacturing Inc.), Dr. Neil Spokes and Dr. L. Manja R. Blazer (CHEMetrics, Inc.), Gunnard Jacobson (RED STAR® Yeast & Products Division of Universal Foods Corporation), John Arthurs (Wine-Art Inc.), Grégoire Guerette (Melvico Inc.), Angel Nardone (The American Wine Society), Ivo Pillan (Enotecnica Pillan di Pillan R.L.I. snc), Ghidi Pier Paolo (Ghidi divisione INOX), Gilberto Marchisio (F.lli MARCHISIO & C. S.p.A.), Alan Doernberg (Fisher Scientific Company L.L.C.), David Logsdon (Logsdons' Wyeast Laboratories), Martha Bannister and Shirley Molinari (Vinquiry, Inc.), Donna DeFalco Hadwen (DeFalco's for Brewers & Winemakers, Ottawa), Alain Girerd (SWENTECH International), Michael Guzy (Ohaus Corporation), John Piazza (Piazza & Associates), Brigitte Batonnet (Comité Interprofessionnel du Vin de Champagne), Paul Labelle Photographe Inc., Dr. Ulrike Prechtl-Fröhlich (ZS Verlag Zabert Sandmann GmbH), Shannon Mahoney (StockFood, Inc.), David Maquignaz (Image Network Inc.), Mick Rock (Cephas Picture Library), Tim Vandergrift (Brew King Ltd.), Charles Plant, Greg Taylor, Angela Campbell, Bruna Ceccolini, Stéphane Roch, and Marc Lavoie. I would also like to acknowledge Bob Robertson (Barrel Builders, Inc.) for his ideas and valuable contribution on the proper care and maintenance of oak barrels and on the use of winemaking cleaning and sanitizing agents, Arthur Pennington for sharing his icewine recipe, and Thomas Bachelder for reviewing the manuscript and for sharing his valuable opinions on the art of winemaking.

This revised edition contains many updates based on my articles that have been published in *WineMaker* magazine. I am grateful to the staff of Battenkill Communications of Manchester Center, Vermont for their support and generosity, and for allowing me to reuse published material. They include: Brad Ring (Publisher), Kathleen James Ring (Editor), Betsy Shaw (Managing Editor), Kiev Rattee (Advertising Sales Director), and Coleen Heingartner (Creative Director).

I am grateful to my cousin's husband, Giacomo Cocci, involved professionally in the wine trade in the Marche region of Italy, who has introduced me not only to the fine art of wine appreciation but also to the craft of winemaking. His astute knowledge of winemaking and of the wine trade has provided me with great inspiration in turning this hobby into a passion. I will forever cherish the memories we shared from our 1983 tour of Tuscan wineries as part of his work itinerary.

I would also like to thank my parents, Rita and Quinto, for allowing me to experiment and practice the procedures and methods described in this book. I trust that my father is now quite content with the quality of the wine he (we) produces. His friends are quite impressed with his newly acquired winemaking savvy.

Most importantly, I wish to thank my wife, Dalia, and my two wonderful sons, Justin and Eric for their patience throughout this seemingly long project. Countless days have been spent away from my family. I hope that Justin and Eric will keep the family tradition going into the next generation. I trust they will learn from my experience and improve the techniques to further facilitate this wonderful art of wine-making.

PREFACE

The objectives of this book are to introduce winemaking methods and products to novice home winemakers while providing serious amateur winemakers with proven and practical methods to produce premium-quality wines that are virtually indistinguishable from their professional counterparts. On occasion, when experimenting or when the year's crop has produced low or average quality grapes, home winemakers will have to make use of methods and products referenced herein to "correct" the wine. Correction is required to achieve balance among aromas, body, taste and colour in the finished wine.

Methods and products include the use of various winemaking equipment, œnological chemicals and ingredients, and vinification (the conversion of grape juice into wine by fermentation) techniques and procedures. The ability to produce a good to superior wine under adverse conditions depends on one's knowledge and experience of these methods and products. Experienced winemakers will know how to vinify must (grape juice) into wine through the various stages such that the probability of defects in the finished wine is greatly reduced. Home winemakers are encouraged to experiment to decide which methods produce a desired wine style.

Many methods and products other than those described here exist. However, since this book was conceived for home winemaking, only those commercially available methods and products for home winemaking are described. To learn more about advanced vinification techniques as well as scientific discussions on the subject, readers can consult the references listed in the bibliography in Appendix E.

All concentrations of ingredients and chemical additives provided in this book should be used as general guidelines. As ingredients and chemical products may vary from one manufacturer to another, readers should always use manufacturers' recommended dosages.

How to use this book

This book can first be read to learn about the science and practices of home winemaking. It can then serve as a reference textbook to determine quantities of ingredients to be added, to review specific advice on winemaking procedures, and to determine the root cause when encountering problems.

Chapters are presented in a logical order by first providing an introduction to winemaking and necessary winemaking equipment. A thorough discussion of must and wine analysis serves as a foundation to understanding winemaking and vinification procedures. A solid working knowledge of sugar and alcohol measurements, acidity, pH, and sulphur dioxide levels is necessary to be able to produce the highest quality wine according to one's desired wine style. Detailed descriptions of winemaking procedures are then presented in the general order that these are performed from fermentation to ageing and bottling.

When used as a reference textbook, readers can consult any chapter or section as these have been laid out independently of one another. This also allows winemakers to pick and choose procedures according to the desired wine style. For example, the section on malolactic fermentation can be skipped entirely if this type of fermentation is not desired. Likewise, the chapter on oak barrels may be skipped if not oak-ageing wine although alternatives to barrels are discussed. Specifically:

Chapter 1 provides an overview of winemaking and winemaking terminology, the various wine types and styles that home winemakers can produce, and the available grape juice varieties. Pros and cons of winemaking from grapes, juice and concentrate are discussed. Winemaking flowcharts are presented to illustrate the complete processes from grape crushing to fermentation, to bottling.

Chapter 2 describes all the necessary equipment for home winemaking and instructions on its proper use for producing premium wines.

Chapters 3 deals with the analysis and control of musts and wines—specifically, sugar and alcohol, acidity and pH, and sulphur dioxide components—which are key in producing the best wines. This chapter explains the significance of measuring and controlling these components and their role in winemaking.

Chapter 4 discusses vinification and winemaking procedures essential to producing premium wines, from crushing and destemming—or, must preparation, in the case of juice or concentrate—to stabilization. Other procedures include maceration, pressing, and alcoholic and malolactic fermentations. The importance of cleaning and sanitizing all equipment and of maintaining a sanitized environment throughout the winemaking cycle is also explained.

Chapter 5 details clarification procedures, namely, racking, fining and filtration. These are discussed separately so that winemakers can decide which method(s) to adopt to produce a desired wine style. Clarification by fining and/or by filtration remain much-debated topics. This chapter provides pros and cons of each process to allow winemakers to make their own choice.

Chapter 6 provides guidelines on the traditional process of blending wines. The practice of blending wines has existed since the early days of winemaking and is still used in modern winemaking in spite of the popularity of varietals (wines from a single grape variety). Blending allows winemakers to take advantage of the individual grape variety characteristics to produce more complex, more interesting wines.

Chapter 7 describes the preparation and maintenance of oak barrels in the wine-ageing process, and how to ferment and age wine in barrels. Barrel spoilage problems, their treatments and preventative measures are also discussed. Alternatives to oak barrels for imparting oak aromas are presented.

Chapter 8 describes the necessary equipment required for bottling wine as well as various techniques used to increase bottling efficiency. This chapter also briefly discusses how to cellar wines to allow them to evolve under optimal conditions until maturity.

Chapters 9, 10 and 11 provide step-by-step instructions on the production of sparkling, port and icewines, respectively, making use of techniques introduced in earlier chapters.

Chapter 12 lists the various vinification problems that home winemakers may come across, and the methods used to resolve them.

Chapter 13 presents the confessions of a passionate home winemaker.

Appendix A lists the conversion factors between Metric and U.S. systems for relevant measurements.

Appendix B provides a very useful conversion table to determine Specific Gravity equivalents as well as Brix and potential alcohol levels for various sugar concentrations.

Appendix C provides a winemaking log chart that can be used to record all winemaking and vinification activities. Keeping records of a wine's progress and treatments are key to successful winemaking.

Appendix D provides a summary chart of winemaking ingredients and chemicals, and concentrations presented throughout this book. It can be used as a quick-reference guide.

Appendix E lists some recommended reading to learn more about grapes, winery technology, the chemistry of vinification, analytical methods in winemaking and oak barrel maintenance.

ABOUT UNITS OF MEASURES

Winemaking, in most parts of the world, is greatly influenced by European methods and processes. Therefore, the use of the Metric system (also known as the International System, or SI) for units of measures has proliferated to most winemaking countries. In the U.S., the Metric system is also widely used in laboratory analysis, but the U.S. system is most often used for winemaking equipment manufactured there. For example, French oak barrels sold in the U.S. are described in litres and American barrels are described in gallons.

Readers are advised to exercise caution with the use of units of measures when obtaining winemaking "recipes" from books and other sources to ensure proper dosage. Many U.S. and Imperial units use the same terms but their quantities are quite different—a U.S. gallon is smaller than an Imperial gallon.

This book provides all measurements primarily using the Metric system as well as the U.S. system for U.S.-manufactured equipment. Fahrenheit conversions are provided since this is the primary unit used in the U.S.

The most often used unit of measurement in laboratory analysis is concentration, the amount of a solid present in a liquid. Concentrations are expressed in grams per litre, abbreviated as g/L, or in grams per hectolitre (100 litres), abbreviated as g/hL or in milligrams per litre, abbreviated as mg/L. Other concentration units used in the industry are percentages (weight to volume, or volume to volume) and parts per million, abbreviated ppm. The ppm unit signifies a volume-to-volume ratio for liquids dissolved in liquids or a weight-to-volume ratio for solids dissolved in liquids. For liquids to be dissolved in liquids, one ppm is equivalent to 1 mL per 1000 L using the Metric system. Using the U.S. system, 1000 ppm is equivalent to 0.13 fl oz/gal.

For solids to be dissolved in liquids, one ppm is equivalent to 1 mg/L using the Metric system. In the U.S. system, 1000 ppm is equivalent to 0.01 lb/gal. These assume a density of solids of 1 g per mL and 1¼ oz per fl oz, respectively. Weight measurements are greatly simplified with these conversion factors since it is easier to measure small volumes as opposed to small weights.

For acidity measurements, concentrations are expressed both in g/L or as a percentage of weight to volume where 1 g/L represents a 0.1% acid concentration. For example, a 0.65% acid solution represents 6.5 g of acid dissolved in 1 L of liquid. This book uses g/L for acid concentrations and can be easily converted to a weight-to-volume percentage by dividing the g/L value by 10.

For sulphur dioxide (SO_2) measurements, concentrations are expressed in mg/L although the industry-accepted measurement is ppm. It can be assumed that 5 mL (1 tsp) of sulphite powder weighs approximately 5 g—an acceptable approximation. SO_2 measurements in ppm can then be easily converted to an approximate mg/L value one for one. For example, 50 ppm is approximately equivalent to 50 mg/L.

For sugar concentrations, Brix is the standard unit of use in commercial winemaking while in home winemaking, Specific Gravity is very often used. Given the wide use of both units, this book provides measurements using both units. Residual sugar concentrations are still expressed in g/L.

In some cases, cup, teaspoon or tablespoon-equivalent measurements are provided, as these are standard and practical kitchen measures.

Appendix A provides the list of conversion factors for Metric, U.S. and Imperial systems.

Although specific measurements are given for each product described, readers should always follow manufacturers' recommended measurements as ingredients and chemicals may be sold with different concentrations or may have different compositions.

1
INTRODUCTION

Home winemaking has gained tremendous popularity as a hobby in recent years. Although the cost per bottle of homemade wine is very low compared to commercial wine, the increase in popularity is really attributed to the pleasure and pride of producing one's own wine. The quality of homemade wines can also match or surpass that of commercial wines.

With the availability of high quality four- and six-week wine kits, more and more novice and serious œnophiles are now becoming home winemakers. These kits can produce very good quality wines easily, quickly and economically. Access to winemaking materials previously not available to home winemakers, coupled with improvements in wine production techniques, are also key contributing success factors.

1.1 WINEMAKING TERMINOLOGY

Winemaking refers to the set of processes, from juice extraction to bottling, for producing wines from fruits such as grapes. The specific process of fermentation, converting fruit juice into wine, is referred to as vinification.

The major steps in winemaking include crushing and pressing of the grapes, maceration, alcoholic and malolactic fermentations, racking, clarification, stabilization, ageing, blending and bottling. These operations are performed differently and optionally in the production of white, rosé, red and sparkling wines. Certain operations may not be required at all depending on the type of juice used. For example, crushing and pressing are not required unless making wine from grapes.

When grapes are first crushed and pressed before fermentation, the extracted juice is referred to as the must, and as a result of pressing, it contains some solids such as pulp. Must, the technically correct word, is often referred to as juice or grape juice. Juice also refers to commercially available fresh juice that has been separated from grape particles. Once fermentation of the must has begun and alcohol is present, the must is referred to as wine. When starting with fresh grape juice or concentrated juice, crushing, pressing and maceration operations are not required.

When grapes are crushed and/or pressed, all grape remainders—skins, seeds and stems—are referred to as the pomace. The process of leaving the must in contact with the pomace for colour, flavour and tannin extraction is referred to as maceration. Maceration is most often used in the production of red wines. During maceration and fermentation, the pomace will start to form a cap that will rise to the top of the container and float on the must.

Alcoholic fermentation is the chemical process of converting fermentable sugars into alcohol and carbon dioxide by the addition of yeast. Fermentable sugars include glucose and fructose that occur naturally in grapes, and dextrose (corn sugar) or sucrose (beet or cane sugar) that are added by the winemaker. The process of adding sugar to the must or wine to increase the potential alcohol content and/or to sweeten a wine is referred to as chaptalization. Although it is possible to make many different types of fruit wines by alcoholic fermentation, this book deals only with wine production from grape juice.

Although wines undergo a single alcoholic fermentation process in the production of still (non-sparkling) wines, it is common to refer to primary and secondary fermentations to describe arbitrary phases relative to the amount of fermentable sugars still present in the must. It is usually related to fermentation vigourousness. The transition from the vigourous primary fermentation to the lesser active secondary fermentation signals the need to transfer the wine to another container. Some literature refers to both fermentations as one, i.e., the alcoholic

fermentation. The latter terminology helps avoid confusion when refer-
ring to malolactic fermentation, quite often referred to as the
secondary fermentation. Malolactic fermentation is a non-alcoholic
fermentation that transforms the sharper malic acid in wines into the
more supple lactic acid and carbon dioxide. Malolactic bacteria are
used instead of yeasts to favour such fermentation. Second fermentation refers to the bottle fermentation process in the production of
sparkling wines. Bottle fermentation is simply an alcoholic fermentation carried out in the bottle to retain the carbon dioxide gas in the
wine.

Recently, consumers have become more aware of the presence
and the role of sulphite in wines. Sulphite plays a key role as an antioxidant and preservative in wines. Sulphur dioxide (SO_2), a component
of sulphite, is both an œnological ingredient and a natural by-product
of fermentation, albeit in small quantities. Sulphite, commonly added
to wines to prevent microbial spoilage, is also used to sanitize winemaking equipment.

Racking is the process of separating wine from its sediment that
has settled at the bottom of the container. Sediment resulting from
yeast activity during alcoholic fermentation is referred to as lees. The
settling action of suspended particles as sediment is referred to as sedimentation.

Clarification is the process of removing particles still in suspension in the wine, affecting clarity and limpidity. Clarification can be
achieved by racking, by fining, using chemicals, commonly referred to
as fining agents, or by mechanical filtration. Fining agents are added
to a wine to coagulate particles in suspension and cause them to sediment. A subsequent racking is required when fining to separate the
sedimented particles, or lees. Filtration is the process of passing wine
through a filtering medium to separate particles in suspension.
Filtration does not involve sedimentation.

Stabilization is the process of readying the wine for consumption or ageing to ensure that clarity and freshness of the wine are
maintained. Stabilization also protects the wine from microbial
spoilage, re-fermentation, premature oxidation, and crystallization of
tartaric acid while the wine is ageing. Stabilization is a necessary step
before bottling or bulk ageing of wine for an extended period of time.

Bottle or bulk ageing refers to the maturation phase of winemaking necessary for wine to develop its character, structure, and to

increase its complexity. Both ageing methods will improve wine; however, bulk ageing in oak barrels will impart a special aroma and taste as the wine will extract tannin compounds from the wood. The ageing period can vary from several months to several years depending on the quality of juice or grapes used, grape varieties, vinification methods, stabilization and preservation techniques, and ageing process, just to name a few factors.

Blending, considered an art in winemaking circles, is the process of mixing different wines to achieve a desired style. The final blend should exhibit the desired organoleptic (colour, taste, smell and feel) qualities inherited from the various blending wines.

Bottling is the final winemaking operation where wine is transferred from bulk containers to bottles for further ageing or for drinking. Bottled wine should be properly sealed with corks to protect it from the elements.

1.2 THE PHILOSOPHY OF MAKING CHÂTEAU-STYLE WINES

In producing premium-quality wines, winemakers follow the evolution of their wines from fermentation to bottling and ageing, and tend them to ensure good structure, great complexity, and organoleptic balance of all components. Beyond this, wines must express the winemaker's individual character. Different winemaking and vinification techniques are used to achieve this individuality, often dictated by the winemaker's beliefs in quality, process experience and preference of wine style. As winemaking is not an exact science but rather a subjective art, techniques will vary greatly depending on the desired style and quality of wine. These techniques are often well-guarded secrets within premium wineries.

There are essentially two opposing mind-sets within the winemaking industry. First, there are the traditionalists who process their wines with minimal or no additives such as sulphites, and limited clarification without filtration. Their primary objective is to produce the best quality age-worthy wines, and they spare no expense achieving this goal. Traditional wine production requires careful and constant monitoring and control to prevent spoilage throughout the long winemaking period. Modern commercial wineries, on the other hand, which have short-term financial objectives and constraints, often use additives and processes for quick commercialization of young, ready-to-drink wines.

For home winemaking, it is recommended to adopt a philosophy that lies between these two approaches. The risk of spoilage or oxidation will be reduced while maintaining a high level of quality. In this case, home winemakers will have more control over expected results and can usually recover from faults when they are detected early.

Readers are advised to follow the procedures described in this book and to experiment within the prescribed bounds to establish a personal preference of wine style.

References 8 [Olney] and 9 [Olney] in Appendix E provide a history and insight into winemaking philosophies at the Domaine de la Romanée-Conti (Burgundy) and Château d'Yquem (Sauternes), respectively.

1.3 WINE STYLES

Wine styles can be categorized according to presence of carbon dioxide gas, colour, sweetness and alcohol level.

Wines are first classified according to the presence of carbon dioxide, characterized by fizziness. Still wines have no carbon dioxide whereas sparkling wines are characterized by the presence of carbon dioxide. Sparkling wines are produced by carbonating the wine or conducting a second fermentation in the bottle or in a closed vat. The second fermentation is achieved by the addition of fermentable sugar. Bottle fermentation is the preferred method to produce the best-quality sparkling wine, and is used in the Champagne region of France to produce the world-famous bubbly known as Champagne. Another well-known bubbly is the vat-fermented Asti Spumante from the Piedmont region of Italy. The carbonation method is not used in the production of premium sparkling wines but is an excellent alternative in home winemaking.

All wines are classified according to colour—white, red or rosé. White wines are produced from white grapes or white-juice red grapes, referred to as *blanc de blancs* and *blanc de noirs* wines, respectively. Red wines are produced from red-juice or white-juice red grapes where the juice is macerated with the grape skins to extract the red colour. Rosé wine, referred to as blush wine in North America, is first produced as red wine, with only a short maceration period to extract a little red colour, and then vinified as white wine.

Wines are also classified according to the level of sweetness. When the must is allowed to ferment until the amount of residual sugar is below a certain level, usually not detectable by taste, the wine is said to be dry. Most commercial table wines are dry wines. Beyond this minimum level, the wine becomes semi-sweet or sweet depending on the amount of residual sugar. Semi-sweet and sweet wines are great for accompanying desserts or can be served on their own as dessert. White wines make the best sweet wines although it is possible to produce sweet red wines.

The last classification includes fortified wines where alcohol, usually a distilled spirit such as brandy, is added to increase the alcohol content of the finished wine. Sherry and port are two popular types of fortified wines.

The types of wine can be blended to produce different styles such as a semi-sweet bubbly rosé or a port-style wine (which is a sweet fortified red wine).

1.4 GRAPES, JUICE OR CONCENTRATE?

Home winemakers have several choices for types of must: grapes, fresh or sterilized grape juice, or concentrated grape juice. Refer to Figure 1-1. Whether one chooses to make wine from grapes, juice or concentrate depends on the desired quality, time and effort that one is prepared to invest, as well as cost and availability of winemaking equipment. Each type of must has pros and cons relative to these.

Sterilized and concentrated grape juice are sterilized by a process called pasteurization to strip the juice of any wild yeast in order to prevent fermentation in the container during its shelf life. Fresh juice from grapes is not pasteurized—that is why it needs to be refrigerated.

1.4.1 Wine from grapes

Winemaking from grapes is the traditional method and the serious alternative to concentrate or juice. Through careful and elaborate winemaking techniques, wines of outstanding quality can be produced from grapes. This method is also the most prone to errors and disappointing results if constant care is not exercised throughout the process.

Grapes are usually available in 16.3-kg (36-lb) cases and, for home winemaking, mainly come from California although grapes from other states and countries are available through special order. One can expect to pay a premium price for special orders. Grapes should be

Figure 1-1: Concentrate, juice or grapes?

bought from a reliable supplier who can guarantee the contents of each case. Cases labeled with a grape variety name may actually contain field blends or a completely different variety (usually inferior) from that which is printed on the outside of the case. If a normally-expensive variety seems surprisingly inexpensive, one should think twice before buying. Grapes should look fresh and healthy, and should not be affected by rot. Choose a supplier with a quick turnover of inventory to guarantee freshness of the grapes.

Depending on harvest conditions, Northern Hemisphere grapes are usually available early September through late October or as late as November. Early to mid-October is the best time to buy grapes for winemaking, as these would have reached an optimum sugar level without being rotted. Establish a good relationship with a reliable supplier who can provide updates on harvest conditions and who can inform you when grapes will be arriving (presumably at an optimum sugar level). Refer to section 3.1 for methods to determine how to best select grapes with optimum sugar levels.

The main advantage of using grapes over other types of must is that both the length and the temperature of the maceration period (and, hence, extraction of colour, flavour and tannins) are under the control of the winemaker, and winemakers can balance the organoleptic qualities to a desired style and type of wine. Wines produced from grapes should be processed minimally to reduce removal of ingredients essential for the wine's evolution. In general, these wines are the most age-worthy as compared to wines produced from concentrate or juice.

The disadvantages of using grapes are that grapes are subject to vintage variations and therefore consistent quality from one vintage to another cannot be guaranteed. Winemaking from grapes can also require a significant cost investment for modest productions, can be more time-consuming, and tends to be messier.

1.4.2 Wine from fresh grape juice

Fresh (non-concentrated) grape juice is typically sold in 20 or 23-L pails, or 100-L containers. It is available as fresh cold-stored juice, but increasingly, consumers should be aware that this cold-stored juice is often frozen to prolong its shelf life especially when shipped from Europe.

Fresh grape juice is simply cold-pressed juice, which is then packaged for sale. In an effort to provide a higher-quality product with year-over-year consistency, producers most often make adjustments to the must. For example, fresh grape juice can contain additives such as sugar or grape concentrate to adjust the sugar level (the sugar level determines a wine's potential alcohol level), and sulphite (also referred to as sulphur dioxide or SO_2—a preservative), and one or more acids to achieve a desired acidity level.

Avid home winemakers often expect not to find any additives in fresh grape juice. They prefer to make any required adjustments themselves. It is therefore wise to read the small print on the container carefully and to question the supplier closely to avoid any disappointment. The addition of acid and sulphur dioxide is not a bad thing in itself, but a winemaker should monitor the sugar, acidity, and free sulphur dioxide (SO_2) levels before adding any more of these substances. Refer to chapter 3 for a complete discussion on the effects of sugar, acids and sulphur dioxide, and how to measure and control these substances.

To make wine from fresh grape juice, the juice is first brought back up to fermentation temperature, and then allowed to ferment by adding yeast or letting the yeast already present in the juice take its course. Since fresh juice is not sterilized, it still contains yeast capable of starting fermentation without addition of other yeasts.

The advantage of grape juice is that there is no need for crushing and pressing, and this reduces production time and effort, and minimizes the investment in winemaking equipment. White wines made from fresh juice have some very real benefits over fresh-crushed grapes owing to the fragility of the latter when shipped long distances and to the fact that the processing time is greatly reduced. White wines are most susceptible to oxidation, and therefore, time from harvest to vinification should be minimized. Also, since the juice has not been sterilized, wines produced from fresh grape juice will generally age better than wines from sterilized types of grape juice.

One important disadvantage of fresh grape juice, especially for red wines, is that it does not allow any further control over the extraction of colour, the level of tannin, flavour, and structure and complexity. Since there is no maceration involved, the grape juice is not allowed to extract the important compounds from grape skins.

Recently, Californian fresh grape juice suppliers have started providing juice with skins. This is an excellent idea enabling home winemakers to have crushed and pressed grapes without the investment in equipment and time. Red wines can now be vinified by maceration to extract tannin, flavours and colour compounds as desired. Juice with skins therefore allows the production of high-quality red wines comparable to wines vinified from grapes.

Fresh juice, like grapes, is also subject to vintage variations and therefore consistent quality from one vintage to another cannot be guaranteed. It is also only available during the fall season following harvest. Some winemaking supply shops may carry fresh Southern Hemisphere (e.g., Chilean) grape juices in the spring. The selection of grape varieties is also more limited or more difficult to find than concentrates.

1.4.3 Wine from sterilized grape juice

Sterilized non-concentrated grape juice, available throughout the year in 23-L format is also a popular choice among home winemakers as it requires no water to be added (unlike concentrates which do). The juice contains its natural water but has been sterilized by pasteurization to eradicate wild yeasts. Sulphite is also added to stabilize the juice and to prolong its shelf life, and allow storage at room temperature. It may also contain concentrated grape juice and/or liquid-invert sugar to achieve a desired sugar concentration, and tartaric acid or a blend of acids to obtain a desired acid level.

To make wine, yeast is added to start fermentation, and wine can be bottled within 2 months. Liquid-invert sugar, which consists of glucose and fructose, will ferment more favourably than sucrose when yeast activity starts. The composition of wines relative to fermentable sugars is discussed in section I.6, and the use of sucrose and dextrose in chaptalization is discussed in section 3.1.2.

Sterilized grape juice kits are also available complete with instructions to ensure problem-free winemaking. Kits are packaged with a fining agent, usually bentonite, and isinglass or gelatin, to clarify the wine, yeast and yeast nutrients (diammonium phosphate to favour a good fermentation), sulphite (to preserve the wine), and a stabilizing agent (potassium sorbate) to prevent re-fermentation once the wine is bottled.

As with fresh grape juice, the disadvantage of sterilized grape juices is that these do not allow any further control over the colour of the wine, the level of tannin, flavour, and structure and complexity. The grape juice is not allowed to extract the important compounds from grape skins. Wines produced from the sterilized juices also do not age as well.

1.4.4 Wine from concentrated grape juice

Today, 4- and 6-week wine kits using concentrated grape juice (typically producing 20 or 23 L) are very popular among wine hobbyists, especially beginners. Wines from kits are meant for quick fermentation and bottling, and are therefore meant to be drunk early.

Concentrated grape juice is processed to remove the majority of the water content and to eradicate any yeast, and then sulphite is added to extend its shelf life. The shelf life can be further extended by storing the concentrated grape juice in cold storage or in a freezer. It is best to use the wine kit as soon as purchased, especially if no "Best before" date is provided. The concentrate may also contain liquid-invert sugar to achieve a desired sugar level in preparation for fermentation. Liquid-invert sugar, which consists of glucose and fructose, will ferment more favourably than sucrose when yeast activity starts. Tartaric acid or a blend of other acids may have been added to adjust the acid level for a balanced wine. Œnological tannin may also have been added depending on the type and style of wine to be produced.

Popular wine kits are packaged in aluminum bags of 5.5 L or 7 kg of concentrated grape juice and come complete with instructions to ensure problem-free winemaking. Similar to sterilized juice, concentrated juice has been pasteurized and then sulphite is added. It may also contain liquid-invert sugar and tartaric acid or a blend of acids. The kits are usually packaged with a fining agent, yeast and yeast nutrients, sulphite, and a stabilizing agent to prevent re-fermentation once the wine is bottled. Depending on the type of wine being produced, some kits may also contain œnological tannin, dried elderberries and banana flakes, and oak chips to impart special aromas to the wine and to add complexity.

Concentrated grape juice is also available in packages of, for example, 8 and 15 L. These are known as semi-concentrates, since they have more water content, and have retained essential compounds contributing to flavour and aromas. For this reason and due to their production process, semi-concentrates are believed to produce higher-quality wines than their concentrate counterparts.

To make wine using a concentrate or a semi-concentrate, water and yeast are added to start fermentation. Sufficient water is added to bring the total must volume to 20 or 23 L as per the manufacturer's instructions.

The advantages of kits are that they require a minimum investment in winemaking equipment, minimum time and effort to produce good quality early-drinking wines, and they are available throughout the year. These kits also provide consistent quality from batch to batch and are therefore ideal for reproducing similar batches of wine. Many different types and styles of wine are now available which are otherwise not available as grape juice or grapes, such as Bordeaux, Chablis, Port and Icewine. With international wine production regulations now restricting the labeling of musts and wines to reflect their true appellation of origin, home winemakers need to inquire or confirm the contents of the concentrate. For example, concentrated grape juice from California or other parts of the world can no longer be labeled Bordeaux-style unless it is truly from this region. Alternatively, different styles can be created with the additives often supplied with the kits.

With the quality of concentrates constantly improving, this winemaking alternative has become a favourite among wine aficionados. For beginners, wine kits are ideal since the risk of failure is minimized as the concentrate does not require any significant correction to ensure balance of sugar, alcohol and acidity in the final wine. These kits are available with all ingredients in pre-measured quantities. Concentrated grape juices are also sold separately without the necessary œnological ingredients. These are recommended for experienced winemakers only, as ingredients need to be selected separately and measured accurately.

Although concentrated grape juices share many of the advantages of sterile grape juices, they have the same disadvantages as they have undergone pasteurization. It should be noted that red wines from concentrate will most often yield lighter-coloured wines. There is, however, a myriad of products available at home winemaking shops to correct the different aspects of wines.

1.5 GRAPE VARIETIES

While it is possible to get grapes from California regions such as Napa and Sonoma as well as from other New World vine-growing regions such as Washington, Oregon, New York (Finger Lakes, Long Island), Virginia, Ontario (Niagara), British Columbia (Okanagan Valley, Vancouver Island), most North American fruit available to home winemakers still comes from California's Central Valley. Such grapes can be decent, but may have a high sugar content with no concentration of flavour because of the too-high vine yields (over-cropping) common to the region resulting from overzealous use of irrigation, unremitting sunshine, and general greediness of growers. Over-cropping also produce diluted, light-coloured wines with less complexity. Special orders of premium grapes from selected growers from other parts of California are available, albeit at higher prices.

In the following sections, typical characteristics of California white- and red-wine grape varieties are listed to help winemakers make the proper selection based on desired wine type and style to be produced. Grapes bought from, say, cool-climate regions (e.g. Riesling from Niagara instead of the Central San Joachin Valley) will have a totally different make-up, and, hence, flavour profile. For a complete discussion on grape varieties and characteristics, consult reference 16 [Robinson] in Appendix E.

All grape varieties listed here are from the European *Vitis vinifera* (*V. vinifera*) species. Alicante Bouschet, a hybrid (a cross between different species) of *vinifera* and non-*vinifera* species, is not classified as a *vinifera* variety in ampelography (the scientific description of the vine). However, owing to its wide use as a *tenturier* (French term for a deep-coloured blending wine used to improve colour in red wines) in France, it is recognized as a *vinifera* variety. Grape varieties from the North American *Vitis labrusca* (*V. labrusca*) species are used in a very small percentage of American Northeast and Canadian wines. This species is grown where weather conditions are harsh, and consequently, do not achieve a desired balance between sugar and acidity. *V. vinifera* grape varieties are the recommended choice for producing premium-quality wines.

From all grape varieties listed, many produce poor wines owing to inadequate colour, low acidity or high pH, lack of fruitiness, low tannin level and low alcohol content. Winemakers are encouraged to experiment with the blending of wines from different grape varieties to balance the organoleptic elements. Many well-known blends such as Cabernet Sauvignon and Merlot and/or Cabernet Franc in Bordeaux, or Sauvignon Blanc and Sémillon in Sauternes, produce exceptional wines. In the Châteauneuf-du-Pape appellation, wineries are allowed to blend up to 13 different grape varieties. It should be noted, however, that grape varieties exhibit different characteristics depending on where these have been grown. Chapter 6 lists some guidelines on blending wine.

Table 1-1 and Table 1-2 list the characteristics of common California white and red grape varieties, respectively, and provide some general guidelines to achieve desired styles. The best way to learn about the different varieties is to experiment, to blend different wines, and to determine one's preference.

Winemakers should consult their local grape suppliers to see which grape varieties are available in their area. Many of the listed varieties are very difficult to find and are often not available as vineyards sell typically their premium harvest to commercial wineries.

1.5.1 White grape varieties

Table 1-1 lists various popular California *V. vinifera* white wine grape varieties and their characteristics. The characteristics should be used to determine the type and style of wine to be produced.

When selecting white grape varieties, characteristics to be considered include:

Table 1-1

California *V. vinifera* white grape varieties

Grape Varieties	Types & styles	Main characteristic(s)	Acidity	Affinity for oak	Ageing potential	Quality
Chardonnay	Dry Sparkling	High % alc./vol. Fruity aroma Buttery texture	Moderate	Excellent	Very good	Excellent
Chenin Blanc	Dry Sweet Sparkling	High sugar content High acidity	High	Poor	Excellent (for sweet wines)	Very good
Colombard	Dry	Low % alc./vol.	High	Poor	Poor	Average
Gewürztraminer	Dry Sweet Icewine Sparkling	High % alc./vol. Spicy aroma and taste Deep colour	Low	Good	Good	Good
Muscat	Dry Fortified Sweet Sparkling	High sugar content Grapey aroma	Moderate	Good	Poor	Good
Palomino	Dry Icewine Fortified	Low sugar content Oxidizes quickly	Low	Not recommended	Poor	Average

Table 1-1, *continued*

Grape Varieties	Types & styles	Main characteristic(s)	Acidity	Affinity for oak	Ageing potential	Quality
Pinot Blanc	Dry Sparkling	High % alc./vol.	Low	Poor	Poor	Good
Riesling	Dry Sweet Icewine Sparkling	High sugar level Fruitiness	High	Not recommended	Excellent	Excellent
Sauvignon Blanc	Dry Sweet	Grassy aroma	High	Good	Good	Very good
Sémillon	Dry Sweet	Grassy aroma Deep colour	Moderate	Good	Excellent (for sweet wines)	Very good
Thompson Seedless (Sultana)	Dry Sparkling	High sugar content	Moderate	Not recommended	Poor	Poor
Trebbiano (Ugni Blanc)	Dry	Low % alc./vol.	High	Poor	Poor	Average
Viognier	Dry	High % alc./vol. Deep colour Fruitiness	Low	Not recommended	Poor	Excellent

Table 1-2
California *V. vinifera* red grape varieties

Grape Varieties	Types & styles	Main characteristic(s)	Depth of colour	Tannin	Acidity	Affinity for oak	Ageing potential	Quality
Alicante Bouschet	Dry Fortified	Red juice	Deep	Moderate	High	Poor	Poor	Average
Barbera	Dry	High acidity	Deep	Low	High	Good	Good	Average
Cabernet Franc	Dry (rosé)	Low % alc./vol. Cedar and green vegetal aromas	Medium	Low	Low	Good	Good	Good
Cabernet Sauvignon	Dry	Blackcurrant and cedar aromas	Deep	High	Moderate	Excellent	Excellent	Excellent
Carignan	Dry	Bitterness	Deep	High	High	Not recommended[1]	Good	Average
Carnelian	Dry (rosé)	Blackcurrant Fruity	Deep	Moderate	Moderate	Not recommended[1]	Good	Average
Grenache	Dry (rosé)	High % alc./vol. Peppery flavour	Light	Low	Moderate	Not recommended	Poor	Good
Merlot	Dry	Fruitiness	Medium	Moderate	Low	Very good	Very good	Excellent

[1]The use of new oak should be avoided with this grape variety when using Central Valley grapes.

Table 1-2, *continued*

Grape Varieties	Types & styles	Main characteristic(s)	Depth of colour	Tannin	Acidity	Affinity for oak	Ageing potential	Quality
Mission	Dry Fortified Sweet	Low % alc./vol.	Light	Low	Low	Not recommended	Poor	Poor
Nebbiolo	Dry	High % alc./vol. Tar aroma	Deep	High	High	Very good	Very good	Excellent
Petite Sirah	Dry	Tough astringency Fruity	Deep	High	Moderate	Very good	Very good	Good
Pinot Noir	Dry Sparkling (white)	Fruitiness Berry aroma	Medium	Low	Low	Very good[l]	Good	Excellent
Ruby Cabernet	Dry	Astringency	Deep	High	Moderate	Good	Good	Average
Sangiovese	Dry	High % alc./vol.	Medium	High	High	Very good	Very good	Good
Syrah	Dry Fortified (white, rosé)	High % alc./vol. Black pepper aroma	Deep	High	Moderate	Very good	Very good	Excellent
Valdepeñas (Tempranillo)	Dry	Low % alc./vol.	Medium	Moderate	Low	Very good[l]	Good	Average
Zinfandel	Dry Sweet (rosé)	Blackberry aroma	Medium	Moderate	Moderate	Good	Good	Excellent

[l]The use of new oak should be avoided with this grape variety when using Central Valley grapes.

- ⟜ Acidity level (low, moderate, high)
- ⟜ Affinity for oak (not recommended, poor, good, very good, excellent)
- ⟜ Ageing potential (poor, good, very good, excellent)
- ⟜ Overall quality of the grape variety (poor, average, good, very good, excellent)

1.5.2 Red grape varieties

Table 1-2 lists various popular California *V. vinifera* red wine grape varieties and their characteristics. The characteristics should be used to determine the type and style of wine to be produced.

When selecting red grape varieties, characteristics to be considered include:

- ⟜ Depth of colour (light, medium, deep)
- ⟜ Tannin level (low, moderate, high)
- ⟜ Acidity level (low, moderate, high)
- ⟜ Affinity for oak (not recommended, poor, good, very good, excellent)
- ⟜ Ageing potential (poor, good, very good, excellent)
- ⟜ Overall quality of the variety (poor, average, good, very good, excellent)

It should be noted that although many red grape varieties have white juice—and as such can produce white (blanc de noirs) wines—only those types and styles worthy of white-wine quality are identified. Grape varieties suitable for rosé wine production are also identified.

1.6 THE COMPOSITION OF WINES

The key to producing well-balanced wines is understanding the components of wines and how to analyze and control them.

Table 1-3 lists the ingredients of œnological significance found in grape juice (must) and wine. Typical concentration ranges are provided for healthy and normal juice and dry table wine.

Figure 1-2 illustrates the relationship between sugar, alcohol and acids, and changes in concentration resulting from vinification and winemaking. An understanding of this relationship will prove useful in predicting and adjusting vinification results.

When grape juice is fermented, fermentable sugars (glucose and fructose) are converted into ethanol (ethyl alcohol). The alcohol

Table 1-3
Key Ingredients in grape juice and wine as an approximate
percentage of total volume

Key Ingredients	Grape Juice	Wine
Water	70-75%	84-87%
Sugars	20-25% Fermentable sugars glucose fructose	<0.2% (dry wines) Non-fermentable sugars
Alcohol (Ethanol)	0%	11-14%
Glycerol	0%	Approximately 1%
(Fixed) Acids	0.6-0.9% tartaric malic citric	0.4-0.7% tartaric malic[2] lactic[2]
Tannin and colour pigments	<0.15%	<0.03% (white wines-no colour pigments) <0.2% (red wines)

[2]Malic acid will not be present in totally malolactic-fermented wines. Lactic acid will be present in either partially or totally malolactic-fermented wines. Refer to section 4.6.

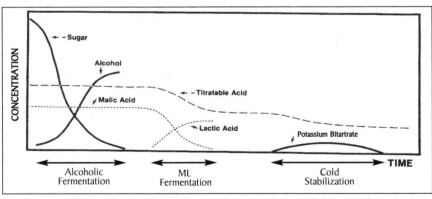

Figure 1-2: Relationship between sugar, alcohol and acids during vinification and winemaking

produced is proportional to the amount of sugar fermented. A by-product of fermentation is glycerol, which affects a wine's perceived sweetness. Glycerol does not affect viscosity—as is often believed—as evaluated from the wine's tears streaming down a glass. When juice is converted into wine, the water content also increases.

The naturally occurring (organic fixed) acids are reduced and transformed to give wine its required freshness. Refer to Figure 1-2. These acids are often referred to as a grouping termed titratable acid. This refers to the total acidity in wines. Of these, tartaric acid (not shown in Figure 1-2) is the most significant—it is the strongest and is present in both grape juice and wine. The second most significant acid is malic acid which is converted into lactic acid in malolactic-fermented wines. Malic acid is found in many fruits and is often associated with the sharp taste and sensation when eating green apples. Lactic acid is found, for example, in sour milk. As the malic acid content is being reduced during malolactic fermentation, titratable acid is also reduced.

Malolactic fermentation is used mostly in the production of red wines, but also in some whites, such as Burgundian Chardonnays, where the acid reduction is a bonus, a beneficial side benefit that brings complexity to their white wines. Malolactic fermentation is discussed in section 4.6.

Grape juice may also contain a very small amount of citric acid—an acid found in many fruits such as lemons—which is usually reduced completely during winemaking.

Titratable acid is also reduced when the wine is stabilized under cold temperature. During cold stabilization, tartaric acid is precipitated as potassium bitartrate and then separated from the wine by racking. Acids and titratable acid are further discussed in section 3.2.

Other compounds, such as tannin, flavours and colour pigments, are extracted from the grape skins, seeds and stems, and play a determining role in the structure, complexity, and ultimately, the quality of the wine. Refer to Figure 1-3 for a cross-section of a grape.

Tannin, flavour compounds and colour pigments belong to a group of substances known as phenols in œnological science. The concentrations of these phenolic substances are significantly different between red and white wines. In the production of red wine, the must is allowed to macerate with the grape skins, seeds and, optionally, the stems. Tannin, flavours and colour pigment extractions are carried out

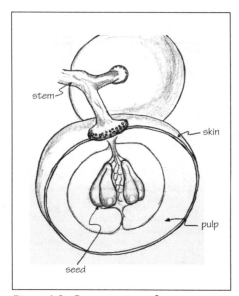

Figure I-3: Cross-section of a grape

until the desired concentrations are achieved. The astringency of the tannins and the alcohol level need to be properly balanced. For example, a highly tannic red wine will be unbalanced, and probably undrinkable, at an alcohol level of 10.0% alc./vol. In the production of white wine, there is minimal or no maceration. The colour of white wine is obtained strictly from the juice. High concentrations of tannin are also not desirable as they impart an astringent sensation that does not marry well with white wines.

The complex transformation of grape acids is further complicated by the presence of minerals and elements in the (vineyard) soil, namely potassium, which affect the acid balance and the wine's ability to protect itself from spoilage microorganisms. These have a direct impact on quality and longevity of the wine. A wine's pH value, which measures the active acidity, gives an accurate indication of chemical stability and protection against spoilage. The precise significance of pH, and how to measure and control it, is explained in section 3.3.

As can be seen, ingredients in juice undergo complex transformations when fermented into wine. Many vinification parameters must be monitored and controlled throughout this process. The quality of the wine is therefore highly dependent on the winemaker's ability to achieve a balance among the many components. A wine's chemical balance of alcohol, sugar, acidity, tannin, flavours and colour will determine its organoleptic balance and the overall quality of the wine.

1.7 WINEMAKING PROCESS

Different processes are used for winemaking from grapes, fresh juice, sterilized juice, and concentrated juice. Differences in winemaking procedures of the different types of musts are highlighted in the following sections and summarized in Table I-4. Each winemaking and vinification

Table 1-4

Summary of winemaking procedures for different types of musts

Type of must	Grapes	Fresh juice	Sterilized Juice	Concent- rated juice	Refer to section
Crushing/ Destemming	Yes	No	No	No	4.2
Maceration	For reds only	No	No	No	4.3
Pressing	Yes	No	No	No	4.4
Alcoholic Fermentation	Yes	Yes	Yes	Yes	4.5
Malolactic Fermentation	Yes	Yes	No	No	4.6
Oak Ageing	Yes	Yes	No	No	7.3

stage for each process is discussed in more detail in subsequent chapters.

This book presents all the winemaking methods and techniques using grapes so that home winemakers can make informed decisions throughout the winemaking process. Many of these methods and techniques will need to be adapted for wines from concentrate or grape juice, or may not be required at all.

1.7.1 Winemaking from grapes

Figure 1-4 and Figure 1-5 illustrate the white and red winemaking processes, respectively, using grapes to extract juice for fermentation. The major differences between these two processes are as follows:

1. In white winemaking, grapes are pressed either as whole bunches with the stems or immediately following the crushing/destemming operation. There is usually no maceration of the juice with the grape solids.
2. Malolactic fermentation in white wines is inhibited except for a few select grape varieties, such as Chardonnay.
3. Bulk ageing of white wines is done in glass or stainless steel containers. Only very few types of grape varieties benefit from oak barrel ageing, particularly in white grape varieties.

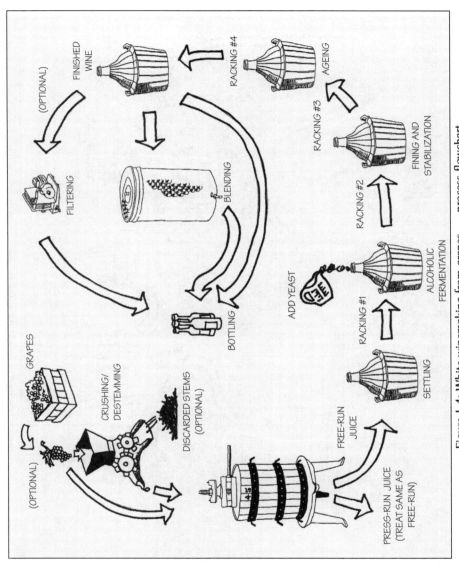

Figure I-4: White winemaking from grapes — process flowchart

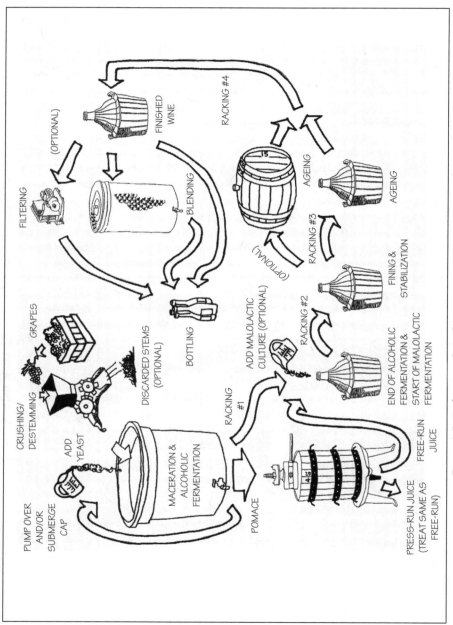

Figure I-5: Red winemaking from grapes — process flowchart

Rosé wine is produced in one of two methods. The first method involves a short maceration period of the must, without fermentation. The second method involves pressing red-juice red grapes. Both methods then use white vinification processing where the light-red juice is transferred to a glass vessel and is readied for yeast inoculation.

Carbonic maceration, or *macération carbonique* in French, is another popular technique used by commercial wineries in the production of young, fruity red wines. Whole grape bunches are put into a fermentor and go through an intra-cellular fermentation. Fermentation is initiated within the berries, without the addition of yeasts (wild indigenous yeasts will cause fermentation), by injecting carbon dioxide in the closed fermentor. This fermentation process produces soft, less tannic, early drinking wines with up-front fruit. They are not meant for ageing and should be drunk within a few months from production.

Carbonic maceration is used extensively in the French Beaujolais region in the production of Beaujolais Nouveau. Pinot Noir and Gamay grape varieties are the most popular and most used in *nouveau* wines vinified using this technique. It is also gaining popularity in North America wineries. Although more difficult to conduct carbonic maceration in home winemaking, a partial carbonic maceration is possible where a portion of the grapes are crushed and destemmed, and the rest are whole-cluster fermented. Figure 1-6 illustrates the red winemaking process from grapes using partial carbonic maceration. Details of the procedure are described in section 4.5.3.

1.7.2 Winemaking from fresh grape juice

Figure 1-7 and Figure 1-8 illustrate the white and red winemaking processes, respectively, using fresh grape juice. Winemaking from fresh juice does not involve crushing, destemming, or pressing operations. No maceration is required either as the juice has already been separated from the grape solids. These are the major differences from grape winemaking. The remainder of the processes is identical to grape winemaking.

1.7.3 Winemaking from sterilized grape juice

Figure 1-7 and Figure 1-8 illustrate the winemaking process using sterilized grape juice for white and red winemaking, respectively. As with fresh juice, this process does not involve crushing, destemming, or pressing operations, or any maceration as the juice has already been separated from the grape solids. The major differences from fresh juice winemaking are as follows:

1. Malolactic fermentation is improbable, as the juice has been completely sterilized, and is not recommended (refer to section 4.6).
2. Ageing in bulk is done in glass or stainless steel containers. Wines from this type of juice do not benefit from extended or oak-barrel ageing.

Sterilized juice can be fermented in a plastic pail, properly protected with a plastic lid, being less prone to oxidation at this vigourous stage of fermentation when lots of carbon dioxide is being given off, forming a protective layer over the fermenting wine.

1.7.4 Winemaking from concentrated grape juice

Figure 1-9 illustrates the winemaking process using concentrated grape juice. This process applies to both white and red winemaking. It requires the addition of water to the concentrate to reconstitute the juice before fermentation. This juice is then vinified in the same manner as sterilized juice.

When possible, add purified water when reconstituting the juice. Distilled water is a popular choice since it is widely available and cheaper. Tap water should be avoided as it contains impurities and chlorine that may affect vinification or the quality of the finished wine.

Concentrated juice can be fermented in a plastic pail, properly protected with a plastic lid, since it is less prone to oxidation at this vigourous stage of fermentation when lots of carbon dioxide is being given off, forming a protective layer over the fermenting wine.

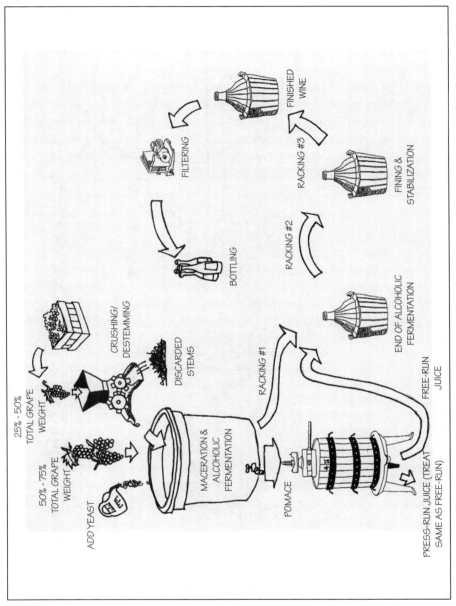

Figure 1-6: Red winemaking from grapes by partial carbonic maceration — process flowchart

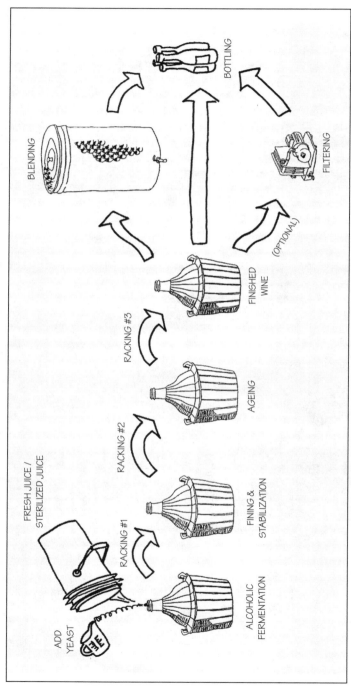

Figure I-7: White winemaking from fresh grape juice or sterilized juice — process flowchart

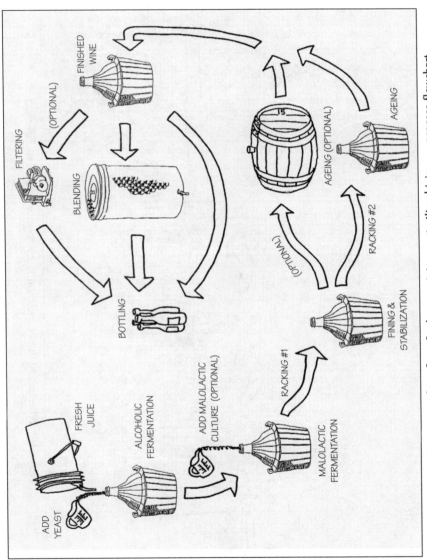

Figure I-8: Red winemaking from fresh grape juice or sterilized juice — process flowchart

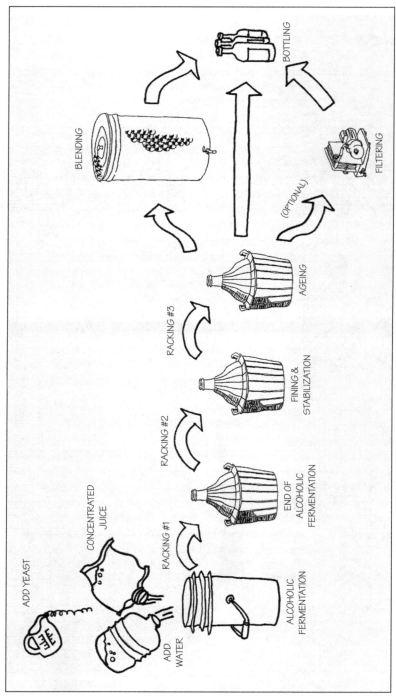

Figure I-9: Winemaking from concentrated grape juice — process flowchart

2
WINEMAKING EQUIPMENT

Winemaking has become a popular hobby with its relatively low cost compared to commercial wines. Winemaking equipment and products that greatly facilitate the production of premium-quality wines are now available to home winemakers. Low-cost, high-quality wines require a small to modest investment, one that will last a lifetime. Depending on the type of must chosen—concentrate, fresh or sterilized juice, or juice from grapes—some equipment may not be required.

2.1 CRUSHER AND DESTEMMER

The crusher is an indispensable tool for serious winemakers. It is strictly used for winemaking from grapes. Its purpose is to break the skin of grapes and to allow the juice to flow out so that it can combine and interact with yeast to start fermentation. The crushing operation is optional for white winemaking where the juice can be extracted from the grapes directly at pressing time, although more difficult to perform. It is necessary, however, for red winemaking to allow the juice to macerate with the grape skins for tannin and colour extraction, except in the case of the carbonic maceration technique.

The crusher consists of a funnel-shaped hopper to receive the grapes and one or two aluminum crushing rolls that rotate in opposite

Figure 2-I: Hand-cranked, double-roll crusher

directions. It is available with a number of options to meet various needs and budgets. For small-scale winemaking, the basic hand-cranked single-roll or double-roll model will serve the purpose. Double-roll models are typically equipped with an agitator designed to facilitate movement of the grapes through the rolls. To create ease and to speed up the crushing process, power-driven crushers are available equipped with a motor. Figure 2-I illustrates a hand-cranked, double-roll crusher.

A choice of stainless steel or enamel-paint model is available. The stainless steel model is costlier but will not rust therefore ensuring that the must and wine are not affected by rust. Wine that has been in contact with rust can become spoiled and undrinkable.

For very serious amateur winemakers, power-driven crushers are also available equipped with a built-in destemmer that removes all stems following crushing. The destemmer is attached to the crusher's exit chute and consists of a rotating screw-fork in a perforated semi-cylindrical drum. As the grapes are crushed, they are channeled and driven through the drum that causes the crushed grapes and juice to fall below into a container. The stems are ejected at the other end for disposal. The perforated drum can be removed when destemming is not required.

Double-roll Crusher with Agitator

Hopper

Destemming Mechanism

Motor

Exit Chute

Figure 2-2: Power-driven crusher/destemmer

Figure 2-2 illustrates a power-driven crusher/destemmer, with the protective cover removed to expose the destemming mechanism. Other power-driven crusher models are equipped with an auger inside the hopper to mechanically feed the grapes through the rolls. This safety feature is very practical.

Grapes can be separated from the stems before or after crushing depending on the desired wine style. Section 4.2 discusses the effects of destemming before or after crushing. At the present time, there is no commercially available tool for home winemakers to destem grape bunches before crushing. A hand destemmer can be built by using a wire mesh framed by wood, with openings large enough to allow grapes to pass through without the stems. This is a labour-intensive task however for anything over a few cases of grapes.

The crusher or crusher/destemmer operation is very simple. The apparatus is positioned over a container capable of receiving all the grapes. The grapes are then dropped gently into the hopper where the crushing rolls can be started manually or with a motor. Vine leaves, that may still be part of the grape bunches, should be removed before crushing. Vine leaves can impart undesirable flavours to the wine and can affect its quality.

2.2 WINEPRESS

The winepress—also known as the vertical winepress—is not an absolute requirement for red winemaking, although very useful, but it is essential for making white wine. It is strictly used for winemaking from grapes. Its purpose is to press the crushed grapes, or grape bunches if not previously crushed, to extract as much juice as desired.

The winepress (see Figure 2-3) consists of a sturdy three-legged tray with a spout used to drain grape juice, a basket consisting of hardwood staves, a jackscrew-driven pressure mechanism, a screw, and wooden pressure discs and blocks. The pressure mechanism operates like a ratchet and can be made to rotate in either direction to exert or release pressure. Direction of rotation is controlled with two metal inserts—known as pawls—within the pressure mechanism.

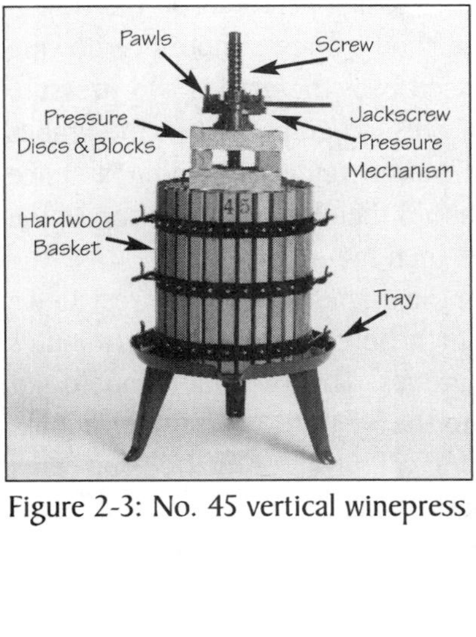

Figure 2-3: No. 45 vertical winepress

The commonly available Italian winepresses are rated according to the inner diameter of the basket, in centimeters. For example, a No. 45 winepress has a 45-cm (diameter) basket. Winepresses are available in sizes No. 15 to 70 in increments of 5, and in size No. 80. Table 2-1 provides approximate winepress capacities in terms of number of uncrushed and crushed 16.3-kg (36-lb) cases of grapes for the given approximate winepress dimensions. A press size No. 45 or 50 is recommended

Table 2-1
Approximate winepress capacities

No.	Basket Diameter (cm)	Basket Height (cm)	Cases of uncrushed grapes with stems	Cases of crushed grapes
30	30	40	1	4 to 6
35	35	45	2	7 to 10
40	40	55	3	11 to 15
45	45	60	4	15 to 20
50	50	65	5	20 to 27
55	55	70	7	28 to 35
60	60	75	9	36 to 44
65	65	80	11	45 to 55
70	70	85	14	56 to 68
80	80	95	20	75 to 99

for serious winemakers. Winepresses smaller than No. 30 are mainly used for fruit wines other than from grapes.

Although the winepress is a heavy-duty tool, it must be operated carefully to avoid damage. With the basket centered on the tray, it should be filled with crushed or uncrushed grapes without overflowing it. The pressure discs should be placed over the grapes and pressure should be exerted to level them. For crushed grapes, when the grapes are being loaded, a pail should be placed under the spout as juice starts to run. The pressure blocks should then be placed on top of the discs and the pressure mechanism is then mounted.

Pressure should be exerted on the grapes until a little resistance is felt. The free running juice can then be collected. A few minutes should be provided until the flow subdues. This operation should not be rushed as it can lead to damage to the winepress. The free running juice is referred to as free-run juice and will produce the free-run wine, or *vin de goutte* in French. The process should be repeated until considerable resistance can be felt when exerting pressure. Pressing should then continue as much as possible, ensuring a few minutes wait between each press cycle. Juice extracted from this pressing is referred to as press-run juice and will produce the press wine, or *vin de presse* in French. Free-run juice should be used to produce the higher-quality wine since press-run juice will be much more astringent. The quality of free-run juice greatly increases when minimal pressure is exerted. The yield of free-run juice will however be much smaller. Section 4.4 discusses the effects of pressing grapes with stems and the vinification of free-run and press-run juices.

Each case of grapes will yield approximately 7 L of free-run juice and 3 L of press-run juice. These quantities and proportions will depend on the grape variety and pressure exerted by the winepress.

For some types of grapes with slippery skins—for example, Muscat—it is advisable to leave or add some stems to the grapes when pressing. Otherwise, the pomace causes the winepress basket to lift making the pressing operation very tedious.

Note: When making both white and red wines, the white grapes should be pressed first so as not to contaminate the winepress with the red pigment that would still be present in the basket's staves. Since whites are pressed on arrival, and reds are pressed after or late in the alcoholic fermentation phase, one usually presses the whites first quite naturally. Therefore this should not be a problem.

2.3 VESSELS FOR FERMENTING, STORING, AND AGEING WINE

Various types of vessels, of different materials, are used in home winemaking. The most popular ones are glass demijohns and carboys, food-grade plastic and cement vats, oak barrels, and stainless steel tanks. Open-top vats are used for maceration of grapes in must and cannot be used for storing and ageing wine. Demijohns, carboys, oak barrels, and stainless steel tanks can be used for fermenting must as well as storing and ageing wine. When containers are used for fermentation, they are referred to as fermentors.

Except for oak barrels, which react favourably with wine, all other containers must be inert so that they do not impart any off-flavour, or worse, spoil the wine. Plastic containers that are not food-grade should be avoided.

Section 4.1 describes how to clean and sanitize containers, in addition to instructions provided in the following sections.

2.3.1 Demijohns and carboys

Glass demijohns and carboys are practical containers for home wine-making. They are inert, fairly inexpensive, and are available in a variety of sizes, shapes and colours. Colour is not an important factor if the wine will be stored for a short time away from light. If wine is intended to be stored for a long time, for example, longer than 6 months, or if the wine is exposed to light, it is highly recommended that tinted-glass containers be used. They are available in brown or green tints to slow down maturation. Clear glass vessels have the advantage of allowing unobstructed visual inspection of the wine, facilitating the monitoring of sediment and the racking operation. Figure 2-4 illustrates a demijohn and carboy.

Demijohns are available in sizes of 5, 10, 15, 20, 25, 34 and 54 L, in clear, brown- or green-tinted glass. They usually come enclosed in a protective plastic cover or straw wickerwork with carrying handles. Straw-covered demijohns are not recommended, as the wickerwork will deteriorate over time and are much more difficult to clean. Clear-glass carboys are available in sizes of 18.9, 20 and 23 L.

Special carrying handles, that fit around the neck of carboys and secured with a wing nut, are available to easily move carboys around. The 23-L carboy shown in Figure 2-4B also illustrates a carboy-carrying handle.

One should always have available different demijohn and carboy sizes, depending on the volume of wine being produced, to ensure wine is always topped up in containers. Topping up is required when fermentation subdues. As the amount of carbon dioxide produced decreases, a small amount of air space will be needed in the properly-locked container. A number of 3.8-L (1-gal) glass containers as well as standard 750-mL and 1.5-L bottles are useful to have on hand to hold small amounts of wine to top up larger containers. Section 5.1.3 discusses the practice of topping up containers.

Figure 2-4: A, 54-L demijohn; B, 23-L carboy

When conducting fermentation, the container should be sized to allow for expansion. For the vigourous phase of fermentation, the container should be filled to approximately 75 percent capacity. When racking the wine to a secondary fermentor to complete fermentation, this will still be quite vigourous so allowance for expansion should be made by filling the container to approximately 90 percent capacity. When the fermentor is properly protected from air, the air cannot react with the wine as carbon dioxide will fill the empty space and protect the wine.

The V Vessel System

Another type of fermentor now available to home winemakers is the V Vessel shown in Figure 2-5. The V Vessel eliminates the need for cumbersome racking from carboy to carboy.

It consist of an inverted teardrop-looking, food grade plastic container with a valve and a ball-shaped collection capsule assembly for "racking" the wine, and a hole at the top for inserting a fermentation lock and bung. The 23-L capacity V Vessel mounts on a wall, at waist height, using the supplied wall bracket.

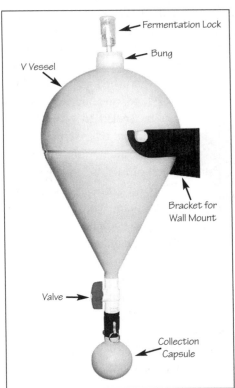

Its operation is very simple. Juice or concentrate is poured into the vessel from the top. The valve in the open position allows the juice to enter the collection capsule. As wine ferments, the sediment will travel to the bottom and into the collection capsule. When the primary fermentation is complete, the valve is closed and the collection capsule is detached to remove the sediment. The capsule is emptied, cleaned and sterilized, and then placed back on the valve assembly to continue with the secondary fermentation. The valve is re-opened and the sediment

Figure 2-5: The V Vessel System

removal procedure is then repeated following completion of the secondary fermentation.

The wine is then fined and/or filtered, stabilized and bottled right from the V Vessel. No need for any racking.

2.3.2 Plastic and cement vats

Food-grade plastic and cement vats are used for macerating grapes in must. While both types of vats can be cleaned easily, plastic vats can be moved easily as opposed to their cement counterparts. Cement vats are still popular in home winemaking and commercial winemaking. Proprietor-made Beaujolais and Bordeaux wines as well as those from Italy, Spain and Portugal are still produced in cement vats.

A container as wide as possible should be chosen so that the crusher rests on it. When using a destemmer, the stems should be discarded away from the container. It is important to have a wide container to maximize the surface area of grape juice in contact with the cap therefore maximizing the effects of maceration. For example, a deeper colour is obtained in a shorter maceration period. Figure 2-6 illustrates a 350-L plastic vat, with a capacity of 20 cases of crushed grapes, used for macerating red wine juice. Containers that can be sealed to protect wine from air are required as fermentors to complete fermentation following maceration or to store and age wine.

Figure 2-6: A food-grade plastic vat for macerating red wine juice

Food-grade plastic vats come in many different sizes depending on one's needs. They can be bulky and cumbersome for storage when not in use. Therefore, when determining capacity needs, future requirements should be considered if one intends to increase production, and to allow for volume expansion of the must during fermentation. Plastic containers should not be used for storing or ageing wine for a prolonged time. Plastic is a permeable material which will cause wine to oxidize.

Warning: Only non-toxic food-grade plastic should be used to avoid spoiling the wine, or even worse, harming oneself. If in doubt, plastic vats specifically designed for winemaking should be selected. Recycled containers, previously used to store olives or unknown substances, should be avoided.

To clean cement vats, they must first be stripped of any tartrate deposit. This is easily accomplished with a light scrubbing using a plastic-bristle brush. It should then be cleaned using a caustic soda solution, and, after cleaning, a layer of tartaric solution should be brushed on before using.

2.3.3 Oak barrels

The use of oak barrels in home winemaking is not a common practice. The most common reason heard is that the use of oak barrels is too risky and should be left to experienced professional winemakers. With very little know-how and routine supervision and maintenance, the use of oak barrels can be made to be risk-free and fun in home winemaking. The quality of the finished wine is well worth the additional investment in time and money.

Oak barrels should ideally be purchased new to reduce any potential problems with used barrels. New barrels can be reused multiple times for several years therefore justifying the investment. Old wooden barrels can be troublesome, as they need to be prepared, cleaned and sanitized carefully before use. Lastly, white wine should never be stored or aged in oak barrels previously used for red wine. The white wine will absorb the red pigments from the wood and will become a reddish colour.

Chapter 7 presents a full discussion on the maintenance and preparation of oak barrels for fermenting and ageing wine, and alternatives to barrels.

2.3.4 Stainless steel tanks

Floating-lid AISI 304 stainless steel tanks, such as the one shown in Figure 2-7A, are an excellent alternative to demijohns and carboys for fermenting wine and for high-capacity, short- and long-term wine storage. The floating-lid design transforms these tanks into variable capacity containers. The lid is simply inserted inside the tank and then allowed to float on the wine surface. A membrane around the lid is

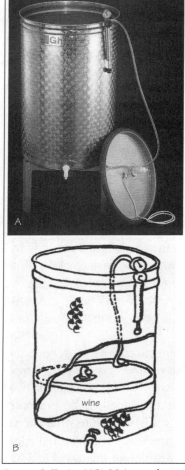

Figure 2-7: A, AISI 304 stainless steel tank and B, floating lid operation

inflated to create an airtight seal to protect the wine, as shown in Figure 2-7B.

The tanks are made from stainless steel, which is inert, and therefore wine will not react with it during prolonged aging. And they are easy to clean and store.

A floating-lid stainless steel tank consists of a fixed-volume tank, which may be equipped with a man door, a sight glass and a three-legged stand, various spigots or valves, and a lid with an inflatable membrane. The lid has an air pump attachment for inflating the membrane.

Tanks are available in volumes ranging from 34 to 1850 L or more, and different steel thickness (gauge) ranging from 0.6 mm (3/128 in) to 1.2 mm (3/64 in).

The lower-gauge steel tanks are more prone to dents from accidental hitting. Opt for the higher-gauge tanks depending on the size you choose and on your budget. Both gauges are commonly available in a metal alloy referred to as AISI 304. This alloy is more susceptible to pitting from sulphur dioxide (SO_2) than the AISI 316 alloy that offers a higher degree of resistance to SO_2, salts and strong, corrosive acids. AISI 316 tanks are usually found in commercial wineries whereas nearly all tanks for home winemaking are AISI 304.

A choice of bright, mirror or marbled exterior finish as well as flat, conical or 5%-slope bottom is available. The exterior finish is simply a matter of personal preference whereas the conical and sloped bottoms simplify drainage of sediment or liquid if the tank is equipped with a bottom valve for this purpose.

Tanks are fitted with a spigot (ball valve) ranging from 1.3 cm (½ in) to 3.2 cm (1¼ in) making winemaking operations, such as racking and filtering, very simple. Larger-volume tanks also have a discharge valve at the bottom.

Some tank types and sizes, shown in Figure 2-8, are equipped with a 30-cm (12-in) man door on the side of the tank near the bottom for easy access for cleaning and removal of grape solids. A sight glass will also prove useful to determine and monitor the volume of wine in the tank; otherwise, it's guesswork. It will be difficult to measure how much wine is in the tank based on the depth of the lid. The sight glass may be equipped with a sample valve for quickly withdrawing a small amount of wine for tasting. The sample valve can also be located on the main body of the tank. The sample valve is a handy feature since the lid does not need to be removed and replaced when sampling wine.

A three-legged stand can be purchased separately, if not already provided with the tank. The tank storage location should be carefully chosen since it cannot be moved once filled with wine. A 200-L tank full of wine weighs over 227 kg (500 lbs)!

The lid is the "heart" of the tank and is what transforms it into a variable-capacity container. Also made of stainless steel, it is equipped with an inflatable membrane on its circumference. The lid is placed inside the tank, on top of the wine, and allowed to float. The membrane is then inflated using the supplied hand air pump to seal the wine from air. The membrane creates a perfect seal on the inner circumference of the tank to protect the wine.

Figure 2-8: Large capacity tanks with man door, sight glass, and wine sampling valve

Useful tip: *When inflating the lid to seal the tank, inflate the membrane partially until the lid can be pulled up without it falling back down. Lift the lid a little, an inch or so, and then pump the membrane up to the recommended pressure. This tip avoids having wine pouring out from the fermentation trap due to the lid's downward pressure on the wine if it is not raised.*

A special fermentation lock on the lid allows carbon dioxide gas to escape but prevents air from entering the tank. This clever contraption, unlike the well-known fermentation lock we all use, operates using two marbles to accomplish this.

The hand air pump is connected to the membrane via a polyethylene tube. A pressure gauge indicates the membrane pressure, which can be adjusted at any time to maintain an airtight seal. The pump has a release valve to deflate the membrane when the lid is to be removed. The manufacturer's recommended maximum air pressure in the membrane should be respected to avoid damaging it. Some retailers suggest that you purchase an extra membrane ... just in case.

Given that tanks are very deep, a cord attachment is used for raising or lowering the lid. The larger volume tanks—over 2000 L— have a lid hoisting attachment fixed to the side and reaching toward the center of the tank. The cord is attached to an eyelet at the center of the lid making the raising/lowering operations cumbersome since the lid will not balance. A newer tank model is now available with three eyelets to keep the lid balanced.

When emptying tanks during such operations as racking or bottling, the lid gasket should be deflated before drawing wine from the tank; otherwise, the tank will implode.

Stainless steel tanks should always be cleaned and sanitized properly before use. Sulfite or bleaching products should **not** be used on stainless steel. These products will pit the surface of the tank and will shorten its life.

The recommended method for cleaning and sanitizing tanks is a hot-water rinse of the entire inside surface, followed by a sodium percarbonate (or sodium carbonate, i.e. soda ash) treatment, followed by a citric acid treatment by dissolving 3 tbsp per 4 litres (I gallon) of water. Sufficient solution should be used to properly rinse the entire inside surface of the tank, and then the sanitization is completed with a thorough water rinse. The lid, spigots/valves, man door and any other parts that will come in contact with the wine should also be thoroughly sanitized.

Refer to section 4.1.4 for more information on the use of these sanitizing agents.

2.4 FERMENTATION LOCKS

The fermentation lock is an essential device in winemaking. Its purpose is to allow carbon dioxide gas to escape from a closed fermentor during fermentation of the must without letting any air come into contact with it. Air is wine's worst enemy and will cause spoilage if in contact with the wine for any significant period of time.

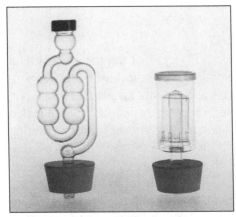

Figure 2-9: Fermentation locks and silicone rubber bungs

There are various types of fermentation locks available. A favourite amongst winemakers is the S-shaped fermentation lock that produces a symphonic sound during the vigourous phase of fermentation. The advantage of the S-shaped fermentation lock is that it prevents sulphite solution from flowing back into the wine under cellar temperature fluctuations. Temperature changes will cause sulphite solution to be forced in or out of the fermentation lock. In the straight-cylinder fermentation lock model, the sulphite solution will contaminate the wine under such conditions. An advantage of the straight-cylinder fermentation lock is its ease of cleaning. Figure 2-9 illustrates two types of fermentation locks fitted with silicone rubber bungs.

A good supply of fermentation locks should be available in stock, as it could prove problematic if caught short when the local supply store is closed.

To use a fermentation lock, a holed silicone rubber bung is first attached and then a sulphite solution (refer to section 4.1.2) is added up to the level indicated on the fermentation lock. The fermentation lock is attached firmly to the wine container. The bottom tube of the fermentation lock should protrude from the bung by approximately 0.5 to 1 cm, and the tube should be approximately 2 cm above wine level. The top portion of the lock, where the carbon dioxide gas escapes, should be protected with a lid to prevent dust and flies from entering the lock. The lid is designed to let the carbon dioxide gas escape freely. Some cotton wool can be put into the opening instead of the lid. The sulphite solution should be replaced every 3 to 4 weeks, as it will lose effectiveness when exposed to air for a prolonged time.

The wine should not be allowed to enter the fermentation lock as it could come in contact with the sulphite solution or become exposed to air. This can be avoided by monitoring the wine level in each container to ensure that it does not rise with temperature fluctuations in the fermentation area or cellar.

2.5 MISCELLANEOUS EQUIPMENT

There are many other miscellaneous devices that will prove very useful and indispensable for home winemaking. These include bungs, siphoning tubes, special sieve and faucet attachments for plastic fermentors, floating thermometers, vinometer, various size funnels, long-handled spoons and stirrer, gravy baster, cleaning brushes and measuring spoons. A portable balance will also come in handy for measuring chemicals to remove guesswork when using kitchen measuring spoons.

Other miscellaneous equipment, such as hydrometer, refractometer, pH meter, and sugar, acid and sulphite analysis kits are described in Chapter 3 as these pertain to the analysis and control of musts and wines.

2.5.1 Bungs

Winemakers should have a good supply of both no-hole and single-hole bungs (stoppers), of varying sizes, for demijohns, carboys and smaller containers. Silicone rubber bungs provide a better airtight seal and are preferred over cork stoppers. Bungs should fit snugly and should be sufficiently inserted into the mouth opening of the container to ease later removal. Bungs are available in sizes No. 2 to 14 including half sizes from No. 5½ to 13½.

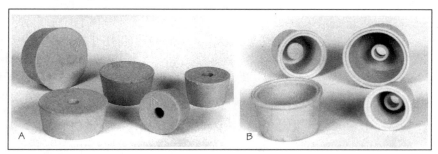

Figure 2-10: A, standard, and B, Buon Vino bungs

Buon Vino Manufacturing Ltd. (Buon Vino) has designed a new type of silicone rubber bungs that incorporate several practical features. The bungs are designed as a mini container to collect any overflow liquid from fermentation locks. A lip at the top of the bung prevents it from falling into the container during insertion, and also allows easier removal. Buon Vino bungs are available in Small, Medium, and Large sizes to fit most types of containers. Being approximately 35 percent longer than standard bungs, fewer sizes are required. The longer taper provides a snugger fit and a better seal. They are also available without or with a hole for a fermentation lock.

Figure 2-10 shows both standard and new Buon Vino bungs. Table 2-2 can be used as a quick reference to determine the proper bung size based on the type and size of container.

Table 2-2 Recommended bung sizes for glass containers

Type and size of container	Recommended bung size number
750-ml bottle	4 or 4½
5-L demijohn 4-L container	6 or 6½
18.9, 20, 23-L carboys	7 or Small
10, 15, 20, 25, 34-L demijohns	9½ or Medium
54-L demijohn	11, 11½, or Large

2.5.2 Siphons

Siphoning equipment consists of a solid clear-glass J-tube with an end cap, or antidregs tip, and a clear, food grade, flexible plastic (polyvinyl) tubing available in various lengths. Popular plastic tube diameters are 6 mm (¼ in), 10 mm (³⁄₈ in), 13 mm (½ in), 19 mm (¾ in), and 26 mm (1 in). The 6 and 10-mm tubings are the standard size for small-capacity winemaking equipment and filtration systems. The 10-mm tubing should be used for quicker transfer of wine from one container to another. The 13, 19, and 26-mm tubings are used on larger-scale winemaking equipment and filtration systems.

The antidregs tip is attached at the bottom of the J-tube and is used to prevent sediment from entering the tube when siphoning wine during the various winemaking operations. Figure 2-11 illustrates a J-tube with an antidregs tip and plastic tubing for siphoning.

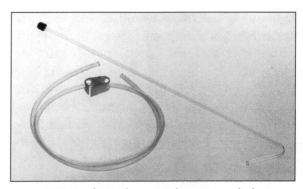

Figure 2-11: J-tube with an antidregs tip and plastic tubing used for siphoning wine

To siphon or rack wine from one container to another, the container with the sediment is placed higher. A height difference of 1 m between the containers will cause a good siphoning action. The J-tube, antidregs tip and plastic tubing assembly are inserted in the container with sediment. Suction by mouth is used to start the flow of wine into the lower container. Containers with wine and sediment should not be displaced for a few days before racking. The siphoning will be a lot more efficient and the racked wine will be clearer with less waste if the sediment is not disturbed. This is especially true if the wine has been fined recently.

Figure 2-12: A, special faucet and sieve, and B, setup in a plastic fermentor

2.5.3 Special sieve and faucet

Although it is possible to siphon red wine from the plastic fermentor, following maceration, to a demijohn or a carboy, this will prove to be a tedious task as the siphoning tube will clog easily with grape skins, seeds and other solids. Also, it is not practical to place the heavy fermentor higher to achieve an effective siphoning action. The best solution involves using a special plastic sieve and faucet that allow drainage of wine from the fermentor without clogging. The special sieve will filter large grape particles allowing the must to flow freely. The faucet, which has a 26-mm (1-in) or 32-

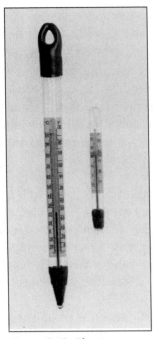

Figure 2-13: Floating thermometers

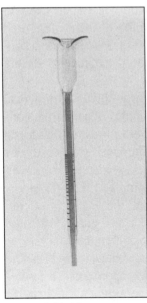

Figure 2-14: Vinometer

mm (1¼-in) diameter, can be opened or closed easily to control the flow of wine.

The sieve is mounted from the inside of the plastic fermentor and is held in place by both a bracket and the faucet that are mounted through a hole in the fermentor. Figure 2-12A shows the special sieve and faucet, and Figure 2-12B illustrates the setup in a plastic fermentor.

2.5.4 Floating thermometer

A floating thermometer is necessary to ensure that the temperature of the must remains within the recommended temperature range before adding yeast to start fermentation. It is also used to monitor the temperature of the must and wine to ensure a proper and consistent fermentation environment. Figure 2-13 illustrates two sizes of floating thermometers for winemaking purpose. The smaller thermometer is most practical when used in clear juice or wine. The larger thermometer is mainly used during the maceration stage. The grape solids would bury the smaller thermometer making it hard to locate. The larger thermometer is sufficiently long to penetrate through the cap to measure the must temperature.

2.5.5 Vinometer

A vinometer is a practical device for the approximate determination of an unknown alcohol content in a finished dry wine. Figure 2-14 illustrates a vinometer. This instrument is not intended for alcohol determination of sweet wines, as the high sugar content will yield false readings.

To determine the approximate alcohol content, a small amount of dry wine is poured in the vinometer opening. When the wine fills up the tiny tube inside, the vinometer is inverted. The wine will flow out and will cease due to capillary attraction. The alcohol content can then be read from the vinometer scale at that point.

2.5.6 Other miscellaneous equipment

Double cheesecloth and a good plastic strainer should be used for separating grape juice from pulp and other unwanted solids when, for

Figure 2-15: Plastic funnel with a removable sieve and large-hole sieve

example, transferring red wine from the one fermentor to another. Metal strainers should not be used unless they are stainless steel.

Plastic funnels, one small and one large, with a built-in removable plastic sieve are useful for transferring must from one fermentor to another. Figure 2-15 illustrates a plastic funnel with a removal sieve and a sieve to separate juice from large grape particles.

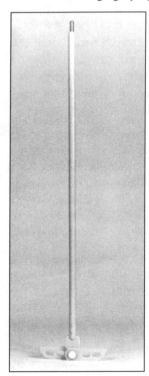

Figure 2-16: Stirring stem

A long-handled plastic spoon is required to stir must and wine for various winemaking operations. A new stirrer easing this operation is now available. A long stem is equipped with 2 stirring paddles that move to a horizontal position when spun fast. An electric drill attached to the top of the stem is used for this purpose. The apparatus is inserted into a container to stir wine. Figure 2-16 illustrates this stirring stem.

A gravy baster or wine-thief is a practical device to withdraw small samples of wine from containers. Small and large polyester brushes with metal handles are useful for cleaning tough stains and sediment from glass containers. A set of measuring spoons from 1/8 tsp (0.625 mL) to 1 tbsp (15 mL) is indispensable for measuring the many powdered chemicals used in winemaking. Figure 2-17 illustrates miscellaneous winemaking equipment.

Measuring spoons commonly used in the kitchen are very handy for quick, approximate measurements of chemicals. When the weight of a chemical can be related to its volume in teaspoon or tablespoon measurements—such as the tables often provided in the appendix of winemaking books—these spoons are very practical. The only problem is that their margin of error may be significant, and this is an important drawback when working with chemicals to be added in accurate amounts.

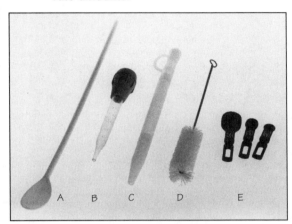

Figure 2-17: Miscellaneous winemaking equipment: A, long-handled stirring spoon, B, gravy baster, C, wine-thief, D, large polyester brush and E, set of measuring spoons

A measuring balance, such as the one depicted in Figure 2-18, will prove to be an excellent investment over time. A portable model operating on either battery or AC power is most practical. They are available in many capacities; 400 g, 600 g or 1200 g balances will meet most winemakers' needs. Some models also provide measurements in various units including grams and ounces. The most important consideration in choosing a balance is its readability or accuracy. A balance with reading in 0.1 g increments is quite sufficient. Higher accuracy balances will commend higher prices. 1-g increment balances might be fine for most measurements; however, in the long run, the 0.1-g will prove to be a better investment.

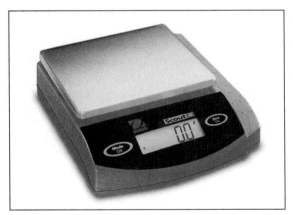

Figure 2-18: A Ohaus SC4010 balance with a 400-g capacity and 0.1-g accuracy

3

ANALYSIS AND CONTROL
OF MUSTS AND WINES

Key œnological ingredients found in grapes are fermentable sugars, (organic fixed) acids and phenols (namely, tannin, flavour compounds and colour pigments). Refer to Table 1-3 on page 39. During vinification of the must these ingredients undergo transformations and are present in the finished wine in different concentrations from their initial amounts. The relative concentration of each ingredient will determine the structure of a wine.

A wine's structure is primarily determined by the alcohol content, the amount of residual sugar, acidity and pH levels, tannin level and colour intensity. These components must be present in balanced concentrations for the desired type and style of wine to be produced. For example, an age-worthy full-bodied dry red wine should have between 12.5% and 14.0% alc./vol. with a residual sugar content less than 2.0 g/L, good acidity with a low pH, a relatively high tannin level and a deep colour.

A wine's quality is judged based on the balance of these components. It is crucial, therefore, to be able to monitor and control the sugar content, acidity and pH levels, tannin level and colour intensity during vinification. Various instruments and chemical analysis procedures exist for the monitoring and control of sugar, acid and pH. No such commercially available home winemaking tool exists for the determination of the tannin level. Winemakers rely on their tasting experience to adjust the tannin level. Similarly, no analytical tool is available for the determination of colour intensity. Colour is monitored and adjusted by visual inspection.

The must and finished wine must also be monitored and controlled to ensure that a sufficient amount of sulphite is present, necessary for preserving and ageing wine. Sulphite can be harmful to health and should therefore not exceed prescribed maximums.

3.1 SUGAR AND ALCOHOL

The amount of sugar present in the must before fermentation determines the potential alcohol content if all the sugar was to be fermented. Determining and controlling the amount of sugar in the must at key stages during vinification are critical steps in winemaking to ensure a proper rate of fermentation. Alcoholic fermentation procedures are discussed in section 4.5.

The hydrometer, depicted in Figure 3-I, is the winemaker's tool for measuring the concentration of fermentable sugars in the must, and

therefore, the potential alcohol level. The hydrometer operates on the buoyancy principle based on a liquid density or concentration relative to the density of another liquid, usually water. Several hydrometer scales can be used to measure sugar concentration. The most common scales used in North America are those measuring specific gravity, abbreviated SG, and Brix degrees, usually abbreviated B° and often referred to as Balling degrees. Other common scales are Baumé and Oechsle used mainly in Europe. Brix and specific gravity scales are used from here on.

Brix is a measure of the amount of sugar, in grams, in 100 g of must. A Brix reading of 23 B° represents a must consisting of 23 percent fermentable sugar by

Figure 3-I: The hydrometer

weight. Specific gravity is a measure of must density relative to the unit density (1.000) of water at a predetermined temperature. Most hydrometers are calibrated for 15.5° C (60° F) while others are calibrated for 15° C (59° F) or 20° C (68° F). As an example, a must with an SG of 1.092 denotes that its weight due to sugar is 1.092 times the weight of water for the same volume when measured at 15.5° C (60° F).

Since consumers are not familiar with Brix or Specific Gravity measurements, concentrations expressed in g/L is used for informing them of the residual sugar content. For example, a dry wine with 2.0 g/L of residual sugar contains 2.0 g in 1 L of wine.

Although the hydrometer does not provide an accurate reading of the sugar level, it is the most practical and most widely used winemaking instrument. Hydrometer readings are affected by both the presence of alcohol and of particles in suspension. The margin of error is small and is within acceptable tolerance. A titration-method sugar analysis kit is an alternative method that compensates for the factors affecting the reading. Section 3.1.1 describes the procedure for using a titration-method sugar analysis kit.

Another very useful piece of instrumentation is the hand-held refractometer also used to measure the sugar content, in Brix degrees (B°), in unfermented musts and other juices. The refractometer, which measures the refractive index of juices, cannot be used with

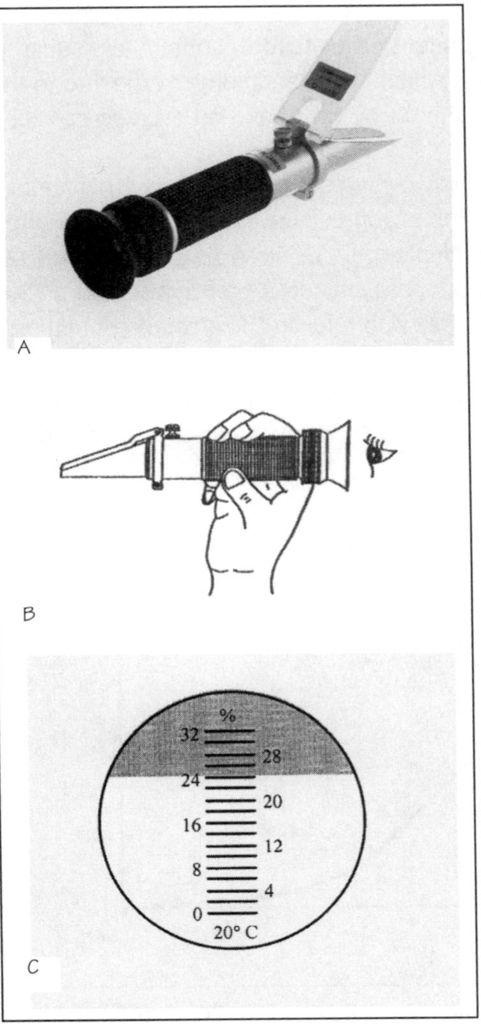

Figure 3-2: A, a hand-held refractometer, B, using a refractometer

musts that have begun fermenting. The presence of alcohol yields false readings.

The refractometer is an expensive instrument but will prove indispensable when the sugar content and the potential alcohol level need to be determined before buying grapes. It is very practical as it only requires a single drop of juice to read the sugar content. Figure 3-2 illustrates a hand-held refractometer and its method of use.

When using a refractometer to determine the sugar level in grape berries, samples should be taken from both outer and inner berries in the grape cluster. Inner berries tend to contain less sugar as opposed to the outer berries, which have had a longer exposure to the sun. Several measurements should be taken and an average can then be computed.

Potential alcohol is most commonly expressed as a percentage of alcohol volume to wine volume, abbreviated % alc./vol. or very often as % alc. v/v or % alc. For example, a 12.5% alc./vol. wine contains 125 mL of alcohol in 1 L of wine, or approximately 94 mL in a standard 750-mL bottle of wine. As % alc. may also refer to the alcohol content as a percentage of weight to weight (% alc. w/w), it is important to know which one is being used as the two measurements are significantly different. This book always uses % alcohol, volume to volume, or % alc./vol.

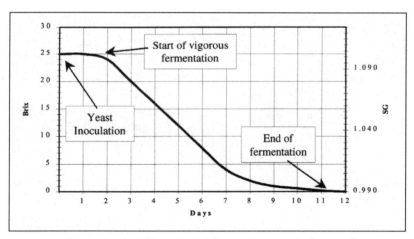

Figure 3-3: Typical curve for a normal fermentation at 20° C (68° F)

Table 3-1

Brix and SG temperature correction factors

T (°C)	Brix (B°)	SG	T (°F)
1	-0.4	-0.002	34
2	-0.4	-0.002	36
3	-0.4	-0.002	37
4	-0.4	-0.002	39
5	-0.4	-0.002	41
6	-0.2	-0.001	43
7	-0.2	-0.001	45
8	-0.2	-0.001	46
9	-0.2	-0.001	48
10	-0.2	-0.001	50
11	0.0	0.000	52
12	0.0	0.000	54
13	0.0	0.000	55
14	0.0	0.000	57
15	0.0	0.000	59
16	0.0	0.000	61
17	0.0	0.000	63
18	0.0	0.000	64
19	0.0	0.000	66
20	+0.2	+0.001	68
21	+0.2	+0.001	70
22	+0.2	+0.001	72
23	+0.2	+0.001	73
24	+0.2	+0.001	75
25	+0.4	+0.002	77
26	+0.4	+0.002	79
27	+0.4	+0.002	81
28	+0.4	+0.002	82
29	+0.4	+0.002	84
30	+0.6	+0.003	86
31	+0.6	+0.003	88
32	+0.6	+0.003	90
33	+0.6	+0.003	91
34	+0.6	+0.003	93
35	+0.8	+0.004	95

Appendix B shows the relationship between SG, B°, potential % alc./vol., and quantity of sugar in a given volume.

The hydrometer is most useful in monitoring fermentation progress and for determining when fermentation has ended completely. The sugar level should be measured at the time of crushing, or pressing for white wine production, and throughout the fermentation period. For musts from concentrate or juice, the first reading is taken before yeast inoculation. If fermentation stops or slows down due to an undetermined cause, hydrometer readings will help identify this abnormality. Readings are plotted on a graph each day and compared to the typical normal fermentation curve shown in Figure 3-3. The curve shown is for a non-chaptalized wine that has been fermented to dryness. Section 12.1 discusses techniques to deal with fermentation problems.

The fermentation curve depicted in Figure 3-3 illustrates the rate of conversion of sugar into alcohol from yeast inoculation to end of fermentation. For the first 24 to 48 hours, there is no significant activity, as the yeast has not started its effect. Once fermentation starts, sugar is converted at a high rate over the next 2 to 7 or more days. As the amount of fermentable sugars reduces and the alcohol content increases, the yeast activity subsides considerably until it stops completely.

3.1.1 Measuring sugar and potential alcohol contents

Before measuring the sugar content, the must should be as clear as possible to obtain a more precise reading. Grape particles and pulp, affecting the hydrometer reading, should be filtered using cheesecloth, or left to settle overnight in a large graduated cylinder, so that clear must can subsequently be poured off into a measuring cylinder, and the Brix (SG) can be read with little interference from suspended solids. A sojourn in the fridge will speed this process up, but the must should be brought up to 15° C (59° F) before measuring, unless temperature corrections are made. The sugar content reading will be inaccurate if the temperature is significantly above or below the calibration point. If so, the reading should be compensated according to the factors provided in Table 3-1. For example, a Brix reading of 22.0 B° at 21° C (70° F) should be corrected to 22.2 B°. Similarly, if using SG as the unit of measure, an SG reading of 1.090 at 21° C (70° F) should be corrected to 1.091.

To measure the Brix or SG, a cylindrical tube should be filled to within 3 cm of the top and the hydrometer is then inserted. The must may need to be stirred with the hydrometer in combination with some heat to remove carbon dioxide and air bubbles to ensure a proper reading. The hydrometer scale should be read at eye level as shown in Figure 3-4.

To determine the potential alcohol content of wine, the hydrometer reading at end of fermentation should be subtracted from the reading at the start. Appendix B provides conversion of Brix and SG readings into % alc./vol. For example:

	B°	SG	% alc./vol.
Initial reading	22.0	1.090	12.0
Final reading	0.0	0.990	0.0
Final % alc./vol.			12.0

Table 3-2 lists suggested initial and final sugar concentrations, recommended alcohol content, and percentage residual sugar for differ-

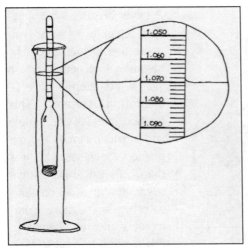

Figure 3-4: Measuring the sugar content with a hydrometer

ent types of wines. For dry wines, the must should be within the suggested Brix (SG) range and the wine transferred to a secondary fermentor when the reading is 7.5 B° (1.030) or lower. Fermentation will be completed for dry wines when the Brix (SG) has reached 0.0 B° (0.990) and remains at that level for at least two weeks. The amount of residual sugar will be less than 2.0 g/L. For medium-sweet and sweet wines, the amount of residual sugar should be in the range 10 to 40 g/L and 50 to 200 g/L, respectively.

Determining the amount of residual sugar in wines can be quickly measured by using CLINITEST® reagent tablets, shown in Figure 3-5, available from drug stores. Each tablet is used to measure the amount of sugar, specifically glucose, between 0 and 20 g/L in increments of 2.5 g/L between 0 and 10 g/L.

Table 3-2
Suggested sugar concentrations for various types of wine

Type of wine	Dry white	Dry red	Medium -sweet	Dessert (sweet)
Initial B°	20.0 - 23.0	21.0 - 25.0	18.5 - 23.0	32.0 - 38.0
Initial SG	1.080-1.095	1.085-1.105	1.075-1.095	1.135-1.153
Final B°	0.0	0.0	4.0	15.0
Final SG	0.990	0.990	1.015	1.060
% Alc./Vol.	10.6 - 12.7	11.3 - 14.1	8.3 - 11.1	10.6 - 13.1
Residual sugar (g/L)	<2.0	<2.0	10 - 40	50 - 200

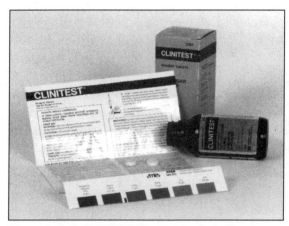

Figure 3-5: A CLINITEST® sugar analysis kit

A tablet dissolved in a specified quantity of wine will cause a colour change. The colour is matched against a set of predetermined concentration colours. This method is quick and simple and provides a gross approximation for wines with less than 20 g/L of residual sugar. If the wine contains ascorbic acid, more commonly known as vitamin C, this method will cause false readings. Refer to section 4.7.1 for more details on the use of ascorbic acid.

To obtain a more accurate reading of the sugar level in musts and dry or sweet wines, a titration-method sugar analysis kit is available in the better winemaking shops. A typical sugar analysis kit, shown in Figure 3-6, can measure sugar concentrations from 1.0 to 200 g/L. Its main dis-

Figure 3-6: A titraton-method sugar analysis kit

advantage is that the measurement procedure requires more time and effort to perform.

The titration-method sugar analysis kit uses copper sulphate-based and thiosulphate-based solutions. The solutions are mixed and boiled, and wine is added incrementally until the blue colour disappears completely. Using a conversion table provided with the kit, the amount of wine used is converted into the amount of sugar present.

3.1.2 Chaptalization—Correcting the sugar content

Chaptalization, the practice of adding sugar to musts or wines to increase the alcohol content and/or to produce a sweet wine, is a shunned procedure among traditional-minded winemakers. However, this practice is perfectly acceptable and is widely used in cooler-climate winemaking regions of the world, such as Burgundy, where grapes may not always reach the desired sugar level.

When chaptalizing the must, it is advisable to add fermentable sugar just after the start of fermentation. The must is richer in yeast content at the start and will therefore favour fermentation of the added sugar. It is then recommended to add sugar in stages to avoid shocking the yeast which could cause fermentation to stop. Successive chaptalization will also have the benefit of prolonging maceration and fermentation periods which will produce a richer, more complex fuller-bodied wine with greater colour and flavour.

When required to chaptalize musts produced from grapes, one should first estimate the total volume of must to be chaptalized in order to add a reasonably approximate amount of sugar. This is required since the volume of must cannot be determined with exactitude until after pressing. A simple estimation rule is to assume a yield of approximately 10 L of juice for every 16.3-kg (36-lb) case of grapes. This estimation depends on the grape variety (certain varieties such as Cabernet Sauvignon have a smaller yield than others), on the amount of pressure exerted during the pressing operation, and on the vintage quality. A wet vintage will produce grapes with a high water content therefore increasing yield.

Appendix B illustrates how to determine the amount of fermentable sugar in a litre or gallon of must based on the Brix (SG) reading. This will provide assistance in measuring the amount of additional fermentable sugar needed to achieve a desired final alcohol level. As a rule of thumb, adding 17 g of fermentable sugar—dextrose (corn sugar) or sucrose (beet or cane sugar)—per litre will raise the alcohol content by 1% alc./vol, or 9.2 g/L will raise the Brix by 1 B°.

Sugar should first be dissolved in a small quantity of warm must and then cooled off before being added into the three-quarter full fermentor. If the must being added is too hot, the resident yeast population (necessary for a successful fermentation) in the fermentor may be shocked. When fermentation begins and becomes vigourous, the sugar should be added progressively in stages all the while ensuring that fermentation continues without any problems especially since chaptalization will raise the fermentation temperature, and too high a temperature can cause fermentation to stop. Also, over-chaptalization may inhibit start of fermentation, as the yeast cannot start activity with excessive sugar. Chaptalization of a fermenting must will cause a lot of foaming. Therefore, containers should be filled to no more than three-quarters to avoid over-foaming, not to mention a messy floor. In addition, total production capacity should be recalculated, as each kg of sugar added will increase the must volume by approximately 0.7 L.

To determine the final % alc./vol. when chaptalizing in stages, the **potential** % alc./vol. must be re-measured and the amount of alcohol produced must be re-calculated before each sugar addition. Here is an example of final % alc./vol. determination when chaptalizing in stages.

	B°	SG	Potential % alc./vol.	Actual change in % alc./vol.
Initial reading	20.0	1.080	10.6	
Second reading	15.0	1.060	7.8	} 2.8
First chaptalization	16.5	1.065	8.6	
Reading	14.0	1.055	7.2	} 1.4
Second chaptalization	15.0	1.060	7.8	
Final reading	0.0	0.990	0.0	} 7.8

The final alcohol content of the chaptalized wine would therefore be 2.8 + 1.4 + 7.8 = 12.0% alc./vol. The non-chaptalized must would have resulted in a wine with 10.6% alc./vol. if fermented to dryness.

To sweeten a wine by chaptalization, non-fermentable sugar should be added once the wine has been cleared and stabilized. Fermentable sugar should **never** be added to a finished wine to produce a sweet wine as this type of sugar may ferment in the bottle and cause it to explode. A wine sweetener-conditioner (made from concentrated grape juice or liquid-invert sugar) should be used and added at a rate of 12-25 mL/L of cleared and stabilized wine. This super-sweet syrup, which reduces the ageing time of the wine, also contains potassium sorbate (refer to section 4.7.1) to prevent renewed fermentation.

The sweetener-conditioner made from concentrated grape juice gives better results as the juice content enhances the flavour and aromas of wine. This is not the case with the sweetener-conditioner made from liquid-invert sugar.

An alternative method to chaptalization for sweetening wines is to stop fermentation so that the finished wine has naturally occurring residual sugar. This method is described in section 4.5.4.

3.2 ACID ANALYSIS AND CONTROL

The concentration of all acids, or total acidity, in wines must be balanced with the sweetness and astringency (from tannins) for each wine style. For example, a dry (no perceptible sweetness) Chardonnay requires less acidity than a syrupy Sauternes or an icewine. Excessive acidity—considered a serious wine fault—will result in a green, tart or acidulous and unbalanced wine, and it will diminish the drinking pleasure. Too little acidity, on the other hand, will cause the wine to be flabby, thin or flat.

The need for balance is essential because acidity, sweetness and astringency represent three of the four primary taste areas on our tongue (the fourth, although not relevant in wine tasting, is saltiness).

Winemakers must therefore strike a balance, which requires the ability to quantify acidity and to control it through all stages of winemaking. This allows a better understanding of the effects of acidity on a wine's evolution and ultimately its sensory evaluation when drinking wine. Acidity is also essential in preserving wine and provides the backbone in age-worthy wines.

Grapes contain many different naturally-occurring (organic or fixed) acids, three of which are of œnological significance: tartaric, malic and citric acids. Lactic acid is only present in trace amounts.

Total acidity is relatively high when grapes first start ripening and then subsides during maturation on the vines as the hard malic acid decreases. Grapes are harvested when the acidity level, established by the viticulturist and winemaker, is typically between 6 and 9 g/L. This represents the acid concentration in grape juice at picking and must be balanced with the sugar content, typically in the range 21 to 23 B° (SG between 1.085 and 1.095).

The amount of sun exposure and rainfall during grape ripening and harvest affect the acid concentration as well as concentration of sugars, aromas, and eventually flavours in the final wine. Failure to harvest at the desired acidity and sugar levels will result in an unbalanced wine.

During vinification and winemaking, the acids change: Tartaric and malic acid concentrations decrease slightly while lactic acid is formed. There are other acids in wine, but they exist in trace amounts only—including citric acid. Therefore, the three acids of œnological significance are: tartaric, malic and lactic.

Tartaric acid is the most significant and the strongest of these acids in both grapes and wine, and is responsible for making a wine lively and fresh. Malic acid imparts a sharp, green-apple sensation. Many winemakers find malic acid undesirable and thus convert it to lactic acid, a much softer acid, by malolactic (ML) fermentation. Citric acid is often undesirable since its sour taste does not complement wines well, and also interferes with vinification processes such as ML fermentation. Refer to section 4.6 for a detailed discussion on ML fermentation.

Acetic acid is another important acid in winemaking and is the main component of volatile acidity (VA). It is produced only in small quantity during the alcoholic fermentation phase if controlled properly using a low-VA producing yeast strain (refer to section 4.5).

A small amount of VA is necessary to appreciate the wine's bouquet. In quantities nearing or exceeding 1.0 g/L, the wine definitely becomes acetic. This fault can be easily detected as the familiar vinegar smell, and indicates the presence of spoilage microorganisms, which is primarily a result of over-exposure to air. ML fermentation will also increase the amount of acetic acid by transforming any citric acid present. For this reason, wines to be ML-fermented should have a low citric acid component.

Home winemakers need not be concerned with measuring VA since a qualitative analysis is sufficient and because it requires extensive laboratory equipment and experience to perform the measurement. A wine affected by excessive acetic acid (a condition known as acetification) should be discarded. It should never be blended as an attempt to improve it—it will not!

Total titratable acidity (TA) is used to quantify a wine's acidity, not including VA, and it represents the concentration of all organic acids in the wine. TA is expressed in grams per liters (g/L) or, quite often, as a percentage of weight to volume. For example, a wine with a TA of 7.0 g/L is said to contain 0.70% total acidity.

Table 3-3
Recommended TA and pH ranges for different types of must and wine

Type of wine	TA range for must (g/L)	TA range for wine (g/L)	pH range for must and wine
Dry white	7.0 - 9.0	5.0 - 7.5	3.1 - 3.4
Dry red	6.0 - 8.0	4.0 - 5.5	3.3 - 3.6
Sweet white	7.5 - 9.0	5.5 - 7.5	3.1 - 3.2

Since all acids are factored into the TA measurement and not all have the same chemical properties, a reference point is used to qualify the measurement. In North America, tartaric acid is used as the reference whereas Europe uses sulfuric acid. This means that, in North America, the TA value represents acid concentration as if it were only tartaric acid. Multiply this value by 0.65 to convert it to TA expressed as sulfuric acid. In this book, all TA measurements are expressed as tartaric acid. In the example above, a TA of 7.0 g/L then represents 7.0 g of equivalent tartaric acid in 1 L of must or wine.

Table 3-3 lists the recommended TA ranges for different types of musts and wines.

Note: *"Total acidity" and "total titratable acidity" are used interchangeably in the winemaking industry although they have different meanings. The former includes volatile acidity whereas the latter pertains to fixed acids only. In this book, total acidity will mean total titratable acidity for brevity and because it is widely used.*

3.2.1 Measuring total titratable acidity (TA)

A wine's total titratable acidity (TA) is measured by a very simple titration procedure, which involves neutralizing the acid content of a wine sample with a base solution (the titrate solution, or simply the titrate). Titrate-method acid testing kits, such as the one shown in Figure 3-7, are readily available in home winemaking shops.

The titration procedure makes use of a colour indicator solution (phenolphthalein) to determine the point where the acid becomes titrated. A sodium hydroxide (NaOH) solution is used as the titrate. It is generally available at a concentration of $0.1N^3$ or 0.2N. The sodium hydroxide solution concentration is often omitted on the product label. It is therefore important to inquire before performing an acid test. The kit also includes 10-mL and 20-mL syringes, an eyedropper and a test tube.

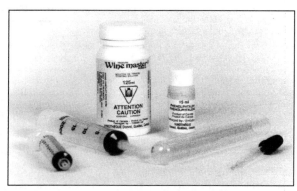

Figure 3-7: A titration-method acid testing kit

To measure the TA of a wine, 15 mL of must or wine should be transferred to a test tube. Any residual carbon dioxide should be removed to ensure a proper reading. Using an eyedropper, 3 drops of phenolphthalein colour indicator solution should be added to the test tube. 10 mL of 0.2N titrate solution should then be measured with a syringe.

The titrate solution is then added to the test tube 0.5 mL at a time until a colour change is noticed. The test tube should be shaken until the colour change is permanent. A **colour change** indicates that the solution is being neutralized. The colour changes to **pink** for **white wines**. For **red wines**, the colour will first turn **grayish green** and then back to a **pinkish** colour signifying the end of titration.

When the colour change has occurred, the amount of titrate solution used should be recorded, i.e., 10 mL less the amount left. Each mL of titrate solution indicates an acid concentration of 1.0 g/L expressed as tartaric acid. For example, if 6.5 mL of titrate solution is used, the must or wine has an acid concentration of 6.5 g/L. When using a 0.1N titrate solution, 20 mL will be required to start the test. The result should be divided by 2 to obtain the acid concentration. Using the above example, 13 mL of titrate solution would be used to obtain the colour change. Therefore, the acid concentration would still be 6.5 g/L.

An alternate, commonly-used method using a 0.1N sodium hydroxide solution to measure TA of wines requires adding 100 mL of

---

[3]N stands for Normality. This is a measurement method in chemistry used to denote the concentrations of solutions used in titration.

distilled water to a 5 mL sample of must or wine in a glass container. Five drops of phenolphthalein should then be added. Similar to the previous procedure, sodium hydroxide is added and the sample is stirred until the colour change is permanent. The amount of sodium hydroxide (NaOH) used determines the TA as follows:

TA in g/L (expressed as tartaric acid) = 1.5 x mL of NaOH used

The generalized equation to determine TA for any volume of must or wine sample and any concentration of NaOH titrate solution is as follows:

$$\text{TA in g/L (expressed as tartaric acid)} = 75 \times \frac{A \times B}{C}$$

where:
    A = mL of NaOH used
    B = Normality of the NaOH solution used
    C = mL of must or wine sample used

The section "*Standardizing sodium hydroxide with potassium acid phthalate*" at the end of this section describes how to compensate for sodium hydroxide solutions that may have lost some strength.

The colour change in red-must or red-wine acid testing may be difficult to notice. A simple trick is to dilute the sample with **distilled** water and viewing it over a bright light. Water addition will not affect the measurement but it will greatly simplify detection of the colour change. Additionally, titration can be performed without phenolph-thalein until the colour changes from red to a greenish blue. Only then is the phenolphthalein added and titration completed until a pink colour persists.

Another simple procedure using a pH meter can be used to measure TA in red wines. Section 3.3 describes the significance of pH in wine analysis and how to use a pH meter.

The pH meter should be re-calibrated using a pH 7.0 buffer solution for an accurate reading. 15 mL of must or wine should be transferred to a beaker. A 10-mL syringe should be filled with a 0.2N sodium hydroxide titrate solution. With the pH meter held in the beaker in the sample must or wine, the titrate solution should be added 0.5 mL at a time while continuously swirling the beaker. The pH

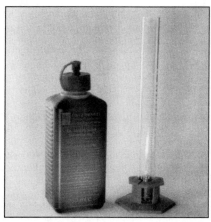

Figure 3-8: Fritz Merkel acid test kit

meter reading will start climbing. Titration is completed when it has reached a pH value of 8.2. The number of mL of titrate solution used can be used to determine the TA, as in the previous procedure.

Fritz Merkel, a German company, now produces a simplified version of the acid test kit for total titratable acidity measurements. The kit, shown in Figure 3-8, sold under the SULFACOR® brand name, consists of 250 mL of an ink-blue test solution and a graduated cylinder. The kit can measure total titratable acidity between 0-15 g/L in 0.5 g/L increments. The TA scale is identified as "Säure g/l" on the cylinder. The test solution should be stored in an airtight container to extend its shelf life.

To measure a wine's total titratable acidity using the Fritz Merkel kit, a must or wine sample should be transferred to the cylinder. As in the previous test method, any residual carbon dioxide should be removed to ensure a proper reading. The sample's meniscus level should be brought to the zero mark located at the bottom of the cylinder. Using an eyedropper, the test solution is added drop by drop to the sample. The cylinder should be shaken after each drop is added to properly stir the sample. Drops should be added until the sample turns to a **dark greenish** colour. Viewing the sample against a white background will greatly help detect the colour change. At that point, single drops of test solution should be added until the sample turns to a **dark blue** colour. The cylinder should be shaken vigorously while covering the opening with the thumb. The test is complete when this colour change occurs. Total titratable acidity can then be measured by reading the sample's meniscus level on the cylinder with the result expressed in g/L.

TA should be measured before start of fermentation, following malolactic fermentation, at the end of fermentation once the wine has been stabilized, and following any acid correction procedures. Measuring during fermentation will not give an accurate reading, as this will be affected by carbon dioxide unless this gas is removed by a vigourous stirring in combination with some heat.

Standardizing sodium hydroxide with potassium acid phthalate

The sodium hydroxide titrate solution must be kept in a properly-stoppered bottle to maintain its shelf life. It should be used within 6 to 9 months from the date of purchase, otherwise it will lose strength. The phenolphthalein colour indicator solution, on the other hand, has a very long shelf life.

The strength of the sodium hydroxide titrate solution can be tested against a standard potassium acid phthalate (KaPh) solution. The test result will help determine if and how to adjust TA results when the titrate solution has lost strength. Alternatively, a new container of fresh titrate solution can be purchased and the old one discarded.

The strength, or Normality (N), of the sodium hydroxide (NaOH) solution is determined by titrating a known quantity of potassium acid phthalate (KaPh) solution and about 5 drops of phenolphthalein. The following equation is then used:

$$\text{Normality of NaOH} = \frac{A \times B}{C}$$

where:

    A = mL of KaPh solution used
    B = Normality of the KaPh solution
    C = mL of NaOH solution used

As with titration for determining TA, the sodium hydroxide solution is added in 0.1 mL increments and then the sample is stirred until the pink colour disappears. Sodium hydroxide is added until the pink colour persists; the titration point has then been reached.

For example, if 5.3 mL of NaOH solution was used to titrate 5 mL of 0.1N KaPh solution, the Normality of the NaOH would be 5x0.1/5.3=0.094 or 0.094N.

A wine's TA can then be corrected using the following equation:

$$\text{Corrected TA in g/L (expressed as tartaric acid)} = \frac{D \times E}{F}$$

where:

    D = Measured TA in g/L expressed as tartaric acid
    E = Normality of the NaOH solution
        (determined above)
    F = Theoretical Normality of the NaOH solution

For example, if the "0.1N" sodium hydroxide has been determined to be 0.094N, and the measured TA of the wine is 6.5 g/L, then the corrected TA is 6.5x0.094/0.1=6.1 or 6.1 g/L.

3.2.2 Correcting total titratable acidity (TA)

The TA of concentrated and sterilized juices is often adjusted during their preparation for commercialization. Generally, home winemakers need not be concerned with TA correction for these musts. It is good practice, however, to always measure TA to ensure a proper balance in the juice. In the case of musts and/or wines produced from grapes and fresh grape juices, the TA should always be measured as it may require adjustments.

The most common methods used to correct the TA in musts and wines are: 1) the addition of acid or an acid blend, 2) the blending of musts or wines, 3) the addition of an acid-reducing solution, 4) malolactic fermentation, 5) cold stabilization, or 6) the addition of water. The processes of increasing and decreasing acidity are referred to as acidification and deacidification, respectively. Deacidification is more commonly referred to simply as acid reduction.

Although all methods increase or decrease total acidity, each method acts on different acids and therefore yields different results in the final acid composition (acid type and concentration) of the wine. Selection of an acidification or acid reduction process should therefore be based on the desired acid to be increased or decreased. As tartaric acid is the most important and most desired acid in wines, the effect of any acid-correcting method on tartaric acid concentration should always be assessed carefully. Paper chromatography tests, described in section 4.6.3, can be used to determine acid components in a wine.

Acidification by addition of acid or an acid blend is an effective method. It is recommended to add acid before the start of fermentation to allow the acid to evolve with the wine and to contribute to its organoleptic qualities. Acid balance affected by alcoholic fermentation can also be corrected when the wine has been stabilized, particularly if acid reduction is required.

The recommended acidification method, however, is to blend a higher-acid wine with the lower-acid one. This method is preferred since it does not use additives and the results are predictable. The only disadvantage is that wines of different TA levels may not always be available when required to perform acid correction. Properly stabilized wines should be used for acid correction by blending.

The addition of an acid-reducing solution is an effective method for acid reduction. The recommended acid reduction methods, however, are to blend a lower-acid wine with the higher-acid one, by malolactic fermentation, or by cold stabilization (refer to section 4.7.2). The addition of water is not a recommended practice as this will dilute the wine and therefore dilute aromas, colour and key ingredients necessary for the wine's stability. This method reduces acidity by diluting all acids present.

Addition of acid or acid blend

To increase the TA using the addition method, tartaric acid only, a blend of tartaric and malic acids, or a 3:2:1 blend of tartaric, malic and citric acids are available. Tartaric acid is the preferred additive, especially if the wine is to undergo malolactic fermentation since the malic acid found in acid blends does not convert, and is highly recommended for high pH wines. As a rule of thumb, 1 g of acid per litre of must or wine increases total acidity by 1 g/L.

Acid blends containing all three acids should be used with caution. These may contain a high concentration of citric acid and, therefore, are not recommended as wine additives. Citric acid has an excessively sour taste and is also partly transformed into the undesirable acetic acid during malolactic fermentation. Acetic acid contributes to volatile acidity. Malolactic fermentation of citric acid will also impart an undesirable off-flavour. Therefore, the use of citric acid is generally not recommended for premium-quality wines.

When adding tartaric acid, wine should be stabilized to prevent acid reduction through precipitation of tartaric acid as tartrate crystals when cold stabilizing. In this case, the most effective stabilization method involves the use of metatartaric acid (refer to section 4.7.2) which prevents crystallization of the tartaric acid. Alternatively, the addition of tartaric acid can be over-compensated to balance crystallization during cold stabilization. This latter method is not recommended if acid reduction and cold stabilization cannot be monitored and controlled accurately.

Tartaric acid crystals are used at the rate of 1 g/L of wine to increase total acidity by 1 g/L. The crystals should first be dissolved in a small volume of wine and then the tartaric acid solution is added to the batch of wine, before the start of fermentation. If the wine will be cold stabilized, the rate of addition can be increased to 2 g/L.

Blending
To increase or reduce acidity in a wine using the blending method, the TA of both wines to be blended must be known. To determine the required volume of wine, of a specific acidity, to correct another volume of wine with a different TA, the following formula (derived from the Pearson Square, refer to section 6.2) can be used:

$$C = \text{Desired TA} = \frac{(A \times D) + (B \times E)}{(D + E)}$$

where:
A = TA of wine to be corrected
B = TA of wine being used as a blend
D = volume of wine to be corrected
E = volume of wine being used as a blend

The required volume E of the blending wine can then be determined by re-arranging the above equation as follows:

$$E = \frac{D \times (C - A)}{(B - C)}$$

For example, to increase the TA of 20 L of wine from 5.0 to 6.0 g/L using a 7.5-g/L blend wine would require approximately:

$$E = \frac{20 \times (0.60 - 0.50)}{(0.75 - 0.60)} = 13.3 \text{ L of blend wine}$$

This example illustrates the importance of maintaining acidic balance during vinification. Acid correction by blending requires a large volume of blend wine to achieve an incremental TA.

Addition of an acid-reducing solution
Acid reduction in a finished wine using an acid-reducing solution uses a potassium bicarbonate or calcium carbonate solution. Both solutions will first reduce tartaric acid. Therefore, care should be taken to prevent reducing the tartaric acid completely. Potassium bicarbonate is excellent for acid reduction, whereas, calcium carbonate is not recommended as it imparts an unappealing earthy taste to wine. It is

therefore important to verify the active ingredient when buying a generic, no-name acid-reducing solution.

Potassium bicarbonate powder should be used at the rate of 2 g/L of wine for a TA reduction of 1 g/L. The potassium bicarbonate powder should first be dissolved in a small quantity of wine (not water) and then added to the batch of wine. The wine should be tasted and re-measured before further additions are made. This method will cause some precipitation of potassium bitartrate solids—which will further reduce the TA—that will need to be separated by racking after 6 to 8 weeks of cellaring. The precipitation period will depend on the cellar temperature. If the wine will be cold stabilized, the rate of addition of potassium bicarbonate powder should be reduced to 1 g/L.

Specially formulated chemicals are also available for reduction of both tartaric and malic acids in musts or wines with a high TA but low tartaric acid content. Such musts or wines may have an unusually high malic acid content as a result of a poor vintage where grapes did not fully ripen. Two such chemical products, marketed under the ACIDEX® and SIHADEX® brand names, can be used to reduce tartaric and malic acids in approximately equal parts by precipitating them in their salt forms—a chemical process known as double salt precipitation. This process involves total reduction of both acids in a calculated, pre-measured must or wine volume, and then blending this volume with the remaining batch. The volume of must or wine to be deacidified is calculated based on the total volume of must or wine, the actual TA, and the desired TA. For example[4], to reduce the TA of 500 L of wine from 12.0 to 7.0 g/L, 278 L should first be deacidified using approximately 1.7 kg of SIHADEX®, and then blended with the remaining volume. The advantage of these products is that the precipitated solids can be separated from the must or wine within 30 minutes of completing the acid-reduction process.

Note: *Manufacturers' instructions for using ACIDEX® and SIHADEX® should be followed carefully to ensure proper results.*

Malolactic fermentation
ML fermentation is a natural and effective method for reducing TA, which converts the harsher malic acid into the softer lactic acid. It is widely accepted by commercial winemakers, including traditionalists.

---

[4]Based on SIHADEX® Technical Information, E. BEGEROW GmbH & Co., Germany.

It is considered a traditional and natural method as opposed to chemical additives.

The only drawback of ML fermentation is in trying to determine the quantitative impact on TA. No readily accessible tools are available to home winemakers to measure the exact amount of malic acid present, which is then converted to lactic acid. Therefore, predicting the change in TA is difficult. It is suggested to allow wine to undergo the ML fermentation and then measure the TA once this fermentation is completed or stopped. The drop in TA is the change between the value at the start of ML fermentation and at the end. Acidity can then be adjusted up or down by other methods described here if the TA is still not at the desired level. If the final TA is within the recommended range, it is best not to alter it at this point.

ML fermentation is discussed in depth in section 4.6.

Cold stabilization

Another natural and effective method for decreasing TA in wines is cold stabilization. It is not usually used specifically to decrease, but rather to prevent precipitation of tartrate crystals once the wine is bottled. These are the crystals found at the bottom of a bottle, which had not been cold stabilized and which has been left in the fridge for too long.

The procedure involves placing the wine in cold storage at a temperature between -4° and 4° C (25° and 40° F) for a minimum of three weeks and then racking it. This has the effect of precipitating some tartaric acid as tartrate crystals (potassium bitartrate salt), which decreases acidity and hence TA.

The precise amount of potassium bitartrate to be precipitated is hard to control because of temperature and duration factors. Therefore, it is recommended to cold stabilize the wine, measure the TA, and then adjust accordingly.

Refer to section 4.7.2 for additional information on cold stabilization.

Note: *Cold stabilization may increase **or** decrease a wine's pH depending on the starting pH level before cold stabilization. Refer to section 3.3.2 for more details.*

Table 3-4
Effects of the different acidification and acid reduction
methods on the different acids in wine

Acidification / acid reduction method	Effect on TA (tartaric acid)	Effect on TA (citric acid)	Effect on TA (malic acid)	Effect on TA (lactic acid)
Addition of tartaric acid	increase			
Addition of tartaric/malic/ citric acid blend	increase	increase	increase	
Blending of musts/wines[5]	increase or decrease	increase or decrease	increase or decrease	increase or decrease
Potassium bicarbonate solution	decrease			
ACIDEX® or SIHADEX®	decrease		decrease	
Malolactic (ML) fermentation		decrease[6]	decrease	increase
Cold stabilization	decrease			
Addition of water	decrease	decrease	decrease	decrease

[5]Effects on acids depend on acid components present in blending wines. [6]ML fermentation reduces citric acid and partly transforms it into acetic acid, therefore increasing VA.

Table 3-4 summarizes the effects on the concentration of each acid component in a wine for each acidification and acid reduction method.

3.3 pH ANALYSIS AND CONTROL

Lisa Van de Water, of the Wine Lab at Napa, best summarized the importance of the effects of pH on wines, as reported by Donald E. Gauntner in the American Wine Society Journal, Winter Issue, 1997.

"At **lower pH**, red wines are redder, fresher, fruitier, younger tasting for their age, slower to age, slower to mature, less complex, less full-bodied, much slower to spoil, and easier to maintain free of spoilage in the cellar because the SO_2 is more active at the lower pH."

"**Higher pH** wines, if they are red, are less red (sometimes brown, sometimes purple), less fresh, less fruity, more complex, more full-bodied, faster to age, faster to mature, easier to spoil, and more difficult to manage in the cellar with SO_2."

The relationship between pH and sulphur dioxide (SO_2) is discussed in section 3.4.

Clearly, pH plays an important role in determining the quality of a wine. Yet, all too often, home winemakers shy away from understanding the effects of pH on wine and from performing measurements to ensure that wines remain trouble-free from vineyard to winery to table.

PH is a close relative of acidity, specifically, total titratable acidity (TA) for wines. TA measures the acid concentration in musts and wines, while pH measures the relative strength of those acids. And the pH of wines depends on the pH of the grape juice (must), which in turn depends on such factors as grape variety, type of soil, viticultural practices such as irrigation, the climate during grape ripening, and the timing of the harvest. For example, soils rich in potassium or grapes harvested during heavy rainfalls will tend to have a higher pH.

Two wines with similar TA measurements but different pH will be very different and will also evolve differently. A wine with lower pH may show a redder colour (in the case of red wines) with greater stability during ageing, and will have more fruit and less complexity and body than the higher pH wine. The lower pH wine will also mature more slowly—and therefore age longer—and will be less susceptible to spoilage. Therefore, TA is not sufficient when evaluating a wine. We also need to understand the relative strength of the acid components, or its pH. It is imperative then to always monitor and control a wine's pH to ensure that it does not fall below or rise above critical thresholds.

Technically, pH is the negative logarithm of the effective hydrogen ion concentration or hydrogen ion activity, i.e. $pH = -\log_{10}[H^+]$. As such, pH is often referred to as active acidity. Great! But what does it really mean?

Solutions (such as wine) can have a pH in the range 0 to 14. A pH of 0 represents a strong acid solution while a pH of 14 represents a strong alkaline solution. Distilled water has a theoretical pH of 7, and wines are in the range of 3 to 4. More specifically, the pH level of musts and wines should be within the recommended range shown in Table 3-3 for a desired style of wine.

The pH level is closely related to TA and they are interdependent. Adjustment of either parameter will typically affect the other; however, their relationship is a complex one. TA and pH are not proportional although, generally, raising the TA will result in lowering of the pH, and vice versa. There are cases, however, in which one can reduce both the TA and pH, for example. Refer to section 3.3.2 on how to reduce both the TA and pH in wine.

A low-pH wine will taste tart, owing to the higher acid concentration. Conversely, a high-pH wine will taste flat and lack freshness. A high-pH wine also will tend to oxidize at a higher rate and therefore will not age as well. It will be more prone to microbial spoilage, thus requiring more sulfite to protect it. High-pH white wines will tend to brown prematurely. In the case of red wines, colour intensity decreases as the pH increases causing the wine to change from a red to brownish-red colour.

The importance of monitoring and controlling the pH level is also illustrated by the fact that a wine with a pH of 3 is ten times more acidic than a wine with a pH of 4. Using more representative pH values for wine, a batch with a pH of 3.2 is approximately 25 percent more acidic than a wine with a pH of 3.3.

Home winemakers need to be concerned with pH levels that fall outside of the recommended ranges, and take corrective actions as quickly as possible. Slight pH variations within the ranges are not as critical, except when adjusting the free sulfur dioxide (SO_2) level. They only become important in specific situations, such as ML fermentation, when the pH level definitely should not fall below the prescribed minimum.

3.3.1 Measuring the pH level

A crude approximation of a wine's active acidity, or pH, can be measured using pH paper. To determine the pH of musts or wines, a strip of pH paper is immersed in the must or wine and the colour of the paper is then matched to a standard set of colours. Each colour corresponds to a specific pH level. PH paper, however, provides results with a wide margin of inaccuracy, ±1 pH unit and is therefore, not a recommended method for precise analysis. The recommended method to measure the pH level is using a pH meter, as the one shown in Figure 3-9, with a resolution of 0.1 and an accuracy of ±0.1 pH unit.

Similar to total titratable acidity, the pH level should be measured before start of fermentation, following malolactic fermentation, at the end of fermentation once the wine has been stabilized, and following any pH correction procedures. PH can also be monitored during alcoholic fermentation since pH is more accurate than TA measurements during this phase. For this purpose, carbon dioxide gas should be removed by a vigorous stirring in combination with some heat to ensure a proper reading. Remember to let the sample cool back down to room temperature before taking a reading.

To measure the pH level using a pH meter, the instrument must first be conditioned and calibrated with pre-measured pH solutions according to the manufacturer's instructions. This involves dipping the pH meter probe in a 7.0 pH buffer solution, waiting for the meter to calibrate, and repeating this procedure with a 4.0 pH buffer solution. After calibration, the probe is simply immersed in a sample of must or wine to take a measurement. Any carbon dioxide present in the must or wine must be removed by stirring and by applying heat to ensure an accurate reading.

Note: Buffer solutions for calibrating pH meters have a limited shelf life. Always use fresh solutions to ensure proper measurements.

3.3.2 Correcting the pH level

As with TA, the pH levels of concentrates and sterilized juices are adjusted during their preparation for commercialization. Generally, home winemakers need not be concerned with pH correction for these musts. Still, it is good practice to keep a log of pH measurements to detect potential problems early. In the case of musts and/or wines produced from grapes or fresh grape juice, the pH level should always be measured as it may require adjustments.

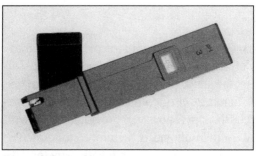

The same methods used to correct the TA are used to correct pH in musts and wines. These methods include: 1) the

Figure 3-9: A pH meter

addition of acid or an acid blend, 2) the blending of musts or wines, 3) the addition of a pH-augmenting solution, 4) ML fermentation, 5) cold stabilization, or 6) the addition of water. It should be remembered that, in general, TA and pH work in opposite directions, i.e., raising the TA decreases the pH, and vice versa. There are exceptions, however, as discussed below.

Although all methods increase or decrease pH, each method acts on different acids and therefore yields different results in the final acid composition (acid type and concentration) of the wine. Selection of a pH-adjustment method should therefore be based on the desired acid to be increased or decreased for a desired pH change. As tartaric acid is the most important and most desired acid in wines, the effect of any pH-correcting method on tartaric acid concentration should always be assessed carefully.

Addition of acid or an acid blend
Tartaric acid addition is an effective method to lower the pH in high-pH wines because it is the strongest acid, it is present in higher concentrations than other acids, and is also easy to control. Tartaric acid addition causes acidity and TA to increase, which in turn lowers the pH. Acid blends achieve the same results; however, they may contain citric acid, which is not a recommended wine additive since it has an excessively sour taste. It is also partly transformed into the undesirable acetic acid, responsible for the vinegary smell and taste, during alcoholic fermentation and ML fermentation. The addition of an acid blend with no citric acid is therefore recommended.

Tartaric acid crystals are used at the rate of approximately 1 g/L of wine to reduce the pH by 0.1 unit. The crystals should first be dissolved in a small volume of wine. The solution is then added to the must, i.e. before the start of fermentation. If the wine will be cold stabilized, the rate of addition can be increased to 2 g/L.

It is important that the tartaric acid addition be done before the start of fermentation. The pre-fermentation acid addition raises the TA, and hence lowers the pH. During alcoholic fermentation and ML fermentation, TA decreases causing the pH to increase. The pre-fermentation addition reduces the risk of the pH increasing above the range where sulphite loses effectiveness. Adding the tartaric acid post alcoholic and ML fermentations, there is a risk of shooting the pH too high. Section 3.4 further explains this relationship between pH and SO$_2$, and discusses its importance.

When adding acid blends, the same rate of addition as tartaric acid should be used, then a measurement should be taken, and adjustments are made as necessary. Trial and error is required when making adjustments because the ratio of acids in the blends is not usually known. However, since they contain malic and maybe citric acid, the blend will be less acidic than a purely tartaric acid blend. The rate of addition would then have to be increased slightly to achieve similar results.

Blending

Blending is a highly recommended method for adjusting pH in wines since it is a natural method not involving the use of chemical additives. It can be used for either increasing or decreasing the pH. Its only drawback is that one may not always have the required wines with the needed pH to obtain the desired result.

Given this drawback, the best way to proceed in making any correction is to blend the wine to be corrected with another wine of known pH. If the wine to be corrected requires the pH to be increased, then a higher-pH wine should be used for blending. Similarly, a lower-pH wine should be used if the pH needs to be decreased.

Mathematical determination of the resulting pH in a blended wine is complex. An easier method is to calculate the TA of the blended wine using the Pearson Square calculation, verifying the calculation by titration, and then measuring the pH. Any required adjustments to achieve the desired TA/pH are made.

On rare occasions, a wine will turn out to have both a high TA and a high pH. The TA may be acceptable, but it may be desired to reduce the pH without affecting the TA. The ideal solution would be to blend this wine with another having the same high TA but a low pH. This is quite a challenge since most home winemakers do not have reserves of that many different wines.

Addition of a pH-augmenting solution

PH in wines can also be increased effectively using potassium bicarbonate or other pH-augmenting agents, such as ACIDEX® or SIHADEX®.

Potassium bicarbonate raises pH by reducing tartaric acid and is therefore recommended for high-TA, low-pH wines. Potassium bicarbonate should be dissolved at a rate of 1 g/L of wine for each 0.1 unit increase in pH. For example, for a 19-L batch of wine with a pH of 3.2, 38 g of potassium bicarbonate is required to increase the pH to 3.4.

Other products, such as ACIDEX® or SIHADEX®, can be used to increase pH by reducing tartaric and malic acids in approximately equal parts by precipitating them in their salt forms—a chemical process known as double-salt precipitation. The advantage of these products is that the precipitated solids can be separated from the wine within 30 minutes. Follow the manufacturer's instructions as each product may have handling differences.

Malolactic fermentation
ML fermentation is usually used to soften a wine by reducing its TA. It is not used specifically to increase its pH, although it could. Home winemakers still need to quantitatively assess the change in pH due to ML fermentation.

As with TA, a drawback of this method is in trying to determine the quantitative impact on pH. No readily accessible tools are available to home winemakers to measure the exact amount of malic acid present, which is then converted to lactic acid. Therefore, predicting the change in pH is difficult. It is suggested to allow wine to undergo the ML fermentation and then measure the pH once this fermentation is completed or stopped. The increase in pH is the change between the value at the end of ML fermentation and at the start. The pH can then be adjusted up or down by other methods described here if it is still not at the desired level. If the final pH is within the recommended range, it is best not to alter it at this point.

ML fermentation is discussed in depth in section 4.6.

Cold stabilization
As with total acidity (TA), cold stabilization is another natural and effective method for increasing pH in wines. The procedure is the same as for reducing TA, described in section 3.2.2.

It should be noted, however, that the cause-and-effect relationship between cold stabilization and pH depends on a wine's starting pH before cold stabilization.

Cold stabilization precipitates some tartaric acid as tartrate crystals (potassium bitartrate salt), which decreases acidity and hence TA. However, potassium contributes to a higher pH, and when it precipitates during cold stabilization, it lowers the pH. This effect actually happens at a pH of 3.65 (use 3.6 when using a 0.1 precision pH meter) or lower because of the relative concentrations of tartrate and potassium in the wine. At a pH of 3.65 or above, cold stabilization will actually raise the pH.

As a guideline, a 0.1 pH unit increase or decrease can be assumed for every 1 g/L decrease in TA. The precise amount of potassium bitartrate to be precipitated is hard to control because of temperature and duration factors. Therefore, it is recommended to cold stabilize the wine, measure the TA and pH, and then adjust accordingly.

Refer to section 4.7.2 for additional information on cold stabilization.

Water addition

Adding water to wine is a simple method for increasing pH. By adding **distilled** water (tap water may have a significantly different pH than the theoretical value of 7.0, and may also contain undesirable substances such as chlorine), the acids are effectively diluted thereby reducing TA and increasing the pH. Many home winemakers use this method, although it is not practiced and is not allowed in commercial winemaking. The major disadvantage is that the flavours, aromas and bouquet also get diluted resulting in a "watery" wine with less complexity. Therefore, this method should only be used when small pH changes are required to avoid adding too much water.

The pH meter probe is simply inserted in the wine and distilled water is then added until the desired pH is reached. The TA should remain within the recommended range. The pH of the water should also be measured before being added to the wine to better predict results. The reason is that the pH of water may actually change considerably depending on how it was stored.

Phosphoric acid

The addition of phosphoric acid is another method for reducing the pH level of a high-pH, high-TA wine. Its use is not recommended as it affects the taste and texture of wine, and it is actually not allowed as an additive in US commercial winemaking. The advantage of phosphoric acid is that it reduces the pH level without significantly altering TA. For home winemaking, it should be used as a last resort when other pH-reduction techniques are not possible.

One or two drops of a 30% solution should be used per litre of wine. After each addition, the pH level should be measured and the wine re-tasted before any further correction.

Table 3-5
Effects of the different methods of increasing or decreasing pH
on the different acids in wines

Method to increase / decrease pH	Effect on pH (tartaric acid)	Effect on pH (citric acid)	Effect on pH (malic acid)	Effect on pH (lactic acid)
Addition of tartaric acid	decrease			
Addition of tartaric/malic/ citric acid blend	decrease	decrease	decrease	
Blending of musts/wines[7]	increase or decrease	increase or decrease	increase or decrease	increase or decrease
Potassium bicarbonate solution	increase			
ACIDEX® or SIHADEX®	increase		increase	
Malolactic (ML) fermentation		increase[8]	increase	decrease
Cold stabilization[9]	increase or decrease			
Addition of water	increase	increase	increase	increase

[7]Depends on pH of each blending wine. [8]ML fermentation reduces citric acid and partly transforms it into acetic acid, therefore increasing VA. [9]Depends on the pH of the wine at start of cold stabilization.

Table 3-5 summarizes the effects on a wine's pH for each recommended method of increasing or decreasing pH and the acid causing the change.

3.4 SULPHUR DIOXIDE (SO₂) ANALYSIS AND CONTROL

In winemaking, sulphite—a sulphurous acid salt—refers to the antiseptic and antioxidant additive used throughout the winemaking process. Sulphur dioxide (SO_2), a gas formed from elemental sulphur burning and easily detectable as a burnt-match smell, is a major component of sulphite. Sulphur dioxide concentrations in musts and wines are important œnological measurements.

Sulphite plays a key role as a wine preservative in preventing microbial spoilage and premature oxidation. For example, an SO_2 deficiency is one reason why white wines turn brown prematurely. Sulphite is also used to inhibit naturally occurring wild yeasts in musts and to preserve wine. SO_2 is also a natural by-product of fermentation, albeit in small quantities. These small quantities, even when occurring naturally during vinification, do not inhibit either cultured or indigenous (wild) yeasts used in fermenting must.

The taste or smell of SO_2 is considered a serious wine fault. It is therefore imperative that SO_2 levels be kept to a minimum without the risk of wine spoilage. Excessive use of sulphite can negatively impact vinification; for example, a worst-case example of excessive sulphur use would be the inhibition of the alcoholic fermentation. A lesser (but still excessive) use of sulphur would be detectable in the bouquet of the finished wine.

Two SO_2-related measurements are used in the winemaking industry: free SO_2 and bound SO_2. A wine's total SO_2 content is the sum of free and bound SO_2 and is mainly the result of sulphite addition and of yeast fermentation. All SO_2 concentrations are expressed in mg/L or parts per million (ppm).

Free SO_2 comes from the addition of sulphite and is also a by-product of yeast (alcoholic) fermentation. This by-product is not due to sulphur used by some shippers when packing the grapes. It is also produced in wines fermented from juice. Alcoholic fermentation can produce up to 10 mg/L of free SO_2 depending on the type of yeast selected.

In excessive amounts, free SO_2 is characterized by the unpleasant and pungent sulphur smell. Free SO_2 is active and, as such, undergoes chemical transformations altering the sulphite content in wines. The two major transformations include the dissipation of active SO_2 and the combining of SO_2, from free SO_2, with aldehyde compounds to form bound SO_2. The net effect is a reduction in the total SO_2 content. Only free SO_2 has antioxidant and preservative properties. Acetaldehyde is the most prevalent aldehyde compound responsible for oxidation in wine, and is easily detected by its peculiar and unmistakable smell in oxidized wines.

With the free SO_2 content decreasing over time due to oxidation and as a result of winemaking operations—such as racking, which favours aeration—the sulphite's antioxidant and preservative properties diminish in effectiveness. Therefore it is imperative to maintain a nominal free SO_2 level throughout vinification and winemaking operations. As a simple rule of thumb, the recommended maximum free SO_2 level is 50 mg/L. Higher levels of SO_2 can be detected by olfaction. Caution should be taken to avoid having a wine's free SO_2 content fall below 25 mg/L. Otherwise, the wine may risk microbial spoilage. Frequent measurements and adjustments are recommended to avoid running this risk.

Bound SO_2 is difficult to detect by taste and is tolerable at much higher levels than free SO_2.

For the above reasons, only free SO_2 concentrations need to be monitored in home winemaking. A free-SO_2 measurement kit is readily available at winemaking shops whereas no such kit is available to measure the amount of bound SO_2. Bound SO_2 measurements can only be performed in a chemistry laboratory.

The amount of free SO_2 in must or wine is a function of a its pH, total SO_2 concentration and temperature. The precise analytical determination of free SO_2 concentration is quite complex and is beyond the scope of this book. Guidelines for estimating approximate free SO_2 concentrations and required sulphite additions are presented. For home winemaking, these guidelines are acceptable yielding very good results. Readers interested in the chemistry of sulphur dioxide, associated reactions and the chemical relationship between free and bound SO_2 can consult reference II [Peynaud] in Appendix E.

Sources of sulphite
As an additive to musts and wines, sulphite is added as potassium metabisulphite or sodium metabisulphite, both often shortened to metabisulphite, bisulphite or simply sulphite. This causes confusion to

winemakers who prefer the use of the potassium form. Some people who restrict the amount of sodium in their diets prefer not adding sodium metabisulphite.

Potassium metabisulphite is available in powder form while sodium metabisulphite is available in either powder or tablet form. Tablets—known as Campden tablets—have the advantage of providing pre-measured quantities of 0.44 g and are most practical when making small quantities of wine. Tablets are costlier and must be crushed before dissolving in water. Powder is more practical in that the required quantity is easily measured and dissolves much quicker in water than tablets.

Approximately half the amount of metabisulphite sourced from potassium or sodium metabisulphite powder or tablet available to home winemakers will actually provide free SO_2. This is a good approximation if the percent free SO_2 provided is not known. Therefore, as an approximation, it can be assumed that from one part of sulphite added to wine, one-half will become free SO_2. For example, to achieve an additional 25 mg/L of free SO_2, 50 mg/L of sulphite will need to be added. If a wine's free SO_2 concentration is 25 mg/L and the desired level is 50 mg/L, then, 50 mg/L of sulphite will need to be added.

A more accurate calculation can be performed if one knows the percentage of free SO_2 that the source of sulphite provides. Most sources of sulphite contain 57% of SO_2, although some, such as Campden tablets may contain 48%. To calculate the amount of sulphite required, in mg, to achieve a desired free SO_2 level, in mg/L, simply divide the latter by the percent SO_2 content in the sulphite source used.

Using the previous example, to achieve an additional 25 mg/L of free SO_2, 25/.57=44 mg of sulphite powder containing 57% SO_2 would need to be added for each litre of wine. For a 19-L batch of wine, 833 mg, or approximately two 0.44-g Campden tablets, would then be needed.

A dilute sulphite solution can also be prepared in advance and then added, as required, to achieve a desired SO_2 level. This method is discussed in section 3.4.2.

Table 3-6 lists guidelines for recommended levels of free SO_2 for the various winemaking operations when using grapes or fresh juice. For concentrates and sterilized juices, the must should be measured, and adjusted, if needed, to bring the total free SO_2 content to 50 mg/L. These juices are commercialized with sulphite already added.

Table 3-6
Recommended levels of free SO_2 for
various winemaking operations

Operation	Free SO_2 (mg/L)
Crushing of grapes	50
Must preparation ⊸ concentrate ⊸ sterilized juice ⊸ fresh juice	50
Stabilization	50
Bottling	50

Warning: *Some people are allergic to sulphur-based additives, even in small quantities. The use of sulphite should be restricted in such cases.*

Warning: *Sulphite solution releases overpowering fumes and can cause respiratory problems. The solution should be prepared and used in a well-ventilated area.*

To use sulphite as a preservative agent, the required amount of potassium (or sodium) metabisulphite powder or crushed Campden tablets should be dissolved into a small quantity of warm water and then stirred gently into the must or wine. Sulphite powder should not be added directly into the must or wine as it may not dissolve properly. If the must is to undergo ML fermentation, the sulphite dosage should be decreased so as not to exceed the prescribed free SO_2 level, usually less than 15 mg/L. This should take into account the amount of free SO_2 produced during fermentation, typically in the 5-10 mg/L range. Refer to section 4.6.1 for sulphite usage in ML fermentation.

SO_2 and pH
As previously stated, free SO_2 concentration depends on the must's or wine's pH. This is because molecular SO_2 is the active component in

free SO_2, and its effectiveness is dependent on a wine's pH. Specifically, at high pH (low acidity), the effectiveness of SO_2 is greatly reduced and wines are therefore not as well protected against oxidation effects. Sulphite additions must therefore compensate for this. A very simple rule of thumb can be used to determine the amount of free SO_2 required to adequately protect a wine having a specific pH. The amount of SO_2 required is approximately [(pH-3.0)x100)] mg/L for red wines; for white wines add 10 to this value. This calculation assumes that the wine has a pH above 3.0. For example, if a white wine has a pH of 3.4, the amount of free SO_2 should be [(3.4-3.0)x100+10]=50 mg/L. The same wine, but with a pH of 3.7, would require 80 mg/L to maintain the same free SO_2 effectiveness. Consult reference 7 [Margalit] in Appendix E for a thorough discussion of pH and molecular SO_2.

Remember: As pH increases, free SO_2 loses effectiveness, and therefore, more sulphite is required to protect the wine.

3.4.1 Measuring the amount of free SO_2

It is good practice to always measure the amount of free SO_2 in musts and wines before and after any winemaking operation. At a minimum, it should be measured before any sulphite addition to avoid over-sulphiting. All musts made from fresh grapes should be tested post-crush, before any addition of sulphite is undertaken. Shippers most often use sulphur when packing grapes to prevent spoilage in transit.

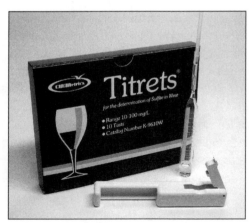

Figure 3-10: A Titrets® sulphite titration kit

The most effective and practical method for determining the amount of free SO_2 is with Ripper-method titration cells that use an iodide-iodate titrant and a starch indicator. The titration cells contain phosphoric acid used to adjust the pH level of the wine sample. Figure 3-10 shows the components of a sulphite titration kit available under the Titrets® brand name and manufactured by CHEMetrics™. This kit can measure between 10 and 100 mg/L of free SO_2, with an error of ±10 mg/L. It includes an ampoule containing the reagent, a valve assembly (shown fitted onto the ampoule) and a Titrettor™, a special holder for Titrets® cells. The Titrettor™ has a bar to control the amount of wine allowed to enter the titration cell. Since the reagent is sealed under vacuum, the titration cells have an unlimited shelf life.

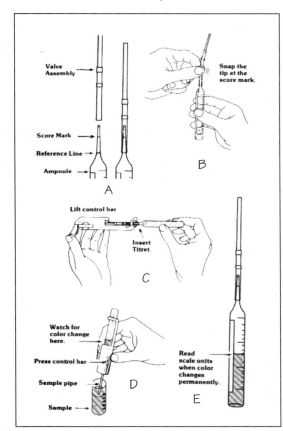

Figure 3-II: How to use a Titrets® sulphite titration kit

Must or wine is allowed to react with the titrant and starch indicator within the titration cell. The amount of free SO_2 is determined by noting the point at which the **deep blue** colour changes to **colourless** for **white** wines, or to the colour of the **red** wine for **red** wines.

Figure 3-II illustrates how to use a Titrets® sulphite titration kit. The valve assembly is first fitted on the ampoule (Figure 3-IIA and B). Once the ampoule is seated in the Titrettor™ (Figure 3-IIC), the tip of the valve assembly is immersed in the test wine sample (Figure 3-IID). The control bar should be pressed firmly but briefly to pull in a small amount of sample. The contents will turn to a deep blue colour. This should be repeated, after waiting 30 seconds, until a colour change is noticed. After each addition, the ampoule should be shaken to mix the content. When the colour of the liquid in the ampoule changes to colourless for white wines, or the colour of the sample for red wines, the ampoule is removed from the Titrettor™. The amount of free SO_2 in mg/L is then read as shown in Figure 3-IIE.

Note: The control bar should not be pressed unless the sample pipe is immersed in the wine sample. Otherwise, air will enter the ampoule and the vacuum may not be sufficient to complete the test.

If the ampoule fills completely without a colour change, i.e., the colour remains blue, the test result is less than 10 mg/L. If the content of the ampoule turns clear immediately—or to the colour of the wine sample—the test result is **greater** than 100 mg/L.

To perform this test for red musts and wines, it is recommended that the must or wine be diluted in water to better see the colour change.

It is recommended to take a measurement at the various winemaking stages for proper free SO_2 content management. Keeping track of all sulphite additions and free SO_2 measurements is a good practice to ensure that musts and wines are within the recommended maximum levels without over-sulphiting. This is specifically important for wines that will undergo malolactic fermentation. This fermentation may not occur if the free SO_2 concentration exceeds the recommended level.

In the case of white wines, this Ripper-method of sulphite content determination is quite accurate. For red wines, the measurement is affected by the presence of phenolic substances—tannin and colour pigments—and ascorbic acid (vitamin C). The free SO_2 content will appear higher than the actual amount present, i.e. it is a false reading. There are no other commercially available methods or products to home winemakers for a more precise determination of free SO_2 content in red musts and wines. Although it is possible to neutralize the ascorbic acid for the test to be valid, the required procedure is beyond the scope of this book. This Ripper-method of sulphite content determination can however be used to confirm the amount of free SO_2 added to musts and wines immediately following sulphiting. For example, if a test measures 15 mg/L of free SO_2 in a red wine (this is a false reading) and 50 mg/L of sulphite are added, a second test immediately following the addition should read $[15 + (50 \div 2)] = 40$ mg/L (only one-half of the sulphite added will become free SO_2).

For vinification where the free SO_2 concentration is critical, e.g. malolactic fermentation, a reading following must preparation or the crushing operation should be taken. The free SO_2 content should theoretically be very low, i.e. less than 10 mg/L, if the must or wine was not previously sulphited, but the test will measure up to 20 or 30 mg/L or more. If adding sulphite before malolactic fermentation and performing another test, the false reading should be subtracted from the new reading to obtain a more precise measurement. For example, when adding 20 mg/L of sulphite to a must with an initial "false" reading of 25 mg/L, the measurement will yield a reading of 35 mg/L ["25" + (20 ÷ 2)]. The actual amount of free SO_2 is 10 mg/L (20 ÷ 2).

3.4.2 Correcting the amount of free SO_2

If the amount of free SO_2 is beyond the prescribed maximum, it can be reduced by successive vigourous aerations until the desired free SO_2 level is reached. Aeration will cause dissipation of free SO_2. This is recommended only if a sulphur smell is detected; otherwise, the procedure will increase the risk of oxidation. Another method is by using hydrogen peroxide. A 1%-hydrogen peroxide solution is added at a rate of 50 g/hL for each 10 mg/L of free SO_2 to be reduced.

Caution: The use of hydrogen peroxide requires chemistry laboratory experience and is therefore only recommended for experienced home winemakers. Excessive addition of hydrogen peroxide can negatively affect the quality of wine. Reference 7 [Margalit] in Appendix E details analytical and laboratory procedures to reduce free SO_2 content.

To increase the amount of free SO_2, the current amount must first be measured, and then sulphite is added until the recommended level of free SO_2 is achieved.

Sulphite additions can be performed by dissolving the required amount of sulphite powder in water (refer to section 3.4 to determine the amount required) or by using a dilute sulphite solution.

For convenience, a dilute sulphite solution can be prepared and stored in a properly stoppered glass container for several months. Beyond one year, much of the SO_2 in the solution is lost therefore rendering it ineffective. A 10% dilute sulphite solution is prepared by dissolving 100 g of sulphite in approximately 500 mL of warm water. When the sulphite has dissolved completely, the total volume of the solution is brought to 1 L by adding cool water, and stirring vigourously. For smaller operations, use 10 g of sulphite in 100 mL of water.

Table 3-7 lists the volume of a 10% sulphite solution, in mL, to be added per litre of must or wine to increase the free SO_2 concentration by the required amount. Each increment of 5 mg/L in the desired free SO_2 concentration will require approximately 0.09 mL/L of must or wine. These amounts are for musts and wines having a pH within the recommended ranges. Adjustments will be required if pH is outside these ranges.

Here are some examples of sulphite additions using a 10% solution to increase the amount of free SO_2:

Example #1
Volume of must or wine = 20 L
Initial free SO_2 concentration in must or wine = 0 mg/L
Desired free SO_2 concentration = 50 mg/L
Required volume of 10% sulphite solution to be added = 20 × 0.88 = 17.6 mL, or approximately 18 mL

Example #2
Volume of must or wine = 20 L
Initial free SO_2 concentration in must or wine = 10 mg/L
Desired free SO_2 concentration = 50 mg/L
Required volume of 10% sulphite solution to be added = 20 × 0.70 = 14 mL

Example #3
Volume of must or wine = 20 L
Initial free SO_2 concentration in must or wine = 10 mg/L
Desired free SO_2 concentration = 25 mg/L
Required volume of 10% sulphite solution to be added = 20 × (0.18 + 0.09) = 5.4 mL, or approximately 5 mL

For sulphite to work properly and effectively, it should be added to must or wine before performing the next winemaking operation. Sulphite's effectiveness would be greatly diminished if it were to be added to must or wine after a racking operation (refer to section 5.1), for example.

It is highly recommended to avoid over-sulphiting and to maintain the free SO_2 content at the prescribed level. Frequent and timely monitoring of musts and wines are required to prevent potential vinification problems due to excessively low or high free SO_2 content.

Table 3-7
SO$_2$ additions from a 10% sulphite solution

Incremental amount of free SO$_2$ (mg/L)	Volume of 10% sulphite solution to be added to each litre of must or wine (mL)
5	0.09
10	0.18
20	0.35
30	0.53
40	0.70
50	0.88
60	1.05
70	1.23
80	1.40
90	1.58
100	1.75

4
MAKING WINE

The general process of making white and red still wines involves a few basic steps. First, all equipment must be thoroughly cleaned and sanitized to avoid any microbial spoilage. The must is then prepared for alcoholic fermentation. When wine is to be made from grapes, crushing, destemming, maceration, and pressing operations will be required before alcoholic fermentation. Maceration is typically used in red winemaking only. Certain types of must can also be malolactic fermented to soften the acidity. The wine is then stabilized to protect it from microbial spoilage, oxidation, renewed fermentation which may occur in the bottle, and cold temperatures. Lastly, the wine is clarified before bottling. Optionally, it can be aged in oak barrels and/or blended with wines from different grape varieties.

The winemaking flowcharts illustrated in Figure I-4 to Figure I-9 on pages 43 to 50 should be used as a reference in the procedure descriptions.

This chapter describes the cleaning process up to, and including, stabilization. Clarification, blending, oak ageing and bottling processes are discussed in chapters 5, 6, 7, and 8, respectively.

4.1 CLEANING AND SANITIZING

The cleaning and sanitizing of winemaking equipment are two vital and compulsory procedures before any must or wine makes contact with equipment and containers including bottles. These procedures are critical in microbial spoilage prevention in wines. Equipment and containers should first be thoroughly cleaned and rinsed with water. These are then sanitized to eradicate microorganisms that could otherwise spoil wine.

*Note: Winemaking literature often refers to **sterilization** as opposed to **sanitization**. Sterilization refers to the process of eradicating all living microorganisms by any of several methods such as filtration or using boiling water. Sanitization refers to the process of eradicating living microorganisms to an acceptably low level such that any remaining microorganisms will not adversely affect the wine. In other words, sanitization is a limited form of sterilization. In wine production, sanitization is sufficient in eradicating unwanted microorganisms.*

The most common and most readily available cleaning and sanitizing agents used by home winemakers are: chlorine, sulphite, two new products sold under the names Bio-Clean and Bio-San, sodium carbonate and sodium percarbonate. The use of soaps and detergents should be avoided on winemaking equipment. These agents leave soap films and residues difficult to rinse away and could therefore affect the taste of wine. The use of chlorine- and sulphite-based products is also not recommended for cleaning stainless steel tanks. A mild household stainless steel cleaner is recommended followed by a thorough water rinse.

4.1.1 Chlorine

A chlorine cleaner, in the form of pink crystals, is available for cleaning glass equipment and is as effective as sulphite as a sanitizing agent without the overpowering smell. The use of a chlorinated cleaner should be avoided on plastic winemaking equipment and oak barrels, which could otherwise impart a bad flavour to wine. To clean such equipment, a sulphur-citric solution is recommended followed by a thorough water rinse.

A chlorine solution is prepared by dissolving chlorine crystals at a rate of 5 mL (1 tsp) per 4 L of water. This solution is very effective in removing stubborn stains on the inside wall of glass containers, and in decolourizing equipment when switching from red to white winemaking. Containers should be filled with a chlorine solution and left to stand overnight to fight tough stains. A simple thorough water rinse removes stains very easily. Containers should then be rinsed with a sulphur-citric solution followed by a thorough water rinse. There should be no trace of chlorine after the water rinse; otherwise, wine will inherit an off-odour and/or off-flavour.

Refer to section 4.1.2 for instructions on preparing a sulphur-citric solution.

4.1.2 Sulphite

Potassium and sodium metabisulphite, also shortened to metabisulphite, bisulphite or more commonly to sulphite, are the most widely used and most effective sanitizing agents. Sulphite can only be used to sanitize—they are not cleaning agents.

To prepare a sulphite solution for sanitization purposes, the powder should be dissolved at a rate of 45 mL (3 tbsp) in 4 L of warm water. The solution should preferably be used within a few weeks as it loses effectiveness over time. To help prolong its shelf life, the container of sulphite solution should be well stoppered.

For sanitizing equipment, adding citric acid will increase the sulphite solution's effectiveness. Equal volumes of critic acid crystals and sulphite powder are dissolved in water to prepare an effective sulphur-citric sanitizing solution.

When sanitizing winemaking equipment, the entire surface should make contact for a few minutes with the sulphite solution and then rinsed thoroughly with water.

Warning: Sulphite solution should be prepared and used in a well-ventilated area.

4.1.3 Bio-Clean and Bio-San

There are now two new environmentally-friendly cleaning and sanitizing products available to home winemakers as an alternative to chlorine and sulphite. Bio-Clean and Bio-San, for cleaning and sanitizing winemaking equipment, respectively, circumvent the unpleasant smell associated with chlorine and sulphite.

The yellow Bio-Clean powder is dissolved at a rate of 15 mL (1 tbsp) per 4 L of warm water. The water will turn to a fluorescent green colour. Winemaking equipment should be thoroughly cleaned with a Bio-Clean solution and then thoroughly rinsed with water until it runs clear. A convenient feature of this solution is that the fluorescent green tracer ensures complete rinsing. For tough stains, an overnight treatment is recommended.

The white Bio-San powder is dissolved at a rate of 15 mL (1 tbsp) per 4 L of hot water. Properly cleaned winemaking equipment should be thoroughly sanitized with a Bio-San solution. The solution should then be drained and any excess should be left to drip out completely. A five-minute waiting period is required before using the equipment.

4.1.4 Sodium carbonate and sodium percarbonate

Sodium carbonate, a white powder commonly known as soda ash, is a cleaner that can be used as a substitute for soap on plastic materials. It also has two other useful properties: it dissolves tartrates and neutralizes acetic acid. For these reasons, manufacturers often recommend soda ash for cleaning oak barrels; however, this should be avoided as essential oak flavour will be leached out and potentially affect the taste of wine. Refer to section 7.1 for a description on how to prepare oak barrels for wine ageing.

Soda ash should be dissolved at a rate of 8-12 g/L of hot water. As soda ash is very difficult to dissolve, it is recommended to dissolve the powder in very hot water and then to dilute the solution to the required concentration. A soda ash cleaning should always be followed by a thorough water rinse, followed by a sulphur-citric rinse, and lastly another water rinse.

Sodium percarbonate, commonly referred to as percarbonate, is a granular-form cleaning agent produced from sodium carbonate through chemical bonding with hydrogen peroxide. Hydrogen peroxide is an effective disinfectant and bleaching agent. Sodium percarbonate can therefore be used to disinfect and bleach winemaking equipment including oak barrels and stainless steel tanks. It is the recommended alternative to soda ash for cleaning oak barrels and to remove excess tannin. Its most common use is in treating barrels affected by spoilage organisms.

Sodium percarbonate is dissolved at a rate of 1-3 g/L of hot water. A sodium percarbonate solution must be properly stoppered in a glass container, as hydrogen peroxide tends to break down quickly. Section 2.3.4 describes how to clean and sanitize stainless steel tanks using sodium percarbonate. Section 7.5.2 describes how to use sodium percarbonate in treating oak barrel spoilage problems.

4.2 CRUSHING AND DESTEMMING

Crushing is the process of breaking the grape skins by mechanical means to expose the juice to yeast for alcoholic fermentation. Crushing of grapes is a necessary operation in red winemaking and does not apply to concentrates, sterilized juices and fresh juices. Although it is optional for white winemaking, crushing is usually performed in home winemaking to ease the pressing operation.

Crushing is the first operation when tannins are extracted. Tannin is a phenolic compound, called phenol (which also include natural colour pigments such as the anthocyanins of dark-skinned grapes and flavour compounds) essential for long-ageing wines. Tannin also has antioxidant and clarifying properties beneficial to wines. However, harsh or excessive tannins can make wines taste overly bitter, astringent and herbaceous. Winemakers therefore need to strike a balance between style of wine and amount of tannin to be extracted.

When whole-bunch clusters of grapes are crushed, tannins are extracted from grape skins, seeds and stems. Of these, stems are the only tannin-imparting component that can be removed prior to crushing. And because stems also cause an increase in pH, which will reduce colour intensity, fruitiness and freshness, this is another reason to remove them. These effects will manifest themselves to a larger extent with green stems than with the more mature woody stems (which usually denotes the full physiological maturity of the grape). In any case, it is far more common to see green stems on California grapes, save for in exceptional years.

Although a small amount of stems may be beneficial to add some tannin, generally, the bulk of the stems are removed before the grapes are crushed—a process known as destemming. Some winemakers destem grape clusters before crushing, and then add in a small amount of stems for minimal tannin extraction. One or two boxes worth of stems for every 10 boxes of 36 lb (16.3 kg) of grapes can be added back in with the grape skins and juice. Stems add bitter and harsh tannins, therefore only a small quantity should be added back. This practice of adding stems back may be beneficial in red wines. On the other hand, white wines become easily unbalanced with minimal tannin, and therefore, stems are usually removed entirely in white wine-making. Destemming can also be done following crushing although more tannin will be extracted because the tannin-imparting stems are crushed along with the grape berries.

Vinification using 100 percent of the stems will yield a highly tannic wine that will take several years to mellow to a drinkable level. This is not recommended for premium-quality wines that will undergo barrel ageing, and nor is it recommended for wines to be aged solely in glass. Highly tannic wines aged in glass containers would display even tighter-wound tannins, for wine aged in glass ages more slowly, not having the benefit of the controlled oxidation of barrel ageing. Therefore, the wine will not achieve the desired organoleptic balance.

The decision to destem before or after crushing depends on the equipment available, not to mention the winemaker's time and patience. Inexpensive crushers (the type without a destemmer) require that stems be removed manually after the grapes have been crushed. This is both tedious and messy. Alternatively, affordable crusher/destemmers can be used to remove the stems efficiently. Their drawback is that they first crush and then destem causing an appreciable amount of harsh tannins to be transferred to the must, and ultimately to the wine. Destemmer/crushers are the ultimate solution, albeit expensive, as they first destem the grape stalks and then crush the grapes.

A manual destemmer can be easily built using a wire mesh (made of non-galvanized metal) in a wooden frame. Holes in the mesh should be just wide enough to allow grape berries to pass through. Stems will not pass through during destemming. The destemmer is placed over a large container and the grape stalks are forced through it with a back-and-forth motion. Grape berries will fall into the container and the stems will remain behind. The grapes are then crushed with any type of crusher. This process is somewhat tedious but achieves good results for those who are patient.

4.3 MACERATION

Maceration is the process of letting the crushed wine berries soak in the grape juice for the purpose of extracting phenols from the grape solids. It is during this process that red wines acquire their structure and colour, and that the wine's ageing potential can be influenced. This process does not apply to concentrates, sterilized juices and fresh juices although purveyors of fresh grape juice now supply grape skins with some juices. Maceration is also the alternative method to using red-juice grapes in the production of rosé wines.

The amount of phenols extracted during maceration depends on a number of factors that will need to be carefully managed and controlled. These include: the maceration period and temperature, and cap management (includes punching down and pumping over operations).

As a general rule of thumb, the longer the juice and grape solids are in contact, the more tannin and colour that will be extracted, and the more full-bodied and coloured a red wine will be. Table 4-1 provides guidelines on maceration periods (which include the fermentation period) for desired wine styles using traditional grape varieties such as Cabernet Sauvignon, Merlot or Syrah. When using very dark-coloured, inky juice grapes such as Alicante Bouschet, these intervals will need to be shortened depending on the desired wine style. Subsequent winemaking operations such as fining, filtering and even ageing need to be considered during maceration. These operations will lighten the colour of red wine, and therefore, more colour may need to be extracted.

The amount of phenol extraction is high in the early days of maceration and continues, albeit at a slower rate, in the final days. Colour extraction, however, happens within the first few days to one

Table 4-1
Recommended maceration periods

Type of wine	Recommended maceration period	Amount of phenols extracted
Rosé	up to 24 hours	very low
Light-bodied, light-coloured	3 - 4 days	low
Medium-bodied, medium-coloured	5 - 7 days	medium
Full-bodied, deep-coloured	up to 21 days	high

week, and then subsides. There is very little colour extraction after the tenth day or so. Refer to Figure 4-1.

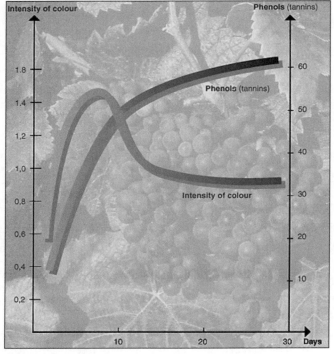

Figure 4-1: Typical rate of colour and phenol extraction

For maximum phenol extraction, the maceration period should be prolonged as much as possible until little or no extraction occurs. The challenge is to retard and slow down fermentation, which would otherwise greatly reduce the maceration period and the level of extraction. The fermentation temperature will rise rapidly up to 32° C (90° F) or more, if not controlled, and will cause a rapid fermentation or may cause a stuck fermentation. The solution is cold soak maceration (pre-fermentation).

Cold soak maceration and cap management

By dropping the temperature of the juice and grape solids down to 8° C (46° F) or lower, maceration is effectively prolonged and fermentation is inhibited (refer to section 4.5 for a discussion on alcoholic fermentation). For a full-bodied, deep-coloured red wine using grapes that have been cold-shipped to their winemaking destination, the juice and grape solids can be cold soaked up to 2 weeks before initiating fermentation by placing sealed freezer bags full of ice into the juice. Freshly picked grapes will first need to be refrigerated in a cooler— not a practical solution for most home winemakers—before cold soak maceration.

The juice and grape solids should be stirred during cold soaking to distribute the temperature evenly, and approximately 50 mg/L of sulfite should be added to prevent volatile acidity (VA) from forming. The grapes should be "punched down" at least twice a day, using a plunger tool (built from a long wooden handle attached perpendicularly, at one end, to a piece of oak wood) to prevent microbial spoilage, as shown in Figure 4-2A. The plunger tool should be sanitized before and thoroughly rinsed after each use. The freezer bags should be reloaded with new ice when the old ice has thawed. The must is inoculated with yeast once ready to start fermentation. The yeast's rate of fermentation is an important factor to be considered when choosing a strain. Too quick a fermentation may considerably shorten the maceration period. Refer to section 4.5.1 for more information on yeast characteristics.

During maceration, the fermentor should be kept covered and properly sealed with a tarpaulin or tank lid to prevent flies from invading the sweet juice. Enough room inside the fermentor should be available for the cap as it starts rising during fermentation. Carbon dioxide (CO_2) gas produced during fermentation will get trapped between the cap (mass of grape solids above the juice) and the cover/lid thereby protecting the juice from oxidation and microbial spoilage. During cold soaking when no gas is produced, CO_2 gas should be injected under the cover/lid from a tank to protect the must from oxidation.

During fermentation, the grape skins will form a cap and

Figure 4-2: Cap management; A, Punching the cap and B, pumping over or *remontage*

rise to the top of the must. To prevent spoilage and to maximize phenol extraction, the cap should again be punched down two or three times a day using a plunger tool until the grape solids are well immersed in the juice. This has the added advantage of evenly distributing the fermentation temperature in the must, as well as encouraging the multiplication of the yeast population in the early stages of fermentation. Separately or in addition to punching the cap, the juice can be pumped over the cap—a process termed *remontage*. Punching of the cap and remontage operations are part of what is known as cap management.

Pumping over involves using an electric pump to re-circulate juice from the bottom of the fermentor to the top over the grape solids as shown in Figure 4-2B. This has the added benefit of also dissipating some heat from the fermenting juice and encouraging yeast multiplication. The entire cap should be doused being careful not to overdo it to avoid oxidizing the wine. It only takes about 20 seconds for 200 liters.

Refer to section 5.3.1 or consult with a retailer about choosing an appropriate pump for this procedure. Not any pump will do since it has to be able to displace grape solids entering it. A 1-hp positive-displacement impeller pump with 1¼-inch tubing is the recommended minimum. If no pump is available, some juice can be collected with a bucket from the bottom of the fermentor and poured over the cap. A fermentor equipped with a spout will prove very practical for cap management procedures.

As the tarpaulin or tank lid will be removed frequently during punching of the cap and pumping over, the protective CO_2 gas will escape. During the vigourous phase of fermentation, sufficient gas is produced to provide adequate protection. When fermentation subsides, CO_2 gas will need to be injected under the cover/lid from a tank.

When fermentation is complete and the Brix level has reached 0.0° (SG below 1.000), an additional week or 10 days of post-ferment maceration will be beneficial in softening the tannins. The wine should be monitored closely during this phase to avoid unpleasant results such as microbial spoilage. Extended maceration is not recommended for high pH wines since these do not benefit as much from long extraction and are more prone to microbial spoilage.

To maximize the benefits of phenol extraction, an inert fermentor that provides an adequate ratio of juice surface to volume should be used. A greater surface allows more juice to be in contact with the grape solids, thereby increasing extraction. Refer to section 2.3 on selecting a fermentor. As a reminder, be sure to account for volume from the rising cap when choosing the size of a fermentor.

Pectic enzymes can be added to the grape juice and solids at crush time to increase the yield of juice and to prevent possible pectin-related problems, such as haze, at bottling time. Refer to section 5.2.7 for instructions on use. Pectic enzymes should not be used if macerating with stems to avoid extraction of overly harsh tannins.

When high colour and tannin extractions are desired without cold soak or extended maceration, fermentation can be carried out at the high end of the recommended temperature range of 22° to 28° C (72° to 82° F). This method can also be used with low-tannin grapes where extended maceration provides no benefit. It also has the advantage of minimizing the risk of oxidation and microbial spoilage since the duration of must exposure to air is reduced. Many great wines are made using "high" temperature fermentation!

White wine maceration
White wines do not benefit from maceration since no colour extraction is required and tannins are not desirable. Some winemakers still allow their crushed white grapes to macerate in the juice for up to 24 hours to give their wines a little more structure and colour. This practice is seldom used in California in modern winemaking although still used in Europe.

For home winemakers, a short maceration period of up to 4 hours is acceptable. Although a longer maceration period of up to 24 hours is used by commercial wineries, it is not recommended for home winemaking, as the wine becomes highly susceptible to oxidation, from exposure to air, and to phenol over-extraction. The must should be sulphited after crushing, and then cooled to a temperature between 10° and 14° C (50° and 57° F) to conduct maceration and to prevent fermentation from starting prematurely.

4.4 PRESSING

Pressing is the process of grape juice extraction by pressure. This operation does not apply to concentrates, sterilized juices and fresh juices.

In home winemaking, the pressing operation should only be performed on crushed grapes. Although whole white grape bunches can be pressed—this will yield clearer juice—it is not recommended on standard home winepress. Only pneumatic or tank presses are able to withstand the high pressure from whole bunch pressing. Pressed, crushed white grapes will yield a cloudy juice that will clarify during the final stages of vinification, i.e., racking, fining and/or filtering.

If the grape bunches are not destemmed, pressing will also yield a more bitter and astringent wine. One advantage of a small proportion of stems added back in is that these will greatly facilitate the pressing operation.

Juice extracted from pressing will not be of consistent quality. The free-run juice extracted by the weight of the must and, optionally, from a light pressing will be of higher quality. Press-run juice will be of inferior quality. This is due to the further pressing of the must that extracts more compounds, namely tannin, from the grape skins, seeds and stems. Press-run juice will have a lower total acidity with an increased amount of volatile acidity and a higher pH. The resulting wine will have reduced colour intensity, fruitiness and freshness, and may lack the required balance to produce a premium wine.

It is recommended to conduct fermentation of free-run and press-run juices in separate vessels, and to blend the finished wines according to the desired quality.

Pressed juice should be sieved using double-cheesecloth to remove as much solids as possible. The juice should be transferred to a glass container and poured against the wall of the vessel. If the juice is poured straight down, the must will aerate and accelerate oxidation.

For white winemaking, the juice should settle for 12 hours before racking to a glass fermentor leaving behind all sediment. Some winemakers believe in a light bentonite fining at this stage (refer to section 5.2.1) to ensure a clean must and a firm deposit for ease of racking. The must temperature should be kept below 15° C (59° F) during this period to prevent fermentation from starting. If fermentation does begin despite one's efforts, it is impossible to rack the clear juice up as the carbon dioxide given off as a by-product of fermentation will disturb the sediment.

The dense juice that has settled can be coarse filtered (refer to section 5.3) to recover some clear juice to be fermented. This process is extremely difficult and requires considerable time and effort as the dense juice contains a very high concentration of solids. Commercial wineries use centrifugal clarifiers for this operation.

For each juice, the fermentor should be filled three-quarters to allow for expansion during fermentation. The amount of volume required depends on the amount of foam expected during fermentation. This depends on the type of yeast chosen.

4.5 ALCOHOLIC FERMENTATION

Alcoholic fermentation, the conversion of must into wine, is the single most vital and critical vinification procedure. The organoleptic qualities of a wine are determined by the winemaker's ability to control the various vinification factors such as temperature, sugar concentration, acidity and pH, SO_2 level, rate of fermentation, tannin level and colour, to name a few. The various transformations and rapid evolution of ingredients require many quick decisions. Constant care and supervision during fermentation is a mandatory practice. Fermentation can progress free of problems if all instructions are followed as outlined.

The qualities of a wine also depend on the quality of the juice or grape variety selected, and on the yeast types used for inoculation. Yeasts are key contributors to the wine's structure, aromas and flavours.

4.5.1 Yeasts and yeast nutrients

Yeasts play a very important part in the fermentation process by converting sugar in the must into alcohol. Once fermentation has begun, yeast cells will multiply and will stimulate a higher rate of sugar conversion. Yeast activity will cease if the fermentation environment does not favour cell multiplication—e.g., low sugar content, not enough oxygen, too low a temperature, or too much SO_2—or if the cell count is low.

Fermentation can be enabled using wild (indigenous) yeasts, which have formed on grape skins, or using cultured yeasts. Traditionalists still use wild yeasts in the production of some wines. These wineries must inevitably invest considerable time and energy to monitor and control the wild-yeast fermentation to prevent any problems. Such fermentations are prone to microbial spoilage if not managed properly. Cultured wine yeasts, on the other hand, allow for a risk-free fermentation with relatively minimal monitoring. For home winemaking using grapes, it is recommended to inhibit wild yeasts and to use selected cultured yeasts specific for a desired wine type. Concentrated

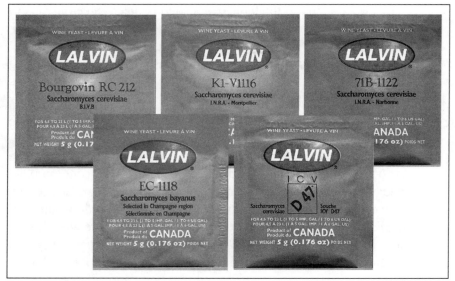

Figure 4-3: Lalvin® cultured wine yeasts

and sterilized grape juices have been stripped of all yeast, therefore, they always require the addition of cultured yeast.

Different cultured yeasts are available for the desired wine type and desired alcohol content. The main wine yeast category is the *Saccharomyces* genus. The most commonly used yeasts are strains from the *cerevisiae* and *bayanus* species. Yeast types are referred to by their genus and species names, i.e., *Saccharomyces cerevisiae* (*S. cerevisiae*) and *Saccharomyces bayanus* (*S. bayanus*). There can be many strains within each species. Each strain has different microbiological and biochemical properties therefore yielding different vinification results.

Lallemand® and RED STAR Yeast & Products Division of Universal Foods Corporation are two major producers of active dry wine yeast—Lalvin®[10] and RED STAR®[11], respectively—for home winemaking. Figure 4-3 illustrates the various Lalvin® cultured wine yeast types and strains available to home winemakers. Table 4-2 provides the characteristics of Lalvin® *S. cerevisiae* and *S. bayanus* yeasts. Table 4-3 presents a quick reference chart for Lalvin® yeast strains for various wine

[10]Lalvin is a registered trademark of Lallemand, Inc.
[11]RED STAR is a registered trademark of the RED STAR® Yeast & Products Division of Universal Foods Corporation.

126

Table 4-2

Lalvin® *Saccharomyces* wine yeast strains and their properties

Yeast strain	Bourgovin RC 212®	ICV/D-47®	71B-1122®	KIV-1116®	EC-1118®
Saccharomyces species	cer	cer	cer	cer	bay
Optimum fermentation temperature range	15-30° C 59-86° F	10-35° C 50-95° F	15-30° C 59-86° F	10-42° C 50-107° F	7-35° C 45-95° F
Alcohol tolerance (% alc./vol.)	14	15	18	18	18
Rate of fermentation	mod	mod	mod	fast	very fast
Foam production	low	low	low	very low	very low
Volatile acid production	low	low	low	low	low
Sulphur dioxide production	low	low	very low	low	mod
Hydrogen sulphide production	low	low	low	very low	very low
Nutrient requirements	normal	normal	normal	very low	normal

Abbreviations: cer, *cerevisiae*; bay, *bayanus*; mod, moderate.

(Adapted from Lalvin® product information)

types, and Table 4-4 lists recommended usage for each strain. Similarly, Figure 4-4, and Table 4-5 to Table 4-7, respectively, present the same type of information for RED STAR® yeasts.

Logsdons' Wyeast Laboratories and White Labs are two other well-known manufacturers of cultured wine yeasts available to home winemakers.

Table 4-3
Recommended Lalvin® yeast strains for various wine types
(Legend: ♥♥♥♥ = strongest recommendation)

Type of wine	Bourgovin RC 212®	ICV/D-47®	71B-1122®	KIV-1116®	EC-1118®
Dry white	♥	♥♥♥♥	♥♥	♥♥♥	♥♥♥
Medium-sweet / Rosé	♥	♥♥♥♥	♥♥♥♥	♥♥	♥♥
Sweet	♥♥♥	♥	♥♥♥	♥♥♥♥	♥♥♥♥
Light young red	♥♥♥♥	♥	♥♥♥♥	♥♥	♥♥
Tannic red	♥♥♥♥	♥	♥♥	♥♥♥	♥♥♥
Sparkling	♥	♥	♥	♥♥	♥♥♥♥

(Adapted from Lalvin® product information)

Table 4-4
Recommended usage for Lalvin® *Saccharomyces*
wine yeast strains

Yeast strain	Recommended for:
Bourgovin RC 212®	Red varieties where full tannin and colour stabilization are desired
ICV/D-47®	Premium-quality white wines; favours malolactic (ML) fermentation
71B-1122®	Fruity wines from concentrates; ideal for rosé and sweet white wines
KIV-1116®	Fruit wines and low-nutrient musts; restarts stuck fermentation
EC-1118®	White and sparkling wines; restarts stuck fermentation; inhibits ML fermentation; ideal for quick fermentations

Figure 4-4: RED STAR® cultured wine yeasts. The packets at each end depict old packaging that might still be sold in certain markets.

When choosing a yeast type and strain, the following fermentation factors should be considered depending on desired results:
- ↶ fermentation temperature
- ↶ alcohol tolerance
- ↶ rate of fermentation
- ↶ foam production
- ↶ volatile acid production
- ↶ SO_2 production
- ↶ hydrogen sulphide production
- ↶ nutrient requirements

The fermentation temperature should always be within the recommended range. Yeast activity can cease if the temperature deviates outside this range and cause a stuck fermentation. The lower temperature-tolerant yeasts are recommended for white wine vinification where fermentation is often conducted at low temperatures, and where a cool fermentation is desired in red must vinification. When a cool temperature cannot be achieved during red wine vinification, higher temperature-tolerant yeasts are recommended because fermentation temperatures rise significantly.

Some strains of wine yeasts can tolerate alcohol levels up to 14% or 15% alc./vol. while other strains can tolerate up to 18% alc./vol. The lower alcohol-tolerant yeasts can cause fermentation to cease when high alcohol levels are required—for example, in the production of Sauternes- or port-style wines. For these types of wines, the higher alcohol-tolerant yeasts are recommended.

A slower rate of fermentation is recommended for vinification of premium-quality wines to favour maximum retention of volatile fruit aromas and extraction of other phenolic compounds. A yeast type with

Table 4-5
RED STAR® *Saccharomyces* wine yeast strains and their properties

Yeast strain	Pasteur Red™†	Montrachet (Davis #522)	Côte des Blancs (Davis #750)	Pasteur Champagne (Davis #595)	Premier Cuvée (Davis #796)
Saccharomyces species	cer	cer	cer	bay	bay
Optimum fermentation temperature range	18-30° C 64-86° F	15-30° C 59-86° F	18-30° C 64-86° F§	15-30° C 59-86° F	7-35° C 45-95° F
Alcohol tolerance (% alc./vol.)	16	13	12-14	13-15	18
Rate of fermentation	fast	fast	slow/ mod	fast	fast
Foam production	low	mod	low	mod	very low
Volatile acid production	low	low	low	low	low
Sulphur dioxide production	low	low/ mod	very low	low	mod
Hydrogen sulphide production	low	high*	low	low	very low
Nutrient requirements	normal	normal	high**	normal	normal

Abbreviations: cer, *cerevisiae*; bay, *bayanus*; mod, moderate. †Pasteur Red™ is a trademark owned by Dr. Lisa Van de Water, The Wine Lab. §Sensitive to temperatures below 13°C / 55°F; fermentation may cease. *Not recommended for grapes that have been dusted with sulphur. **Requires nutrient addition for Chardonnay fermentations. (Adapted from RED STAR® product information)

a slower rate of fermentation should be selected. This factor should be assessed in conjunction with fermentation temperature to achieve the desired vinification environment. For example, too high of a fermenta-

Table 4-6
Recommended Red STAR® yeast strains for various wine types
(Legend: 🍇🍇🍇🍇 = strongest recommendation)

Type of wine	Pasteur Red™	Montrachet	Côte des Blancs	Pasteur Champagne	Premier Cuvée
Dry white	🍇	🍇🍇🍇🍇	🍇🍇	🍇🍇🍇🍇	🍇🍇🍇
Medium-sweet / Rosé	🍇	🍇	🍇🍇🍇🍇	🍇🍇	🍇🍇
Sweet	🍇	🍇	🍇🍇🍇🍇	🍇🍇	🍇🍇🍇🍇
Light young red	🍇🍇🍇	🍇🍇🍇	🍇🍇🍇	🍇🍇🍇	🍇🍇
Tannic red	🍇🍇🍇🍇	🍇🍇🍇🍇	🍇	🍇🍇	🍇🍇
Sparkling	🍇	🍇	🍇🍇🍇	🍇	🍇🍇🍇🍇

(Adapted from RED STAR® product information)

Table 4-7
Recommended usage for RED STAR® *Saccharomyces*
wine yeast strains

Yeast strain	Recommended for:
Pasteur Red™	Full-bodied red wines where varietal (especially Cabernet-family grapes) fruit flavours and complex aromas are desired
Montrachet (Davis #522)	Full-bodied intense-colour red and white wines. Good tolerance to free SO_2
Côte des Blancs (Davis #750)	Red, white and sparkling wines as well as wines with residual sugar
Pasteur Champagne (Davis #595)	All white and some red wines. Not recommended for sparkling wines. Restarts stuck fermentation. Good tolerance to free SO_2
Premier Cuvée (Davis #796)	Red, white and especially sparkling wines; does not favour ML fermentation; restarts stuck fermentation; good tolerance to free SO_2

tion temperature will cause a yeast with a slow rate to still ferment rapidly.

Four- and 6-week wine kits are commonly packaged with a *S. bayanus* yeast type for a fast and safe fermentation. It is generally held that *S. bayanus* yeasts, however, do not yield as complex a wine as those from *S. cerevisiae.*

Foam production is an important consideration in the selection of fermentation vessel capacity. Musts inoculated with higher foam production yeasts should be fermented in higher-capacity vessels to avoid overflowing. Foaming is also greatly affected by the solids level in must as well as protein fractions.

Volatile acids affect the quality of wines and potentially cause spoilage. In large quantity, these acids are undesirable, and a yeast type that inhibits the production of volatile acidity should be selected. Note, however, that in small quantities, volatile acidity is a vital component of a wine's bouquet.

Although minute quantities of SO_2 are produced during fermentation, a yeast type with very low SO_2 production should be selected. This is particularly recommended when SO_2 levels cannot be measured and when the wine is to undergo malolactic fermentation.

Hydrogen sulphide (H_2S, a sulphur-based compound known as a mercaptan) in excessive amounts can be detected as an unpleasant rotten-egg smell. Both *S. cerevisiae* and *S. bayanus* yeast types, even when properly fed, may produce minuscule quantities of hydrogen sulphide that cannot be detected by smell and are not harmful to wine. Another source of hydrogen sulphide is the condition or quality of the juice, which may contain residual elemental sulphur from late applications of vineyard sprays.

Nutrient requirements is an important consideration when producing wines where the yeast will be subjected to adverse fermentation conditions, or as a preventative measure when the source and quality of fruit or juice cannot be ascertained, or when the grapes are deficient in yeast nutrients. Grapes from a poor, rainy, or gray rot-affected vintage will typically be deficient in yeast nutrients. In such cases, yeast nutrients are recommended to favour yeast multiplication and fermentation.

Yeast nutrients are available in powder form and are premixed with all the necessary ingredients. These include either diammonium phosphate or a mix of sodium phosphate and ammonium sulphate, thi-

Table 4-8
Recommended strains for wines to be ML-fermented

Type of wine	Lalvin® strain	RED STAR® strain
White*	ICV/D-47®	Côte des Blancs
Red	Bourgovin RC 212®	Pasteur Red™

*Recommended for Chardonnay

amin (vitamin BI) and other vitamins such as biotin and riboflavin, and other ingredients. Thiamin is the most important vitamin in yeast nutrients for these to feed yeasts in a successful fermentation.

The addition of yeast nutrients is always recommended when making wine from concentrate or sterilized juice. These types of musts are deficient in yeast nutrients resulting from pasteurization and/or sterilization. Yeast nutrients are not required, although recommended, when using fresh juice or grapes. Most often, yeast nutrients are used when fermentation is stuck—along with fresh healthy yeast—or when fermentation is to be carried out in a high-sugar or a high-alcohol environment. As yeast nutrients will favour fermentation of sugar into alcohol, the finished wine will be of higher alcohol content. Yeast nutrients should be dissolved in water and added at a rate of 10-20 g/hL of must. When required to add nutrients under normal conditions, these should be added before the start of alcoholic fermentation, e.g., at yeast inoculation.

The above fermentation factors are however subjective as they are inter-related, e.g., the rate of fermentation is a function of temperature and nutrient requirements. The chemical behavior of these factors also depends on the composition and quality of the must. As such, these factors should be used as guidelines in choosing cultured wine yeasts for desired wine types.

In addition to the above fermentation properties, other factors such as a strain's ability to inhibit wild yeasts, its tolerance to SO_2, and whether it favours malolactic (ML) fermentation (refer to section 4.6) should be considered. For example, to produce an ML-fermented red wine with inhibited wild yeasts, the must can be inoculated with a Lalvin® or a RED STAR® strain as per Table 4-8.

Many other specialized yeast strains are available to make Sauternes-style, Champagne-style and port-style wines, for example. Although these strains are marketed under the wine-style name, such strains contribute to the wine's flavours and aromas but do not necessarily affect the sugar and alcohol contents, acidity, pH, or tannin level. Flavours and aromas are determined by both the selected yeast strain and the vinification and winemaking techniques used. Therefore, when selecting strains with generic names, one should inquire and establish the yeast type (genus and species) and specific strain. For example, a Sauternes-style wine—a late-harvest sweet white wine produced from shriveled sugar-rich grapes affected by "noble rot" (*Botrytis cinerea* fungus)—will contain approximately 14% alc./vol. and a residual sugar content greater than 100 g/L. A yeast strain labeled "Sauternes" will impart typical flavours and aromas found in Sauternes wines. However, winemakers must ensure that the yeast strain can survive in a sugar-rich must and be able to convert the sugar into alcohol. They must also be able to cease fermentation when the desired alcohol and residual sugar contents are achieved. The yeast strain alone cannot produce the labeled type of wine on its own.

Cultured wine yeasts are available in both dry and liquid formats. The recommended and most popular cultured yeast format is dry vermicelli-shaped granules, often referred to as active dry wine yeast. Its advantage is that it has a long shelf life, approximately 2 years, if kept away from moisture and refrigerated between 4° C and 10° C (40° F and 50° F). It is also more stable than its equivalent liquid format. When properly handled, dry yeast cultures now provide fail-safe fermentations when the manufacturer's recommendations are followed.

Active dry yeast is available in 5-g packets—good for 4.5 to 23 L of must. One packet should be rehydrated in 50 mL of water at a temperature between 38° and 42° C (100° and 108° F) for 15 minutes. These temperature recommendations should be strictly followed to avoid killing the yeast. Also, the yeast **should not** be rehydrated longer than the yeast manufacturer's recommended time. A container with a capacity of at least double the water volume should be used, as rehydrating yeast may bubble up.

The active dry yeast can be rehydrated by adding it to the water and stirring lightly. Manufacturers mention that there is no need to stir; however, a gentle stir ensures that all the yeast will be rehydrated. After the rehydration period, the yeast culture, referred to as the inoculum, is stirred and added directly to the must. Stirring in the yeast culture is again optional but recommended. The process of adding yeast to the must is referred to as inoculation.

The use of a yeast starter is often recommended as an inoculum to favour a successful fermentation when using grapes or when fermenting under difficult conditions, e.g., where the cellar temperature is rather cool.

A yeast starter is prepared by using a small volume of must from concentrate, fresh juice, or grape juice and adding yeast to start fermentation. This is done several days before inoculation of the entire must to be fermented. A starter volume of 2 percent of the must to be inoculated is recommended. For example, 1 L of yeast starter should be prepared to inoculate a 54-L batch. Meanwhile, the bulk of the must will be undergoing a beneficial pre-fermentation maceration (cold soak). Optionally, yeast nutrients can be added if a difficult fermentation is anticipated. The yeast starter should be at room temperature, and once fermentation is vigourous, it is added to the bulk of the must.

4.5.2 Conducting alcoholic fermentation

Conducting the alcohol fermentation is a simple and trouble-free operation when basic precautions are followed. The chemistry of fermentation is a well-understood science, and various œnological chemicals and techniques are now available to ensure successful fermentations in home winemaking.

In white winemaking, musts should always be fermented in a properly air-locked glass container to minimize the risk of oxidation. As white winemaking from kits is more tolerant to the effects of oxidation, manufacturers often instruct that the vigourous fermentation should be conducted in an open container. Undoubtedly, closed-container fermentation reduces any risk of oxidation. This is the recommended practice. In red winemaking, the vigourous phase of fermentation is carried out in an open container. To minimize the effects of oxidation, to reduce the risk of spoilage and to keep dust and fruit flies away from the fermenting must, the open container should be covered with a heavy plastic sheet or tarpaulin. This will help maintain a protective layer of carbon dioxide over the fermenting must therefore minimizing the risk of oxidation or spoilage. Fermentors should allow for must volume expansion during fermentation to prevent overflowing. A good rule of thumb is never to fill a vat/container[12] more than three-quarters full.

[12]Refer to section 7.2 for a discussion on barrel fermentation.

During the alcoholic fermentation phase, temperature should be maintained within the recommended range for the wine type being produced and based on the yeast strain selected. As fermentation is an exothermic process (evolves heat), it is good practice to place a floating thermometer in the must for the duration of the vigourous phase when the temperature can rise significantly. The temperature should be monitored continuously and should be adjusted as required to maintain a proper fermentation environment. Fermenting red must can exceed the prescribed maximum temperature very quickly if not controlled and, therefore, can inhibit yeast activity. When yeast activity ceases, fermentation becomes stuck.

Fermentation should start within 48 hours following inoculation, or earlier if the temperature is higher than the recommended range. Since temperature of the must will rise appreciably during fermentation, if adjustable, the room or wine cellar temperature should be set at the low end of the recommended range and should be re-adjusted, if required, once fermentation has begun. When the fermentation becomes vigourous, the room temperature can be lowered to between 10° and 14° C (50° and 57° F) for white wines. Red wines should be fermented between 22° and 28° C (72° and 82° F), or as low as the yeast strain will allow if a cooler fermentation is desired. A slow and cool fermentation is key to producing premium-quality wines. Refer to section 4.3 for more information on cold soak maceration and cool fermentation.

Fermentation activity should be monitored on a daily basis by taking two Brix (SG) measurements to ensure it is progressing well. Monitoring the change in sugar concentration is the best indicator of fermentation progress. Fermentation should progress according to the curve shown in Figure 3-3 (page 74). It is good practice to record all must measurements and quantities of chemicals and ingredients added so recipes could be adjusted in the future. If something should go wrong, the evolution of the wine can be traced from these records.

Caution: *Fermentation of large volumes of must (e.g., 200 L) will release asphyxiating quantities of carbon dioxide. To eliminate any health hazards, the fermentation area should be well ventilated to the outside.*

When fermentation has subdued and the sugar concentration has reached 0.0 B° (between 0.990 and 0.995), the wine should be racked and transferred to another fermentor. If the reading is higher than 0.0 B° (1.000), fermentation should be allowed to continue until the sugar concentration falls below this level.

For wines having fermented in a closed container without maceration, it is recommended to let the wine stand for a minimum of two additional weeks and then to re-measure the sugar concentration. Fermentation is complete when the sugar concentration readings are stable during this period.

For red wines having macerated and fermented in an open vat, these should be racked and the grape solids pressed immediately when fermentation is complete to minimize tannin extraction. If the wine can be properly protected against oxidation and microbial spoilage, an extended post-ferment maceration can be carried out to extract more tannin.

In either case, the wine should not be left for too long on its gross lees (the heavy sediment formed during fermentation) to avoid potential spoilage from a reaction known as autolysis. This reaction is a result of the decaying of the dead yeast cells. The gross lees consist mainly of dead yeast cells, and grape solids when vinifying from grapes (although fresh juices do include some grape solids in suspension). The length of time a wine spends on the gross lees is also dependent on the health of the grapes at crush or harvest. Wines that are issued from a vintage with a high percentage of rot, for instance, should be separated from the gross lees as soon as possible. Sediment formed after the removal of the gross lees are referred to fine lees.

Unlike gross lees, fine lees are beneficial to wines, adding flavour and complexity, when left in contact for up to 6 months. This short fine lees contact period will cause autolysis to a very small extent—a desirable reaction in this case. This procedure is encouraged and used extensively in the production of Champagne and "Sur-Lie" wines of Muscadet de Sèvre et Maine to make for a more complex wine. Fine lees will also be required for wines that will undergo malolactic fermentation to serve as nutrients.

During this period of fine lees contact, the lees should be stirred on a weekly basis for the first couple of months and then monthly. The process of lees stirring is referred to as *bâtonnage* in

French and is essential in creating wines with added flavour and complexity.

Throughout the fermentation period up until completion, the wine should be tested for the presence of hydrogen sulphide, detectable by a rotten-egg smell. If detected early, this potential problem can be easily corrected by racking with aeration, without adversely affecting the quality of the finished wine. Otherwise, prolonged presence of hydrogen sulphide can ultimately spoil the wine. Refer to section 12.7 for a description of how to treat hydrogen sulphide.

When fermentation has completed, it is good practice to measure the TA, pH and free SO_2 content to determine the level and timing of any adjustment that may be required. TA and pH will have decreased and increased, respectively, while the free SO_2 content can be expected to have increased slightly. If the must or wine has been subjected to racking operations, the free SO_2 content may have decreased.

At this point, the wine can be clarified and stabilized; however, it will improve greatly if first allowed to age for up to 6 months in a cool place. If a wine has been aged, it should be racked again before clarification. During the ageing period, the sulphite solution in the fermentation locks should be changed monthly. The wine level in all containers should be monitored for proper topping. If the cellar temperature rises, some wine should be removed, as it will expand when it gets warmer. When this happens, there is a danger the wine will come into contact with the sulphite solution in the fermentation lock as it overflows and spills. The wine can spoil if the sulphite solution has not been changed as it may have developed spoilage organisms.

4.5.3 Simplified partial carbonic maceration

Alcoholic fermentation can be carried out using the carbonic maceration vinification process in the production of young, early-drinking, fruity Beaujolais Nouveau-style wines. A simplified variation of carbonic maceration, known as partial carbonic maceration, is the easiest and most practical method for home winemakers for producing this style of wine. The difficulty with full carbonic maceration is in producing and injecting carbon dioxide gas to start fermentation. The simplified partial carbonic maceration technique described here does not require any carbon dioxide addition, and unlike Beaujolais carbonic maceration, it makes use of cultured yeast to start fermentation.

For partial carbonic maceration, a portion of the grapes (between 25 and 50 percent of the total weight) should be crushed and destemmed into an open plastic fermentor (vat) and inoculated with a red wine yeast culture. The remaining grapes are added as whole clusters in the same vat. The vat should be tightly covered with a thick plastic. This is particularly important if the cap will not be submersed by punching it down. The carbon dioxide gas produced from fermentation will protect the grapes from microbial spoilage if the plastic is tightly secured. If punching down the cap, this should be done gently so as to let the berries burst by themselves. This is a result of intra-cellular fermentation and is what gives the wine its desired softness, fruitiness, and low tannic content. If not all the berries burst, it should not be a cause of concern, as they will burst during the pressing operation.

During the maceration/fermentation phase, temperature should be kept at around 30° C (86° F). Fermentation will occur within the berries, but only a small amount of fermenting juice (wine) will be produced as most of it will remain in the berries. Fermentation should be carried out to dryness which can take between 4 and 11 days. The small amount of wine should then be drained and transferred to a glass container. The "fermenting" grapes may still very much look like whole berries. These should all be transferred to the winepress for pressing. The grape bunches should be handled carefully to avoid breaking the berries and having the wine flow out. The press-run wine should be transferred to a glass container, sealed with a fermentation lock, and fermented to dryness if there is still an appreciable amount of sugar present. Free-run and press-run wines can be vinified separately.

4.5.4 Stopping fermentation

When producing wines that require naturally occurring residual sugar, for example, a sweet dessert wine or a fortified sweet port, there are various methods available to stop fermentation. For home winemaking, only two methods are available: 1) deep cooling of the wine and 2) alcohol fortification.

Potassium sorbate, used to prevent re-fermentation in a finished wine, cannot be used to stop an active fermentation. Refer to section 4.7.1.

Stopping fermentation by deep cooling

Stopping alcoholic fermentation by deep cooling is a tedious and cumbersome task for home winemakers as this method requires the wine to be placed in a cold refrigerator or a freezer at a temperature between –5° and –2° C (23° and 28° F). This is the ideal temperature range to quickly stop fermentation although a temperature of up to 4° C (40° F) will work. This method can only be done practically in small quantities.

To stop an active fermentation, an environment favouring yeast inhibition must first be created. At the start of alcoholic fermentation, only half the inoculum amount should be used. Yeast nutrients should not be added which would otherwise encourage fermentation and making it more difficult to stop. Fermentation should be conducted at the low end of the recommended temperature range. When fermentation is to be stopped, the wine should be placed in cold storage, and sulphited to achieve a free SO_2 level of 100 mg/L. Since fermentation will not cease spontaneously, cooling of the wine should be performed at a slightly higher Brix (SG) than the desired final Brix (SG). The time required for fermentation to completely stop depends on the temperature, the amount of sulphite present and the alcohol content. Stopping fermentation by deep cooling will require some testing and experience to determine when the cooling operation should be performed.

After two weeks, it is recommended that the wine be racked, clarified and stabilized. Following stabilization, the wine can be clarified by sterile filtration (refer to section 5.3) to remove any active yeast still present. As a last step, the wine should be stored in a cold environment, such as a refrigerator, at a temperature between 5° and 8° C (41° and 46° F) for up to 6 months before bottling. The wine can be further chill-proofed by adding metatartaric acid (refer to section 4.7.2).

Chapter 11 details this method of stopping fermentation to produce homemade Icewine from grape juice.

Stopping fermentation by alcohol fortification

Stopping fermentation by alcohol fortification is an effective method although the resulting wine is of a very different style. Distilled spirits, such as brandy, can be added to the fermenting wine. The addition of a high-alcohol spirit will typically result in a wine with an alcohol content greater than 16% alc./vol. Most yeasts cannot survive at such a high alcohol level therefore halting fermentation. The finished wine will consequently have a higher residual sugar content. Alcohol fortification is the key and most critical step in the production of port wines.

To stop an active fermentation, the desired residual sugar level should be first determined and the current alcohol content should be noted before adding a distilled spirit. When a distilled spirit is added, fermentation will cease quickly, depending on the amount of active yeast and fermentable sugar left over, the must temperature and the alcohol concentration of the distilled spirit. The alcohol content will be slightly higher than measured before fortification, as fermentation will not cease spontaneously. Refer to section 6.1 to determine how to calculate the final alcohol content.

The resulting wine will also become lighter in colour since the high-alcohol spirit acts as a clarifying agent and also dilutes the wine colour.

4.6 MALOLACTIC (ML) FERMENTATION

Musts and wines need to be protected from undesirable bacteria that could cause microbial spoilage. There are bacterium species, however, which are beneficial in the vinification of musts. One such species, *Leuconostoc oenos* (*L. oenos*), becomes active in an environment rich in malic acid. *L. oenos* bacteria convert the sharper naturally occurring malic acid into the softer lactic acid therefore making wines more approachable and giving them an added dimension. Carbon dioxide gas is a by-product of this conversion process and is allowed to escape. This conversion process is termed malolactic fermentation— abbreviated as ML fermentation or MLF—and is very often referred to as the secondary fermentation.

ML fermentation can only occur naturally without the addition of bacteria in fresh grape juice; however, indigenous bacteria may impart off-flavours and cause spoilage at low free SO_2 concentrations. It is best to add an ML culture to ensure a successful ML fermentation.

ML fermentation should not be attempted in kit wines because these types of juices have been tartrate-stabilized during their production and thus contain a very high proportion of malic acid, which would be converted to lactic acid. The wine would have very little acid, and a pH above 3.8 making it very susceptible to bacterial infections.

ML fermentation lowers a wine's total acidity and raises its pH level. It is therefore recommended for wines with high TA (total acidity)—due to malic acid—and low pH. Musts with a low acid concentration should not be subjected to ML fermentation, which would otherwise render the wine too flat. As explained in section 3.2, one must always determine the types of acid present in a wine and their relative concentrations before proceeding with any acid-reduction process such as ML fermentation. This is to ensure that a proper balance between TA and pH is maintained. The reason is that different acids, contributing to the wine's TA, have different strengths, i.e. pH.

ML fermentation also adds complexity to a wine and is most beneficial in red wines. Red wines vinified by carbonic maceration will not benefit from ML fermentation. Highly tannic red wines can be drunk earlier if the acidity has been reduced by ML fermentation. The astringent sensation imparted by tannins is softened appreciably. It is generally not recommended for white wines, except for Chardonnay and highly acidic grape varieties. Highly acidic white wines can benefit from ML fermentation in reducing the acid concentration in conjunction with an acid-reducing solution. Conversely, if the acid concentration following ML fermentation is below the desired level, tartaric acid can be added. Acid blends containing fermentable malic acid should not be used to avoid the possibility of restarting a second ML fermentation.

ML fermentation does however have drawbacks and dangers for home winemakers.

Citric acid is partly transformed to acetic acid during ML fermentation, which will increase the level of volatile acidity (VA)—an undesirable effect. The level of citric acid in grapes and wines is usually low and should not be of concern. However, acid blends containing citric acid should not be used when required to perform acid addition to avoid increasing VA.

Progression of ML fermentation also requires careful monitoring and control. If allowed to progress to an unusually high pH level, the wine will oxidize prematurely and will become prone to bacterial infection. Paper chromatography techniques are used to monitor progression, however the kits are hard to find in home winemaking shops. Specialty wine analysis laboratories will carry paper chromatography apparatus and chemicals. Section 4.6.3 describes the paper chromatography procedure for the determination of malic acid presence in malolactic-fermented wines. Rudimentary guidelines to monitor and control ML fermentation are also provided below.

4.6.1 Conducting ML fermentation

It is recommended that the ML fermentation be conducted immediately following the alcoholic fermentation. Two methods are used to conduct the ML fermentation: 1) the spontaneous method without the use of an inoculated ML bacteria culture and 2) by the inoculation method using an ML bacteria culture. In the spontaneous method, the must is allowed to ferment to completion and stored in a cold room or cellar during the winter months. As the cellar temperature rises in the spring months, the must temperature rises to a level favouring ML fermentation. This explains why carbon dioxide bubbles re-appear in the spring. This method poses a potential microbial infection risk, as the wine is stored for several months at a low sulphite concentration. Undesirable bacteria may spontaneously carry out the ML fermentation giving off-flavours and aromas. In the inoculation method, selected bacteria capable of converting the malic acid are used as the ML culture. This method allows winemakers more control, and the ML fermentation period is usually much shorter. Therefore, it reduces the risks of unsuccessful ML fermentation or microbial infection.

Both methods require a proper environment for the ML fermentation to be successful. There are several initial conditions that must be respected. First, the must's free SO_2 content should be less than the maximum prescribed for the selected ML culture. The maximum is typically in the range from 5 to 15 mg/L. Therefore, at crushing and/or pressing, the must should be sulphited very lightly within the prescribed maximum. Second, the pH level should be higher than the prescribed minimum, typically 3.2. Third, the must should be at a temperature between 15° and 18° C (59° and 64° F) throughout this phase. A cool cellar should be heated accordingly, or alternatively, the wine can be moved to a warmer room. Another option is to wait until spring warms up the cellar. ML fermentation will still proceed at a temperature as low as 12° C (54° F), albeit very slowly. Lastly, the presence of fine lees is very important for a successful ML fermentation, especially if an ML culture is not added. Bacteria used in ML fermentation work most favourably when feeding on the nutrients found in the lees.

It should be noted that the above conditions also favour growth of spoilage organisms. Winemakers must therefore use extra sanitary precautions to avoid such problems.

Oxygen requirements of the selected ML strains should also be verified as different strains have different needs. Most selected ML cultures grow and survive much better with very little or no oxygen present. Anaerobic species should be protected from exposure to air (for example, wine should not be racked during the ML fermentation phase).

The manufacturer's recommendations should be adhered to strictly as different ML cultures may have different environmental requirements. For example, many manufacturers specify a maximum alcohol content for a successful ML fermentation.

TA and pH levels should be measured once the ML fermentation has completed to determine the extent of acid reduction. TA and pH levels can be adjusted, if desired, following cold stabilization of the wine. When a wine's TA is abnormally low (high pH), acidity should be increased before ML fermentation to avoid any potential spoilage problems. Preferably, acid addition should actually be done before alcoholic fermentation. Refer to sections 3.2 and 3.3 for more details.

An ML-compatible yeast strain—refer to Table 4-8 (page 133) —should be used during the alcoholic fermentation. These strains will ensure a successful ML fermentation under proper ML environmental conditions.

The must should be inoculated with an appropriate type of ML culture immediately following alcoholic fermentation while ensuring the temperature is maintained within the prescribed range. ML cultures are available in either liquid or freeze-dried format.

A popular type of liquid ML culture readily available at winemaking shops is a blend of OSU (Oregon State University) Er1a and Ey2d *L. oenos* strains. This blend, produced by Logsdons' Wyeast Laboratories and marketed under the Vintner's Choice™ brand name (see Figure 4-5), is particularly effective at lower pH and temperature levels. Vintner's Choice™ ML cul-

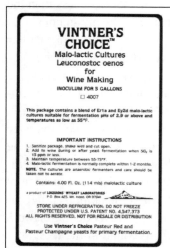

Figure 4-5: Vintner's Choice™ ML culture.

tures are commonly available in 114 mL (4 fl oz) packages that can be used for up to 20 L (5 gal) of must.

Figure 4-6: A, Vinquiry MCW and B, Uvaferm® MLD *L. oenos* ML cultures.

Liquid cultures are however unstable and may yield unpredictable results. Active dry (freeze-dried) ML cultures are the recommended alternative. Freeze-dried ML cultures should be stored in a freezer and are viable for up to one year. Recommended freeze-dried ML cultures are the *L. oenos* MCW, MLD, and OSU Er1a and Ey2d strains. Figure 4-6 depicts the Vinquiry MCW and Uvaferm® MLD packets of freeze-dried ML cultures.

The Vinquiry MCW strain has a superior tolerance to low temperatures, to pH below 3.0, and to alcohol levels up to 15%. These characteristics make this strain suitable for the most difficult ML fermentations. For home winemaking, this culture is available in a 2-g format for preparing 19 L of starter. It is also available in liquid format.

The Uvaferm® MLD freeze-dried format is a direct inoculum bacterium with a high alcohol tolerance. It enhances a wine's freshness and fruity aromas while producing low volatile acidity. No carbon dioxide is produced during ML fermentation and as such, progress is not visible. For home winemaking, this culture is available in a 3-g format for up to 227 L of wine. It is not available as a liquid culture.

The Lalvin® OSU strain is a popular choice of freeze-dried ML culture. It is available in a 2-g format for inoculating between 20-50 L of wine. The culture can also be prepared to inoculate up to 250 L of wine. For such a large volume, instructions (using apple juice) for a difficult ML fermentation should be followed.

For a favourable ML fermentation environment, the content of the packet should be poured in 25 mL of distilled water at 25° to 30° C (77° to 86° F). The inoculum should be stirred lightly following a 15-minute rehydration period. It is then added directly to the wine when the Brix

Table 4-9
Lalvin® OSU environmental conditions

	Favourable MLF environment	More difficult MLF environment
Method	Distilled water	Distilled water + apple juice
Volume to be inoculated using 2 g of ML culture	20 - 50 L	50 - 250 L
Temperature	20° - 25° C 68° - 77° F	<16° C <61° F
Free SO2	<10 mg/L	>10 mg/L
pH	>3.2	<3.2
Alcohol content	<12.5% alc./vol.	>12.5% alc./vol.

(SG) is less than 5 B° (1.020). The wine should be at a temperature between 20° and 25° C (68° and 77° F), have a free SO2 level less than 10 mg/L, a pH greater than 3.2, and an alcohol content less than 12.5%.

Under a more difficult ML fermentation environment—where one or more of the above conditions are not met—the Lalvin® OSU inoculum should be conditioned before adding it to the wine. The inoculum is first prepared with distilled water, as described above, and the suspension is then added to 25 mL of commercial apple juice, **containing no preservatives**. The container should be loosely covered and there should be little air space between the inoculum and the cover. The inoculum should be held at room temperature for 2 to 4 days and then added directly to the wine. Table 4-9 summarizes requirements for a favourable and a more difficult ML environment when using 2-g packets of Lalvin® OSU ML culture.

When several batches of wine need to be inoculated, a sample of wine undergoing ML fermentation can be used as inoculum. The sample should be withdrawn approximately 2 weeks after start of ML fermentation. Batches should be inoculated with approximately a 2 percent sample volume. For example, approximately 1 L of ML-fermenting wine should be used to inoculate a 54-L batch. This method of cross-inoculation reduces the cost of ML cultures to be used but does not always work as reliably as straight inoculation.

In commercial winemaking, ML fermentation is conducted in either stainless steel tanks or in oak barrels. Oak-barrel, ML-fermented wines are considered to be more complex than their stainless steel tank counterparts.

Oak barrels used in ML fermentation will become heavily populated with ML bacteria. Successive vintages can be ML-fermented in these same barrels without any addition of bacteria. The winemaker's challenge is to prevent formation of other spoilage bacteria. To minimize the risk of spoilage, many winemakers will re-inoculate the wine each year when it is to be aged in the barrel for an extended period of time. Oak barrels used for ML-fermented wines should not be used for wines for which ML fermentation is not desired.

The production of tiny and rapid-forming carbon dioxide bubbles should be noticed during ML fermentation, which will normally complete within approximately one to three months if temperature is held between 15° and 18° C (59° and 64° F). If ML paper chromatography equipment and procedures are not readily available, the absence of any carbon dioxide activity should be used to confirm completion of ML fermentation. The technique of observing bubbles during ML fermentation should be confirmed with the manufacturer's instructions as newer cultures on the market behave differently.

When the ML fermentation is completed, the wine should be sulphited and returned to the cellar for storage at a cooler temperature.

Warning: When using anaerobic species for ML fermentation, the wine should NOT be racked as aeration will adversely affect the ML culture.

4.6.2 Inhibiting ML fermentation

ML fermentation is often not desirable for certain grape varieties, or winemakers simply prefer wines that have not undergone this fermentation. In such cases, ML fermentation must be actively inhibited.

There are several methods, used independently or in combination, to inhibit ML fermentation. The most effective method involves sulphiting the must beyond the prescribed maximum before alcoholic fermentation, followed by a racking using the recommended schedule (refer to section 5.1).

An alternative method for white winemaking is to conduct alcoholic fermentation at a temperature between 10° and 14° C (50° and

57° F), i.e., which is below the normal range for ML fermentation. Both white and red wines must be stored within this temperature range during the maturation and ageing processes. The alcoholic fermentation can also be carried out with an ML fermentation-inhibiting yeast culture such as the Lalvin® EC-1118® or the RED STAR® Premier Cuvée. The strains in these cultures are more competitive for nutrients, produce higher amounts of SO_2, and may produce compounds that help halt ML fermentation.

Sterile filtration can also be used to strip the wine of any yeast or bacterium that might otherwise favour ML fermentation. Refer to section 5.3 for a description of sterile filtration.

Although the pH level is another parameter that can be controlled, it is not recommended to alter a wine's pH to inhibit ML fermentation unless necessary.

When it is desired to reduce malic acid concentration by ML fermentation, it is recommended to blend a completely ML-fermented wine with an ML-inhibited wine. Inhibiting a partially completed ML fermentation will result in a wine with a high ML bacterium concentration. Such a wine will be very unstable and can become problematic.

4.6.3 ML determination by paper chromatography

The ability to monitor and control ML fermentation progression is critical in achieving the desired quality and style of wine. ML fermentation is complete when malic acid is totally converted into lactic acid. ML determination by paper chromatography is a qualitative, industry-accepted analytical procedure to detect the presence or absence of malic and lactic acids. When used carefully, quantitative determinations of acid concentrations can be made. The procedure is based on the ability of separating the acid components in wine, namely tartaric, citric, malic, and lactic acids. Separation can be accomplished regardless of the number of components and their respective concentrations. It is based on the relative adsorption of each acid component.

The procedure, often referred to as vertical-style chromatography, involves the use of cellulose chromatography paper, specifically manufactured for this purpose, immersed in a solvent (also referred to as reagent) containing a colour indicator. The chromatography paper is "spotted" with reference acid solutions and samples of wines to be analyzed. As the solvent is absorbed and travels up the paper, acid components in the reference solutions and wine samples are absorbed at different rates and cause spots to form. The spots become visible as the paper is allowed to dry. Based on the relative absorption rate of each component, a qualitative identification of components is possible as well as fairly good quantitative results. The different absorption rate of each component will cause spots to travel different distances up the paper.

Paper chromatography procedure
The following laboratory apparatus and chemicals are required to perform vertical-style paper chromatography tests:
- ⊹ 20 cm x 30 cm Whatman® #1 chromatography paper
- ⊹ 4-L wide-opening jar with a tight-closing lid
- ⊹ disposable micropipets (capillary tubes are very expensive)
- ⊹ chromatography solvent (a solution of n-butanol, formic acid and bromocresol-green indicator)—colour of solvent is orange
- ⊹ 3.0 g/L (0.3%) malic-acid solution
- ⊹ 3.0 g/L lactic-acid solution
- ⊹ 3.0 g/L tartaric-acid solution (optional)
- ⊹ 3.0 g/L citric-acid solution (optional)
- ⊹ a small sample of each wine to be tested and analyzed

Inexpensive paper chromatography kits, such as the one produced and assembled by Presque Isle Wine Cellars shown in Figure 4-7, comprising of all necessary material and chemicals are available from specialized laboratories or winemaking supply shops providing wine analysis products. Assembling all required material and chemicals individually can be very costly and a challenging task. Another advantage of kits specifically designed for wine analysis is that the chromatography solvent is ready to use. References 3 [Boulton, Singleton, Bisson and Kunke], 7 [Margalit], and 10 [Ough and Amerine]

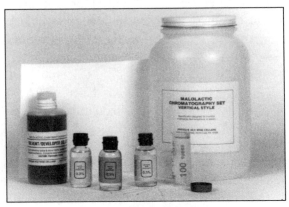

Figure 4-7: Paper chromatography kit

in Appendix E provide detailed instructions on how to prepare the chromatography solvent.

Caution: *Chromatography solvent involves the use of dangerous chemicals and requires knowledge and experience in laboratory procedures. One should not attempt to prepare the solvent unless very familiar with the handling of these chemicals. Chromatography tests should always be conducted in a well-ventilated area as the solvent has a very powerful and irritating smell.*

Using a **lead pencil** (ink will run when absorbed by the solvent), the Whatman® #1 paper should be labeled as shown in Figure 4-8 with a reference dot or "x" marked on the line for each sample to be used. The reference dots are labeled as "T" for tartaric acid, "C" for citric acid, "M" for malic acid, "L" for lactic acid, and WS for each wine sample to be tested. Tartaric and citric acid reference dots are optional. Dots should be spaced at a minimum of 2.5 cm from paper edges and from adjacent dots. The line with reference dots should be at least 3 cm from the bottom edge of the paper.

Using a different micropipet for each solution and wine sample, the micropipet should be immersed in the solution or wine sample to withdraw a small amount. Each reference dot should then be spotted with the correct reference solution or wine sample. Each dot should be spotted 4 times ensuring to let each spot dry before re-applying. This will provide better results. If excessive volume is used for spotting, or if spots are not allowed to dry, these will become large and will make the analysis of results more difficult.

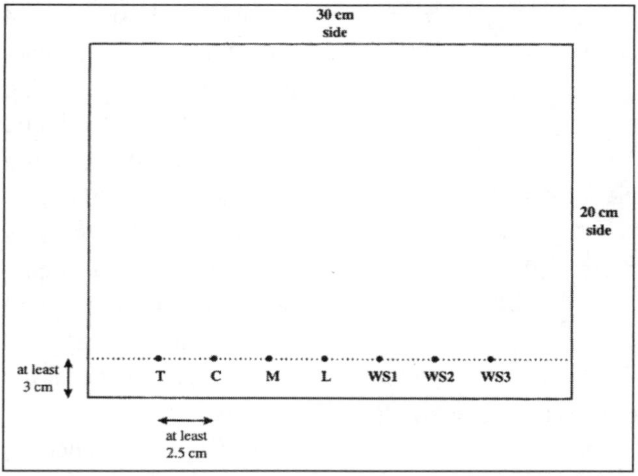

Once the paper has been spotted, it should be left to dry for approximately 15 to 30 minutes. It should then be curled into a cylindrical shape with the axis along the 20-cm side of the paper. The two 20-cm ends should be held together, *without overlapping,*

Figure 4-8: Labeling Whatman® #1 paper for spotting

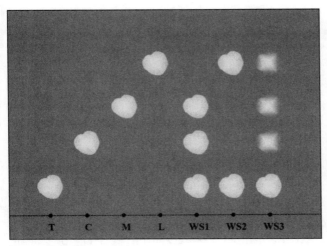

Figure 4-9: Chromatogram

and then stapled. Approximately 100 mL of the solvent is then poured in the jar. The paper should be inserted in the jar and immersed in the solvent. The line drawn on the chromatography paper should be above the solvent level for the test to work properly. Lastly, the jar should be closed tightly with a lid.

The solvent will start traveling up the chromatography paper and will cause separation of acid components. Spot formation will not be visible yet. The solvent should be allowed to reach the top of the paper, which may take up to 6 hours. The paper can be left in the jar safely overnight. When completed, the paper should be removed from the jar and then uncurled. It should be hung to dry in a warm, well-ventilated area to volatilize the solvent and to allow spot colours to form. The left-over solvent can be returned to its original container and be reused for other chromatography tests.

After approximately 3 hours, yellowish spots will appear on the paper. Although results will be visible, spots will become much clearer after several hours or as much as one day when the paper becomes completely dry. At that point, the paper will become blue-green while the spots will have a yellowish colour. Using a blow dryer will accelerate the drying time.

Interpreting chromatography results
The chromatography result is referred to as a chromatogram. Figure 4-9 illustrates a typical chromatogram showing how the spots have traveled and formed. To interpret the results, the following relationship applies relative to distance traveled:

tartaric < citric < malic < lactic

This relationship indicates that tartaric acid spots will travel the least distance while lactic acid spots will travel the most distance. The size of each wine sample acid spot can also be compared to the reference acid solution. A spot smaller in size and of lower intensity than the reference spot indicates that the acid concentration in the wine sample is less than 3.0 g/L. Similarly, a more intense and larger spot indicates an acid concentration greater than the reference 3.0 g/L-solution. This quantitative analysis is only valid if the same precise volume of each sample is used in the spotting process. The acid concentration of samples will be different when different volumes are dispensed, even if by a single drop.

In Figure 4-9, the chromatogram confirms that wine sample WSI has not started ML fermentation, as a malic acid spot is present and there is no lactic acid spot visible. WSI also contains tartaric acid as well as citric acid. Wine sample WS2 has completed ML fermentation due to the absence of a malic acid spot and the presence of a lactic acid spot. There is no citric acid present in sample WS2. In wine sample WS3, ML fermentation has begun but is not complete. The malic acid spot has started disappearing while the lactic acid spot has started appearing. Citric acid concentration is also less than 3.0 g/L. As wine contains many other different acids, other spots may become visible depending on the acid concentrations. The spots will typically be very small or not visible as concentrations of secondary acids are very small.

It should be noted that, due to the different chemical structure of malic acid additives, any must and/or wine acid correction using malic acid will yield invalid chromatography results. Acid correction using malic acid additives should therefore be performed post-ML fermentation if desired. Tartaric acid is, however, the preferred and recommended choice for acid correction.

Note: Although a malic acid spot may be absent, a small amount may still be present in the wine. Therefore, it is recommended to let ML fermentation carry on for another week or two before stabilizing the wine.

4.7 STABILIZATION

Stabilization is an important winemaking procedure following alcoholic and ML fermentations. It can also be performed during or following the clarification (fining) operation, but always before filtering and bottling operations. It is required:

1. to eliminate the risk of microbial spoilage,
2. to reduce the effects of oxidation so wines do not age prematurely,
3. to ensure fermentation does not re-occur in sweet wines once bottled,
4. to maintain colour stability and clarity throughout the ageing process, and
5. to prevent adverse effects when wine is subjected to very low or very high temperatures.

Although wines may be clear with a brilliant colour when bottled, they can become cloudy during ageing if not previously stabilized.

There are two common and complementary stabilization procedures for home winemakers that should always be followed: 1) stabilization using preservatives—the most common preservatives being potassium or sodium metabisulphite and potassium sorbate, commonly referred to as sorbate—and 2) cold stabilization.

4.7.1 Preservatives and stabilizing agents

The most common preservatives and stabilizing agents used in home winemaking are sulphite, ascorbic acid and potassium sorbate, or products which combine one or more of these agents with other œnological products such as tannin. Tannisol is one such product.

Sulphite
Potassium metabisulphite, or sulphite, is the industry-accepted chemical additive for preserving wines.

As a preservative, sulphite powder should be added to achieve a maximum free SO_2 level of 50 mg/L by first dissolving it in a small quantity of warm water and then stirring it gently into the wine. Sulphite powder should never be added directly to wine as it may not dissolve properly. Alternatively, Campden tablets can be used. Section 3.4 discusses specific sulphite properties and applications of this chemical.

Note: Sodium metabisulphite is another source of sulphite, in Campden tablets or as a powder, used as a preservative. Some winemakers opt for the potassium form of sulphite to minimize the amount of sodium introduced in their wines. They prefer to limit the amount of sodium intake in their diets for health reasons.

Ascorbic acid (vitamin C)

Ascorbic acid (vitamin C) is an ingredient often used in home winemaking for its antioxidant properties; however, its use is not well understood.

Ascorbic acid only has an extremely transitory antioxidant effect on wines. It fixes to dissolved oxygen in wine and quickly converts to dehydroascorbic acid—a weak organic acid—within 3 or 4 days. Following this oxidation, ascorbic acid is exhausted and serves no further function. It is mainly used to scavenge oxygen in wine before bottling or other operations where the wine will be subjected to little and temporary aeration.

Another function of ascorbic acid is in preventing a condition known as ferric (iron) casse, caused by oxidation of iron present in wine. Ferric casse will cause wine to become cloudy and hazy when there is a high concentration of oxygen (typically from excessive exposure to air) in high-iron content wines. High-iron content wines that are handled with minimal exposure to air do not need to be treated with ascorbic acid.

Ascorbic acid crystals are added at a rate of 2-3 g/hL of wine just before bottling. The crystals should first be dissolved in water. Dosage should never exceed 10 g/hL to avoid imparting an off-taste to the wine. It should never be used without sulphite or without the recommended minimum level of free SO_2; otherwise, it may actually favour oxidation of the wine.

Potassium sorbate

Potassium sorbate—a salt derived from sorbic acid and often referred to as sorbate—is a widely accepted food and beverage additive used to inhibit growth of yeast and mould. Its main application is in stabilizing wines having residual sugar, and is most effective at higher alcohol concentrations. It is added to wine prior to bottling to prevent renewed yeast activity and bottle fermentation because of sugar still present. If wine starts re-fermenting, it can cause bottles to explode. It is therefore good practice to use potassium sorbate in making sweet wines. It is not required for properly sulphited dry wines where the residual sugar content is too low and alcohol level sufficiently high for yeast to restart fermentation.

Home winemakers who prefer to accelerate the winemaking process for early bottling and drinking should always use potassium

Figure 4-10: Tannisol tablets

sorbate to stabilize wine. As a precautionary measure, wine should be stabilized with potassium sorbate if the amount of residual sugar cannot be determined. Wine kits very often include potassium sorbate as novice winemakers often unintentionally do not ferment the wine to dryness and then bottle prematurely. The quantity of potassium sorbate supplied with kits, however, is often not adequate and it may not prevent renewed fermentation if the level of residual sugar is too high.

Potassium sorbate is commonly available as vermicelli-shaped crystals and should be dissolved at a rate of 10-20 g/hL of wine. The higher rate within the recommended range should be used as a wine's pH approaches or exceeds 3.5, or when the alcohol level is relatively low. The sorbate solution should be stirred vigourously for it to be effective.

A sorbate treatment should always be preceded by a sulphite treatment. This stabilization treatment should be done following clarification or before bottling.

An alternative method to prevent re-fermentation is sterile filtration.

Note: *Potassium sorbate CANNOT be used to stop an active fermentation.*

Caution: *Potassium sorbate should NOT be used to stabilize a wine having undergone ML fermentation. Sorbic acid in potassium sorbate reacts negatively with lactic bacteria resulting in a geranium-like odour—a serious wine fault.*

Tannisol
Tannisol, shown in Figure 4-10, is a product that packages potassium metabisulphite, ascorbic acid and tannin into a convenient format for home winemaking. It is available in a package of 10 tablets each weighing 10 g and consisting of 95% potassium metabisulphite, 3% ascorbic acid and 2% tannin. The recommended dosage is 1 tablet per hL of wine to be preserved. The dosage can be increased to 2 tablets for

wine with faults needing a higher concentration of sulphite. For sweet wines, the dosage can be increased to 3 tablets per hL of wine. Tablets can be easily split into halves or quarters for 54-L and 25-L batches, respectively.

Tannisol should first be crushed down to a powder and then dissolved in a small quantity of warm water. The Tannisol solution should then be stirred in the wine and mixed thoroughly.

4.7.2 Cold stabilization

Note: This section details cold stabilization methods. For a discussion of the impacts on TA and pH, refer to sections 3.2 and 3.3.

Cold stabilization is the process of cooling wine down to a temperature favouring tartaric acid crystallization (tartrate crystals). This process is often referred to as chill proofing. A cold-stabilized wine will not cause tartaric acid crystallization if subjected to low temperatures for an extended period of time. Although not harmful, tartrate crystals—a potassium bitartrate salt—affect the appearance of wine by precipitating at the bottom of the bottle when the wine is chilled for an extended time. Cold stabilization is optional for wines where acidity does not require any adjustment as tartaric acid crystallization causes the TA to drop. Adding metatartaric acid when the cooling temperature cannot be achieved can also be used to prevent tartaric acid crystallization. Despite the fact that it is considered a safe, common additive in European wine regions, its use in commercial wines is illegal in the U.S. and Canada. The main reason is that the effect of metatartaric acid cannot be guaranteed for any extended period of time unless the wine is continuously stored at cold temperatures, e.g., 0° C (32° F). Otherwise, the wine's acidity will start increasing in just a few months as the temperature rises. Cold stabilization should be chosen as the preferred method whenever possible.

Cold stabilization is carried out by placing the wine in cold storage at a temperature between –4° and 4° C (25° and 39° F) for approximately 3 to 6 weeks. The lower temperature is more effective and faster. The wine does not require racking before cold stabilization. When the recommended low temperature cannot be achieved, wine can be stored in a cool wine cellar to precipitate tartrate crystals although this will take considerably longer. If wine will never be stored for an extended time at a temperature lower than cellar temperature, cold stabilization is not required, as the wine will not precipitate tartrate crystals. It is good practice however to always cold stabilize wines as future storage conditions can never be guaranteed.

To prevent precipitation of tartrate crystals by the addition method, metatartaric acid powder should be added at a rate of up to 10 g/hL of wine. This is accomplished by dissolving 2.5 mL (½ tsp) of metatartaric acid powder in 25 mL of cold water and stirring well. This solution should be added at a rate of 1 mL/L of wine just before bottling or filtration and then stirred well. Ideally, the wine should be at cellar temperature to increase the effectiveness of this operation.

Metatartaric acid is a strong chemical that should be measured carefully and used diligently. Metatartaric acid powder should be stored in the refrigerator to prolong its shelf life. It quickly (approximately 2 months) loses effectiveness if stored at room temperature. For this reason, wines treated with metatartaric acid should be cold-cellared and should be consumed early, before the cellar temperature starts rising.

Cold stabilization may require acid correction since tartaric acid is precipitated therefore reducing total acidity. Therefore, if wine has undergone ML fermentation and acid correction is required, the wine should be cold stabilized before adding any acid. Only one acidification procedure will be required.

Note: *Home winemakers should NOT cold stabilize wine in oak barrels. In such a case, it would be extremely difficult, if not impossible, to remove tartrate crystals from the inside wall of the barrels.*

5
CLARIFICATION

Cloudiness and haze are considered serious wine faults as these affect the physical appearance of wine. Wine can only be fully appreciated if it is clear and free of particles in suspension. Traditional clarification of wines is achieved strictly through sedimentation and racking. Wine can also be clarified by using fining agents, which coagulate particles in suspension and precipitate them, and optionally by filtration. Filtration is more commonly used for producing wines to be commercialized quickly.

Clarification of wines by fining or filtration is a much-debated topic in winemaking circles. Traditionalists believe in natural winemaking methods without the use of chemicals and/or mechanical processing. They maintain that such processing alters the wine's structure, taste and colour. Modern winemakers, on the other hand, advocate the use of fining agents to clarify wines but do not filter their premium wines. In general, filtration is a shunned practice for premium wines. Many commercial premium wines are now labeled as unfiltered. This is a marketing tactic to promote unfiltered wines as being of higher quality. However, Emile Peynaud, one of the greatest œnologists of the twentieth century, commented on "the sensory consequences of filtering" in his book *Knowing and Making Wine* [reference 11], "that the mechanical action of filtering has never had a negative influence on quality."

Clarification by fining is carried out after fermentation has been completed. It is however possible to prepare the must or wine, before or during fermentation, for eventual clarification. Proper clarification by fining followed by careful racking will always yield a very clear wine. A clear wine does not imply that there will be no further sedimentation, causing a deposit at the bottom of the bottle. This applies generally to red wines where the concentration of particles is very high causing sedimentation during storing and ageing.

Clarification by filtration is performed following stabilization to filter particles resulting from this operation.

If the wine will be aged in oak barrels, clarification can be carried out following the ageing process, as the tannins will clarify the wine. Tannin acts as an excellent clarifying agent.

5.1 CLARIFICATION BY RACKING

Fermentation, fining and stabilization winemaking processes produce sediment that needs to be separated, or racked, from the wine. Racking wine from its sediment is key to producing clear and stable wines free

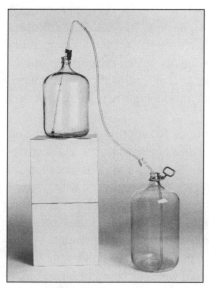

of substances that might otherwise interact with the wine when bottled. Racking is performed either by gravity by siphoning wine from one container to another or by using a pump. Figure 5-1 illustrates the setup to rack wine from its sediment by gravity. Section 2.5.2 describes the siphoning procedure.

Although wine can be racked as often as the winemaker deems necessary, notwithstanding the negative effects of over-processing and extended exposure of wine to air, a clear wine requires a minimum recommended racking schedule. White and red wines require slightly different racking schedules. It is important to rack at the recommended intervals as the wine could develop bad flavours

Figure 5-1: Setup for racking wine by gravity

(autolysis) if it is left in contact with the gross lees for an extended time.

5.1.1 Recommended racking schedule for white wines

For white wines, the first racking is performed after a 12-hour period following the pressing operation when the mud-like sediment (gross lees) has settled to the bottom of the container. The first racking takes place before yeast inoculation and the start of alcoholic fermentation, and is only required for winemaking from grapes.

A second racking is recommended at the end of the alcoholic fermentation phase that produces heavy sedimentation, or gross lees. Wines to be ML-fermented can either be racked once, following both fermentations or can be racked just before starting the ML fermentation. The latter is recommended as the finer lees are most beneficial for ML-fermented wines. Racking can be performed when the Brix (SG) has stabilized at 0.0 B° (between 0.990 and 0.995) for at least 2 weeks.

The third racking follows fining and stabilization procedures, and prepares the wine for bulk ageing. The amount of sediment depends on the extent of the fining procedure, the fining agent used, and on whether the wine is subjected to cold stabilization.

A fourth and final racking is required after the wine has aged for 6 to 12 months, before bottling or filtration. The amount of sediment is relatively smaller than in previous rackings although it may still be significant depending on vinification and winemaking methods used.

5.1.2 Recommended racking schedule for red wines

For red wines, the first racking is performed from the primary fermentor to closed containers following maceration, alcoholic fermentation, and post-ferment maceration phases. It can also be done at any time during one of these phases when the desired level of phenolic extraction is obtained. The leftover pomace is transferred to a winepress for pressing, and the press-run juice is transferred to closed containers. A warm ambient temperature should be maintained if the wine will undergo ML fermentation.

A second racking is required following the end of alcoholic fermentation if the wine has completed fermentation in a closed container. Wines to be ML-fermented can either be racked once, following both fermentations or can be racked just before starting the ML fermentation.

The latter is recommended as the finer lees are most beneficial for ML-fermented wines. Racking can be performed when the Brix (SG) has stabilized at 0.0 B° (between 0.990 and 0.995) for at least 2 weeks.

The third racking follows fining and stabilization procedures, and prepares the wine for bulk ageing. As in white winemaking, the amount of sediment depends on the extent of these two procedures.

A fourth racking is required after the wine has aged for 6 to 12 months, before bottling or filtration. If the wine is to be oak-aged, an additional racking is recommended every 3 to 6 months. Extracted oak tannins will act as clarifying agents causing suspended particles to sediment. Heavily fined oak-aged wines will throw a heavy deposit requiring very careful racking. This fourth racking is not required for red wines vinified by carbonic maceration, as they will not undergo any ageing. The wines will be bottled immediately after fining, stabilization and filtering operations.

Figure 5-2: Private Reserve® for protecting wines from oxidation

5.1.3 Topping up

The racking operation always results in a smaller volume of clear wine as the sediment volume is separated and discarded. The lost volume should be replaced using a procedure referred to as topping up.

The practice of topping up wine in containers and oak barrels is required to minimize exposure of the wine to air that could cause spoilage. By maintaining a minimum air space—known as ullage—between the bung and the wine surface, the risk of spoilage is greatly reduced. Through careful planning and management of total wine production capacity, using different size containers will ensure that these are always topped up. Small quantities of wine left over following a racking operation can be stored and topped up in a small container. If this is not possible, wine of the same variety and quality from a previous vintage can be used to top up. Unless done in very small proportions, water should not be used to top up as this will dilute the wine. Wine dilution will result in a thin wine with diluted flavours and aromas.

Alternatively, when a container cannot be fully topped up, the wine can be stored under a layer of non-toxic inert gases—a technique used by commercial wineries—to protect the wine from oxidation. Private Reserve® cans, shown in Figure 5-2, containing a blend of nitrogen, carbon dioxide and argon gases are available from wine shops or liquor stores. This blend is tasteless and inert, and therefore does not alter the composition or organoleptic qualities of the wine.

Failure to regularly top up containers may cause excessive oxidation resulting in acetic spoilage and/or mycoderma.

Acetic spoilage, or acetification, is caused by acetobacter, vinegar bacteria responsible for acetic acid. Acetic acid, the main component of volatile acidity (VA), is the product of ethanol oxidation. Acetobacter grow in an aerobic environment and can be prevented by keeping containers topped up.

Mycoderma is the more-advanced and irreversible condition of excessive oxidation resulting from the presence of film-forming yeasts from the *Mycoderma* genus. This condition will manifest itself by a white film forming on the wine's surface. Keeping containers topped up can prevent such a condition.

5.2 CLARIFICATION BY FINING

In home winemaking, clarification by fining is usually required for wines produced from fresh juice or grapes. The high-protein content in these wines can cause clarity instability. Fining in wines produced from kits is only required to accelerate the clarification process. In either case, excessive fining should be avoided to minimize stripping of the wine's colour.

When selecting a fining agent, the compactness of the lees should be taken into account in the fining process as some agents will make the racking operation easier than others. Compactness is rated in terms of lees density as either poor or good. For example, a fining agent with a poor lees compactness rating will cause a greater volume of sediment to form and/or may require a second racking as sedimentation is less effective. Fining agents with a poor lees compactness rating will result in an appreciable reduction (for example, 5 percent) of wine volume. Carboys, barrels or other containers should not be moved before racking to minimize such reduction.

Table 5-1
Recommended fining agents and their compactness rating

Fining agent	White wine	Red wine	Lees compactness
Bentonite	Yes	Yes	Poor
Casein	Yes		Good
Egg whites		Yes	Good
Gelatin	Yes*	Yes	Good
Isinglass	Yes		Poor
Kieselsol	Yes	Yes	Good
Pectic enzymes	Yes	Yes	Good
Sparkolloid®	Yes	Yes	Poor

*Requires the addition of tannin. Refer to section 5.2.4 - Gelatin

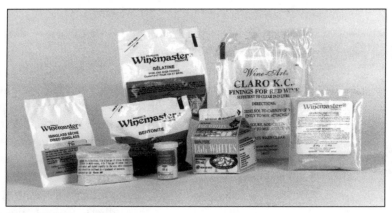

Figure 5-3: Fining Agents

Table 5-1 lists the recommended commercially available fining agents for clarifying white and red wines. Lees compactness of each fining agent is also rated. Figure 5-3 illustrates these fining agents.

Before addition to the wine to be clarified, fining agents in solid form must be dissolved in **water**, unless specified otherwise. Fining agents lose their effectiveness if dissolved or introduced directly into the wine.

Kit wines should stand for a minimum of 2 weeks following fining and before stabilization. This is to allow sedimentation of particles in suspension. The sedimentation period should be extended to a minimum of 4 weeks for wines from grape juice and 8 weeks for wines from grapes.

Although grape tannin is not classified as a fining agent, clarification is often dependent on the presence of tannins. Powdered grape tannin is available as an additive to wine. Refer to section 5.2.9.

5.2.1 Bentonite

Bentonite, an absorptive clay, is a highly-recommended clarifying agent for white wine musts as it inhibits haze caused by naturally-occurring proteins in the must. Bentonite's clarifying effectiveness makes it a popular choice as a fining agent amongst winemakers. It is also recommended for red wines.

For optimal results, it is recommended to add a bentonite solution to the must before the start of alcoholic fermentation. Optionally, it can be added to the fermenting wine after its first or second racking, or before cold stabilization.

Bentonite is added at a rate of 25-100 g/hL of must or wine. To prepare a bentonite solution, the bentonite powder should be added to a volume of warm water, in mL, approximately 10 to 15 times its weight, e.g., 30 g in 375 mL. The solution should be shaken vigourously for a few minutes, and then left to stand for 24 hours. The bentonite solution should be stirred occasionally during this period. The solution should then be added at a rate of 10 mL/L to the must or wine, and stirred well. Using the above example, this rate provides 0.8 g (30 g × 10 mL ÷ 375 mL) of bentonite per litre of must or wine, or 80 g/hL. One half of the recommended quantities should be used if adding bentonite at the end of fermentation. Wines treated with bentonite should be stored at a temperature between 15° and 25° C (59° and 77° F) during the fining period.

To ensure a good effervescence and a good refermentation in the bottle when making sparkling wine, the concentration should be reduced by approximately one-half.

5.2.2 Casein

Casein, a phosphoprotein of milk, is primarily recommended for clarifying white wines. It is available as a powder and is added at a rate of 50-100 g/hL of wine. It can also be used to improve colour in white wines, resulting from oxidation, by using the maximum recommended dosage.

Casein powder is dissolved in a small quantity of cold water and then added quickly to the wine while stirring vigourously. A bentonite treatment is recommended following the casein fining.

Warning: Although most of the casein is removed by racking prior to bottling, care should be taken as some people may have allergic reactions to this substance.

5.2.3 Egg whites

Fining with egg whites, a traditional method of clarifying red wines, is still widely used in modern winemaking as it proves to be an excellent fining agent. An important advantage of egg white as a fining agent is that the loss of colour is minimized. Being rich in albumen, egg white has the added advantage of softening a wine's astringency and is therefore most appropriate for highly tannic wines or wines undergoing barrel ageing. Egg white fining is mainly used for wines produced from grapes.

In preparing egg whites for clarification, the egg white must be separated from the yolk and then added to salted water. The recommended dosage is 5-10 g/hL of wine, or 1 to 2 egg whites per 100 L. Alternatively, pure, refrigerated egg whites can be used. Typically, approximately 30 mL (2 tbsp) of pure egg white is the equivalent of 1 large egg white.

For each egg white, a pinch of table salt should be dissolved in 100 mL of water and then combined with the egg white. Egg whites can be added to the wine directly into the barrel and mixed well. The wine should be racked in 1 to 2 weeks, no later.

5.2.4 Gelatin

Gelatin, obtained from animal tissues and available as a powder, is a good fining agent for red wines. It is usually not recommended for fining white wines as it will reduce the amount of tannins, and in fact, may not fine adequately if the tannin content is too low. To avoid over-fining in white wines, grape tannin powder should be added before gelatin fining. For excessively tannic red wines, gelatin is an excellent fining agent. Red wines vinified by carbonic maceration will benefit from a gelatin fining as their tannin content may be too high.

Gelatin powder is added at a rate of 1-5 g/hL of wine, or up to 25 g/hL for wines having a higher-than-normal concentration of suspended particles or having high pectin content. To prepare a gelatin solution, (unflavoured) gelatin powder should be soaked in approximately 25 times its weight of warm water. For example, if 10 g/hL of gelatin is desired in 20 L of wine, then 2 g of gelatin should be dissolved in 50 mL of warm water. The gelatin should be stirred thoroughly until dissolved completely. Some gelatin manufacturers may recommend soaking the gelatin in cold water and then heating it to parboil.

The warm gelatin solution should be mixed with a little wine—about twice the amount of water used—and then added to the rest of the wine. The wine should be mixed thoroughly and then racked from its sediment in 2 to 3 weeks time.

5.2.5 Isinglass

Isinglass, a very pure gelatin prepared from the air bladders of fish, is a popular fining agent amongst home winemakers as it proves to be very effective in a short time. It is recommended mainly for white wines. One disadvantage of isinglass is that it produces a heavy deposit.

Isinglass is available either in powder format, added at a rate of between 1-3 g/hL of wine, or as a liquid added at a rate of up to 1 mL/L of wine. The powder format has proven to be more effective. Liquid isinglass should be diluted in a small quantity of **wine** and stirred into a wine batch after fermentation is complete. Isinglass powder should be completely dissolved in water at a temperature between 16° and 18° C (61° and 64° F) and stirred thoroughly. The solution should stand for 15 minutes and then stirred again for 2 minutes. The solution should then be added to the wine and stirred vigorously for 2 or 3 minutes. The sediment should be allowed to settle at the bottom of the container for 2 to 3 weeks before racking.

5.2.6 Kieselsol

Kieselsol, a silicate suspension, is used in conjunction with gelatin to increase its effectiveness. Kieselsol/gelatin is an excellent clarifying agent for both white and red wines. It is specifically effective in wines with low tannin content. Therefore, wines produced from concentrate, sterilized or fresh juice can be clarified effectively with kieselsol. Wine-Art currently markets kieselsol under the Claro K.C.® brand name. A package contains both the kieselsol and gelatin. Separate packages are required for white and red wines as the necessary gelatin quantities are different.

Kieselsol should be added at a rate of 25-50 mL/hL of wine. Using Claro K.C.®, 11 mL of kieselsol per 20 L of wine is added directly to the wine and stirred gently. The fermentation lock should be replaced on the container. After 24 hours, gelatin should be added directly to the wine. For white wines, 100 mL of gelatin is used per 20 L of wine while 50 mL is used for red wines. The wine should be stirred gently and then the fermentation lock should be replaced. A minimum of 1 to 2 weeks should be allowed before racking.

5.2.7 Pectic enzymes

Wine contains pectin that may cause cloudiness and, therefore, would require to be clarified. Pectic enzymes are added to wine to remove excess pectin and are especially beneficial for press-run wines (from grapes) being richer in pectin content. They are used to fine both white and red wines. Pectic enzymes can also be used at crushing to increase the yield of free-run juice.

Pectic enzymes powder is added at a rate of 1-2 g/hL of white wine and 2-4 g/hL of red wine by first dissolving the powder in cool water. It is recommended to add pectic enzymes following the crushing operation, as a preventive additive, although they can be added during the fining operation. The must or wine should be at a minimum temperature of 27° C (80° F) for pectic enzymes to be effective.

If cloudiness persists after fining, this indicates that the wine may contain excessive pectin. To test for the presence of pectin, 50 mL of wine is added to 200 mL of methanol. If heavy whitish sediment forms, the wine contains excessive pectin and should be treated again with pectic enzymes. Mechanical filtration may be required to further clarify the wine.

Note: The manufacturer's prescribed dilution rate should be observed as pectic enzymes are sold in different concentrations.

5.2.8 Sparkolloid®

Sparkolloid®, an alginic acid salt, is also a popular fining agent amongst home winemakers and is used primarily for red wines although suitable for white wines. Although Sparkolloid® is a very effective fining agent, it has disadvantages. It will tend to throw very heavy sediment causing an appreciable loss in wine. More important, fining with Sparkolloid®

requires a much longer period of time—up to 6 months—to allow proper sedimentation of particles in suspension. To accelerate the fining operation for earlier bottling, a second fining agent recommended for red wines can be used. The second fining should be performed at least one month following the Sparkolloid® fining.

Sparkolloid® powder is added at a rate of 10-40 g/hL of wine. To prepare a Sparkolloid® solution, water must first be brought to a boil in an enamel, stainless steel or other heat-resistant saucepan. The Sparkolloid® powder should then be added to the boiling water and stirred well. The solution should be left to boil for 20 minutes while stirring continuously to dissolve all the powder. The hot Sparkolloid® solution should be added to the wine and stirred well. The wine should be left to clarify for approximately 6 months before racking.

When using Sparkolloid® to clarify white wines, grape tannins may need to be added to the wine, several days before fining, if the tannin content is too low.

5.2.9 Grape tannins

Tannin is a key œnological ingredient contributing to a wine's structure and taste. It is also required to age wine for an extended period of time. The lesser-known application of tannin is in the fining operation.

When a wine to be fined with gelatin or Sparkolloid® has a low tannin level, grape tannins can be added to facilitate fining. In this case, grape tannins should be added a few days before fining.

Grape tannin powder is added at a rate of 10-30 g/hL of wine, or up to 50 g/hL when fining with gelatin where the pectin content is high. A tannin solution should be prepared by dissolving the powder in warm wine and then adding it directly to the wine batch and stirring well.

5.3 CLARIFICATION BY FILTRATION

The effects of wine filtering on its quality are a much-debated topic amongst winemakers. Premium-quality wines are seldom filtered, as fining is deemed sufficient. Filtering is believed to strip wine of key organoleptic ingredients as well as altering its colour. The industry consensus is that premium wines will retain their high quality over a longer time when fined only; a claim not supported for filtered wines. Many traditional winemakers still opt for natural winemaking and forego both fining and filtering operations.

Young wines produced for quick commercialization must however be filtered. Otherwise, unfiltered, fined young wines will still throw a deposit. Consumers do not accept sedimentation in young wines made for the mass market, although perfectly acceptable in premium or older vintage wines, and these types of wines are perceived as of much higher quality. Sedimentation is therefore a secondary issue if not a characteristic of premium wines. For a similar reason, home winemakers filter their wines so they can be drunk early with little or no sediment forming in the bottle.

Although the effect of filtering is not an exact science, it is proven that filtering will yield a lighter-coloured wine. The major drawback of filtration involves the additional processing time that may expose the wine to air and therefore accelerating oxidation. This is the reason why the free SO_2 content is always verified and corrected before and after filtration.

Normally, the filtering operation is performed in lieu of fining, following stabilization and ageing of the wine. Filtration of fined wines is a common practice among home winemakers. This is not recommended for age-worthy wines. Home winemakers should opt for either fining or filtration but not both. It is acceptable, however, to fine a wine which has been coarse filtered to remove large unwanted particles.

5.3.1 Filtration equipment and systems

There are various types of wine filtration systems available depending on one's budget and the quantity of wine to be filtered. A pressurized-wine filtration system, which forces wine through a filter medium (e.g. pads) by air pressure, is very popular for kit wines but has the major drawback of accelerating wine oxidation, and is for this reason not recommended for premium wines. Suction or vacuum-type filtration systems are costlier but provide better results. These are the most popular systems in home winemaking.

In the suction-type filtration system, wine is forced through the filter medium by a suction force and transferred into an open-glass container. The pump used in this system can also be used for racking operations. The recommended method, using a vacuum-type filtration system, creates a vacuum in the container receiving the filtered wine, therefore, minimizing the wine exposure to air.

The main components of a filtration system are the pump, the filter medium, and the filtration device housing the filter medium. The most popular and effective filtration devices used by home winemakers are the round filtration plates and the plate-and-frame type systems. Similarly, the filter medium of choice is cellulose fiber pads. Other media, such as diatomaceous earth (DE) and membrane filters, are commonly used for commercial winemaking but rarely for home winemaking.

Gravity-flow and venturi filtration systems should be avoided as these unnecessarily prolong the filtering operation and hasten oxidation. Such systems make use of gravity and water pressure, respectively, and are not efficient for filtering.

Pumps

The choice of a good pump is essential for efficient filtration. There are several considerations when purchasing a filtration system equipped with a pump. The most important factors are the type of pump, priming requirements, and the rate of fluid displacement. Another consideration is whether the pump is to be used for racking operations.

Pumps are classified into two general categories according to the fluid displacement method and priming requirements. The two categories are positive displacement and centrifugal pumps. Priming refers to the process of filling a pump's cavity with the fluid to be displaced prior to the pumping operation. Pumps can be classified as unprimed or self-priming.

Positive displacement pumps, commonly used for small-scale filtration, consist of pistons or diaphragms capable of displacing a liquid by suction without the need for priming. Such pumps are termed self-priming. Although priming is not required, some positive displacement pump types cannot run dry. These pumps are often referred to as wet pumps or water system pumps as they require a liquid to be displaced for proper operation. Pumps capable of running dry are termed vacuum-type pumps owing to their ability to create a vacuum in a container. This is another important consideration in the purchase of a pump. Very often, the pump will inadvertently be left to run dry. A vacuum-type pump will not be damaged if this happens.

Newer intermittent-use water system pump models designed to also run dry for an extended time are now available. They can be used for both suction- and vacuum-type filtration. This type of pump, when

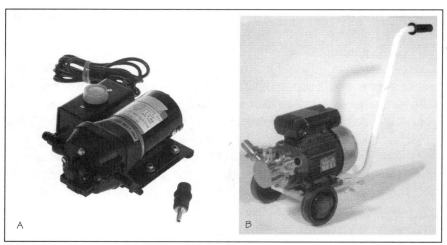

Figure 5-4: A, A water system pump and B, a positive displacement stainless steel pump with rubber impellers

run dry must be able to operate at a minimum manufacturer-specified pressure to properly filter as a vacuum-type system.

A water system pump, shown in Figure 5-4A, is an indispensable tool for both racking and filtering operations. This pump can be used in either a suction or vacuum system. It is equipped with a ¼-horsepower, variable-speed motor capable of displacing 10 to 15 L of wine per minute. It is also equipped with inlet and outlet adapters of varying diameters for connecting to various devices such as racking tubes and filtration plates. A useful add-on is the pump pre-filter, shown in Figure 5-5. It is specifically designed for use with the type of pump shown in Figure 5-4A. It is placed at the input side of the pump to restrict large particles such as oak chips, grape skins and tartaric crystals from entering the pump. This will preserve and lengthen the life of the check valve in the pump.

For larger productions, a high-throughput positive displacement or centrifugal pump is recommended. The positive displacement pump, shown in Figure 5-4B, is equipped with a 1½-hp motor and rubber impellers, and is capable of displacing up to 100 L of wine per minute.

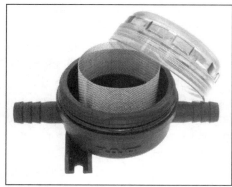

Figure 5-5: A pump pre-filter

Centrifugal pumps generate their pumping action by imparting a centrifugal force to the liquid to be displaced as opposed to a suction force in positive displacement pumps. The pump's cavity must be filled with a liquid before the pump can reach its normal operating pressure and start displacing the liquid. A centrifugal pump requiring manual priming is termed unprimed, whereas a self-priming pump will automatically fill its cavity prior to displacing the liquid. Centrifugal pumps will generally displace liquids at a higher rate than positive displacement pumps. As such, medium- and large-scale filtration systems will generally be equipped with centrifugal pumps.

Plate and plate-and-frame filtration systems
Many types of filtration systems are now available for small, medium, and large-scale home winemaking. Plate and plate-and-frame systems remain the most popular and most efficient models. The choice of a filtration system depends on one's capacity needs. The two major considerations are the type—white or red—and amount of wine to be filtered in one operation. These will determine the required filtration surface area, and therefore, will also determine the number of filter pads for any specific system. Filtration systems are equipped with a pump to match the filtration capacity.

Two popular and practical filtration systems for small-scale home winemaking are the round-and-grooved plate model and the Buon Vino Mini Jet plate-and-frame model.

The round-and-grooved plate model consists of two plates allowing wine to enter a chamber and to be forced through two parallel filter pads. The filtered wine is then collected in a second container. When assembling the unit, one filter pad per plate should be used with the rough side of the pads facing each other. The smooth side of each filter pad should face the grooves in each filtration plate.

The filtration plates typically have a single 8-mm (5/16-in) inlet used to force unfiltered wine through the rough surface of the pads and out to two 6-mm (1/4-in) outlets connected to a T-connector to the inlet of the pump assembly. These plates can be configured in either a suction or vacuum configuration. Figure 5-6 illustrates a filtration unit using round plates and the required filter pads.

The Buon Vino Mini Jet filtration system, shown in Figure 5-7, consists of a plate-and-frame assembly with an integrated water system

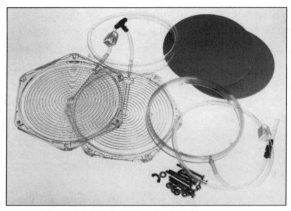

Figure 5-6: Filtration plates and filter pads

pump, and uses three filter pads. This system operates in a suction configuration.

These two types of filtration systems can be used to filter an average of 25 L of clarified wine. The quantity that can be filtered depends on the amount of solids still in suspension, and will therefore be smaller for red wine as opposed to white wine.

For medium-scale filtration, e.g., 50-100 L, a plate-and-frame filtration system such as the Buon Vino Superjet (Figure 5-8) or the Pillan F.6 system (Figure 5-9) is recommended.

The Buon Vino Superjet system uses an integrated water system pump with filter pads and plates anchored in a frame assembly. Three filter pads are used allowing for increased filtration capacity. It comes equipped with a pressure gauge used to determine when the filter pads are becoming clogged and needing replacement. The inlet and outlet are equipped for 10 mm ($3/8$-in) plastic tubing.

The Pillan F.6 system is equipped with an unprimed centrifugal pump, a plate-and-frame assembly for six filter pads, and a pressure gauge. The inlet and outlet are equipped for 13 mm ($1/2$-in) plastic tubing.

Figure 5-7: Buon Vino Mini Jet filtration system

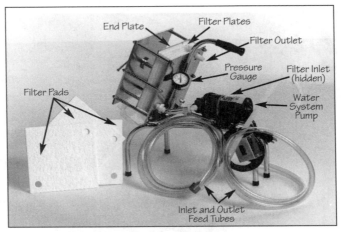

Figure 5-8: Buon Vino Superjet filtration system

Higher-capacity plate-and-frame filtration systems using 10, 20 or 30 filter pads are also available, albeit very expensive, for large-scale filtration. Manufactured by Pillan, the F.10, F.20 and F.30 models are equipped similarly to the F.6 model but are set on casters for ease of mobility. The Pillan F.20 system shown in Figure 5-10 can filter on average in excess of 300 L of wine. The filtration system's inlet and outlet are equipped for 20 mm (¾-in) plastic tubing.

Depth filter pads

The most commonly available filter pads for home winemaking filtration systems are depth filter pads manufactured from cellulose fibers.

Depth filter pads operate on the absorption principle by filtering both on the pads' surface and depth. Therefore, pads are rated according to their total volume in addition to the maximum particle size allowed through the pads, often referred to as the nominal retention rate. Pads for home winemaking filtration are available in standard 4-mm ($^5/_{32}$-in) thickness. The

Figure 5-9: Pillan F.6 filtration system

175

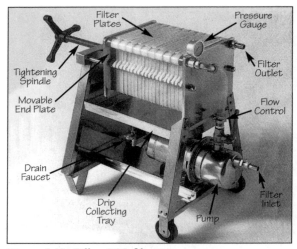

Figure 5-10: Pillan F.20 filtration system

surface area is therefore a deciding factor when choosing a filtration system as greater surface area pads will filter more effectively and more volume than the smaller surface area pads.

Filtering rate—defined in litres per hour—is also a key factor in choosing an appropriate system. Unfortunately, it is very difficult to quantify filtering rates for different systems. Filtering rates depend on the pump characteristics, filtration type (a function of filter pad rating), clarity of the wine, and type of wine, i.e. white or red wine. Therefore, selection of a filtration system should not be based strictly on filtering rate.

For any given system, selecting the filtration type is key to an efficient filtering operation. The filtration type—coarse, clarifying (polishing) or sterile—defines the rating relative to maximum particle size for cellulose-fiber depth filter pads. Invariably, this rating is designated by a simple numbering scheme—No. 1, 2, 3, 4 and 5. The highest number indicates a finer filter. Table 5-2 lists a typical mapping from filter pad No. to filtration type and typical maximum particle size (nominal retention rate) allowed through the filter pads. The maximum particle size is measured in micron units where 1 micron is defined as 10^{-6} meter. This table can be used as a guideline when selecting depth filter pads. The choice of pads should also be based on whether one is filtering

Table 5-2
Depth filter pad ratings

Filter pad number	Filtration type	Typical particle size (microns)
1	Coarse	10
2	Clarifying	5
3	Clarifying	2 - 3
4	Sterile	1 - 1.5
5	Sterile	0.6 - 0.8

Table 5-3
Pillan depth filter pad ratings

Filter Pad ID	Filtration Type
CKP V4	Coarse
CKP V8	Coarse
CKP VI2	Medium polishing
CKP VI6	Polishing
CKP VI8	Medium sterilizing
CKP V20	Sterilizing
CKP V24	Sterilizing in critical conditions

white versus red wine, and the clarity of the wine to be filtered. One should always inquire about particle size when selecting depth filter pads as the rating varies among manufacturers.

The No. I pads are mainly used for coarse filtration of wines with a high concentration of suspended particles. These pads will not show a significant change in the wine. They are used to collect and/or break down large particles. No. 2 pads are finer and are used for the brightening and polishing of wine. These will show a significant change in the wine's clarity and brightness. No. 3 pads will further enhance the clarity and brightness of wine. These should be used before bottling to minimize sediment forming at the bottom of the bottle. A clear white wine can typically be filtered once only using No. 3 pads. A clear red wine will require a first filtering using No. 2 pads. Nos. 4 and 5 pads are used for sterile filtration to remove any active yeast and prevent re-fermentation, or to remove other spoilage organisms in suspension.

In general, successive finer filtering should follow filtration with lower-numbered pads. Otherwise, the filtering operation will take a very long time or may not be possible at all if the pads clog. For example, a wine to be sterile-filtered using No. 4 pads should first be filtered with No. 2 pads followed by No. 3 pads. The need for coarser filtering should be evaluated based on the amount of particles in suspension.

Table 5-3 lists filter pad IDs and terminology used on the commonly-available Pillan depth filter pads.

Reminder: Filter pads have a smooth side and a rough side. For proper filtration, wine should always be forced into the rough side of the filter pad and out from the smooth side. Filter pads are not reusable and should be discarded after use.

Black carbon-type filter pads are also available and are used to increase the effectiveness of the filtering operation. They are used mainly for wines contaminated with unwanted particles. Carbon-type filter pads should not be used for healthy wines as they will be excessively stripped of colour and flavour compounds.

Table 5-4 summarizes key characteristics of the various filtration systems presented in this section.

5.3.2 Filtration

Figure 5-II illustrates setups for the most common wine filtration systems used in home winemaking. Figure 5-IIA and B illustrate the use of a round-plate system in a suction-type and a vacuum-type configuration, respectively. Figure 5-IIC illustrates the setup for plate-and-frame systems.

To create a complete vacuum, the system shown in Figure 5-IIB requires a special bung assembly, shown in Figure 5-12, on the container receiving the filtered wine.

The special bung assembly allows the pump to withdraw all the air and create a vacuum in the container to receive the filtered wine. The filtration system then forces the wine through the filter pads under

Table 5-4
Key characteristics of popular filtration systems

Model	No. of pads	Type of pads	Size of pads (cm)	Approximate total pad surface area (cm^2)
Buon Vino Mini Jet	3	rectangular	14.5 x 13.0	525
Round plate system	2	round	22	760
Buon Vino Superjet	3	square	20 x 20	1,200
Pillan F.6	6	square	20 x 20	2,400
Pillan F.10	10	square	20 x 20	4,000
Pillan F.20	20	square	20 x 20	8,000
Pillan F.30	30	square	20 x 20	12,000

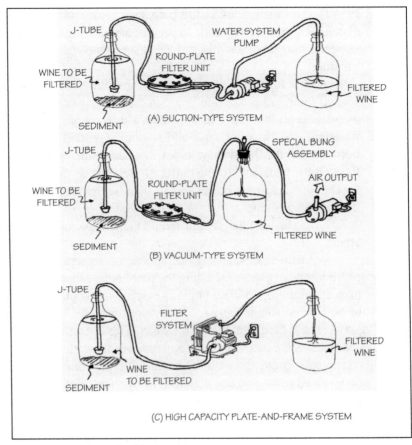

Figure 5-11: Setups for filtering wine using various systems

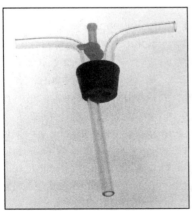

Figure 5-12: Special bung assembly

vacuum. The wine is totally filtered under vacuum and is therefore protected from oxidation effects.

For a round-plate filtration system, a filter pad should be inserted into each filtration plate with the smooth sides of the pads positioned against the plate grooves. The pads should be saturated with water and any excess should be left to drip. The pads should be fitted tightly in the plates to minimize leakage and maximize filtration efficiency. The two plates are secured togeth-

179

er with the rough sides of the pads facing each other. The wingnuts should be tightened by hand. To prevent any wine leakage from the unit, opposite wingnuts should be tightened simultaneously and with uniform pressure.

For a high-capacity plate-and-frame filtration system, a water-soaked filter pad is inserted between each filter plate. Pads should be aligned according to the manufacturer's instructions to ensure proper filtration. Pads have a coarse and smooth side, and so must be positioned correctly. If pads have holes to enable wine flow from the inlet, through the pads, and to the outlet, these must be positioned correctly. The filter pads and plates should then be tightened properly within the frame assembly.

The chosen filter system should then be assembled according to Figure 5-II.

As with all winemaking operations, it is imperative to sanitize the entire filtration system, including the pads, before filtering wine. To sanitize an entire round-plate filtration system, the container labeled wine to be filtered should be filled with approximately 20 L of water. The pump should then filter out all the water. This operation ensures that all components are properly rinsed and removes the carton flavour from the pads, which could otherwise be imparted to the wine. This step should be repeated with approximately 10 L of sulphite solution to sanitize the entire system. A small amount of citric acid (just discernible to the taste buds) can also be added to the sulphite solution to increase its effectiveness. The resulting drop in pH of the solution increases the SO_2 effectiveness, but the addition of citric acid also "sweetens up" the pads and avoids any cardboard taste.

Lastly, the system should be flushed using approximately 10 L of distilled water, preferably, to rinse out any sulphite solution remaining in the filtration system. The system is then ready for wine filtering. It is recommended to filter wine when cold, e.g., at cellar temperature, for a more effective filtration operation. Plate-and-frame filtration systems are sanitized in the same fashion.

For a round-plate filtration system, when starting the filtering operation, the control clip should be locked to restrict flow of wine into the upper outlet so that the filter unit fills up. When the filter unit is full, the clip can be opened. When the filtering is completed, the clip should then be locked to drain the remaining water out of the filter unit.

Before filtering, a small amount of sulphite can also be added to the wine to protect it from oxidation, particularly when using suction-type systems.

The sediment at the bottom of the container should not be disturbed while filtering wine. If sediment is allowed to pass through the filter pads, they will clog the pads and slow down the filtration process. One set of pads will therefore filter a much smaller volume of wine. Also, the first half to one litre of liquid to pass through the system may contain water. The volume of diluted wine depends on the amount of water left in the unit during the flushing operation. The diluted wine should be discarded and not be mixed with the wine. The wine can be tasted and as soon as it tastes a full wine, the tube can be placed back into the receiving vessel.

If the filtration system is equipped with a pressure gauge, the manufacturer's recommended maximum pressure should be observed to determine when the filter pads become clogged and need to be replaced. Typically, as the pressure mounts, it is because the pads are clogged and will then begin to leak and spray.

When filtration is completed, the filter pads should be discarded, and the entire system should be rinsed again with water, with a sulphite solution and again with water.

Note: *Once the pump is turned on and filtering has started, the operation should not be interrupted by turning the pump off/on. This will greatly decrease filtering efficiency and may affect the wine's clarity.*

6
BLENDING

Traditionally, wines were commonly a blend of two or more varietals (wines produced from a single grape variety). The final blend was subject to regional winemaking laws and/or local traditions. Winemaking laws in Europe date back to the early twentieth century. These were created to mandate and control the types of blend and percentage of each used in the final wine. Blending, known as *assemblage* in French, is used to produce different styles of wine. Each variety contributes its specific characteristics to achieve a desired style. In vintage wines, only wines from the same vintage can be used for blending. In non-vintage wines, different vintage wines can be blended. Non-vintage blending is a practice mainly used to maintain a consistent level of quality from year to year.

Blending of wines from different varietals is still practiced widely. Premium Bordeaux red wines—blends of two or three varieties—still command very high prices on the open market and at auctions. More recently, consumers' increased awareness of wines and associated varietals coupled with new marketing tactics from wineries have led to varietal wines. These single-variety wines have become very popular in New World wine-producing areas such as Australia, California, Chile and South Africa. Popular white wine varietals are Chardonnay and Sauvignon Blanc. Popular red wine varietals are Cabernet Sauvignon, Merlot and Pinot Noir. Zinfandel has recently become another popular Californian red wine varietal but was made famous in the U.S. as a White Zinfandel in blush, sweet wines.

This practice is not limited to blending of different varietals. It includes blends of one or more varietals that have been vinified using different techniques. For example, an oak-aged wine having an affinity for oak may be blended with a wine that has benefited from ML fermentation. The resulting wine has an oak aroma with reduced acidity and greater complexity. It is a superior wine as each blending wine has been vinified to highlight its distinctive characteristic. Once combined, the blending wines will marry into one and enhance the complexity of the final wine. In addition to creating a superior wine, a proper balance of the following elements must be achieved and/or maintained:

- fruitiness
- complexity of bouquet and taste
- intensity in the mouth
- body (mouth-feel)
- length and intensity of finish
- colour intensity
- residual sugar content
- alcohol content
- acidity
- pH
- tannin level
- oak character

Winemakers must be able to select the appropriate varietals and to be able to control the many parameters of each varietal in producing a specific style. A specific style will be achieved through extensive tasting of the endless combinations and permutations of blends. The challenge is also not to disturb the balance of each wine when blending. Often when trying to balance one element, another element may become unbalanced, and the blended wine may not meet expectations. For example, if an oak-aged wine is blended with a very fruity wine, the final blend may have the desired oak aroma but it may also hide the much-desired fruitiness. For these reasons, blending has become an art requiring skillful craftsmanship and experience. Blending will require extensive experimentation until the final desired result is achieved.

Blending is also used to correct or mask wine faults. The objective is still to produce a wine of higher quality than the individual wines. If a fault can be corrected or masked, blending is recommended. It is not recommended if a wine has fault that cannot be corrected, i.e. it is spoiled. A spoiled wine blended with a sound wine will spoil the final blend. Chapter 12 describes procedures to prevent and to correct wine faults without the use of blending.

Table 1-1 and Table 1-2 on pages 34 and 36, respectively, describing the characteristics of the various varietals, can be used to select wines for blending to produce a desired style. This will greatly simplify this task for novice winemakers.

It is recommended to blend wines according to well-established classical blends to become acquainted with this art. This will reduce the probability of producing undesired results as many varietals are not well suited to blending, and others should only be blended.

Following is a sample of classical blends for white and red wines:

- Chardonnay and Pinot Blanc
- Sauvignon Blanc and Sémillon
- Cabernet Sauvignon, Cabernet Franc, and Merlot
- Barbera and Nebbiolo

These varieties can be blended in any proportion of each variety. For example, Château Pétrus (Pomerol) typically uses 95% Merlot and 5% Cabernet Franc, while Château Mouton-Rothschild (Pauillac) typically uses approximately 80% Cabernet Sauvignon, 10% Cabernet Franc, 8% Merlot and 2% Petit Verdot (a *V. vinifera* variety), and Château d'Yquem (Sauternes) most often uses 80% Sémillon and 20% Sauvignon Blanc. Pomerol, Pauillac and Sauternes are Bordeaux appellations.

Blending can be performed at any stage of the winemaking process, including the blending of must from crushing or pressing. It is highly recommended, however, to blend wines as a last step before bottling when the wines to be blended have been clarified, stabilized and oak-aged. This will ensure that no further changes in the wine's structure will occur after blending, and also provides more control over the final blend.

6.1 BLENDING PROCESS

Blending requires careful planning and preparation. First, a desired wine style should be established and the component characteristics of each blending wine should be assessed. The residual sugar content, alcohol content, TA and pH should be assessed quantitatively. Fruitiness, colour intensity, tannin level and oak character can be assessed qualitatively. Many tasting glasses should be available to taste the various test blends. Tasting should be conducted at room temperature, if possible, with even lighting to verify the colour intensity.

The required wines to achieve the desired style are then blended in small and increasing proportions. Blends with different combinations and permutations of varietals and proportions should be tasted.

The residual sugar content, TA and pH can be measured repeatedly until the desired level of a specific element is achieved. The alcohol content can be calculated for each blend. The desired level of fruitiness can only be determined by olfaction. The level of oak flavour can be determined by olfaction and gustation whereas the tannin level can only be determined by gustation. Colour intensity can be determined by visual inspection.

When blending wines of different alcohol contents, the final alcohol content of a blended wine can be determined as follows:

$$\% \text{ alc./vol. of blended wine} = \frac{(A \times D) + (B \times E)}{(D + E)}$$

where:

A = % alc./vol. of first wine
B = % alc./vol. of second wine
D = volume of first wine
E = volume of second wine

For example, if 10 L of a 12% alc./vol. wine is blended with 5 L of a 13.5% alc./vol. wine, the resulting blended wine will have an alcohol level of:

$$\frac{(13.5 \times 5) + (12 \times 10)}{(5 + 10)} = 12.5\% \text{ alc./vol.}$$

When the desired style is achieved, a sample of the blend should be set aside in the cellar for up to four weeks. This is important as the blend may evolve and taste different from when first assembled. Following the storage period, the blended wine should be re-tasted and re-adjusted as required. The final blend may then be aged and/or bottled.

All wines selected in creating the final wine should be blended in a large container capable of holding the total volume. Each bottle of wine will then be of consistent quality. Large variable-capacity AISI 304 stainless steel tanks are very practical for blending.

6.2 THE PEARSON SQUARE

The Pearson Square is an easy-to-use tool to calculate the number of parts of solution (i.e. wine) of a given concentration required to bring the concentration of another solution to a desired level. This tool can be used in lieu of the mathematical relationships presented earlier in the determination of total acidity and alcohol concentrations.

There are five parameters involved:

A = concentration of the wine to be used
B = concentration of the wine to be "corrected"
C = calculated or desired concentration
D = number of parts of wine to be used and is equal to C-B
E = number of parts of wine to be "corrected" and is equal to A-C

By placing these parameters in the following Pearson Square, any parameter can be determined if the other four are known quantities.

A		D
	C	
B		E

Using the example in section 6.1, where a final alcohol level of 12.5% is desired by blending two wines having 12% and 13.5% alcohol, respectively, the Pearson Square could be used to determine the required volumes as follows:

13.5		0.5
	12.5	
12		1.0

The value of D and E are 0.5 and 1.0, respectively, meaning that for every litre of the 13.5% alc./vol. wine, 2 L of the 12% alc./vol. wine are required.

Similar calculations can be performed for total acidity determination in blended wines. Using the example in section 3.2.2 on page 90, to increase the TA of 20 L of wine from 5.0 to 6.0 g/L using a 7.5-g/L blend wine, the Pearson Square can be used to determine how many parts of each wine that would be required.

7.5	1.0
6.0	
5.0	1.5

Therefore, for every 1.5 L of the 5.0-g/L wine, 1.0 L of the 7.5-g/L wine would be required. Then, for 20 L of 5.0-g/L wine to be increased to 6.0 g/L, 20/1.5=13.3 L of the 7.5-g/L wine would be required.

7
OAK BARRELS

Oak barrels are seldom used in home winemaking. Their high price, and perceived high maintenance and high risk of wine spoilage have made oak barrels unattractive to amateur winemakers. Yet, barrels have been used since the early days of winemaking. It is well known that oak-ageing benefits far surpass the perceived disadvantages. Some knowledge and experience of barrel maintenance coupled with the wine's new organoleptic dimensions should make their use very attractive and the investment worthwhile.

A wine's quality, complexity and ageing potential are greatly enhanced by ageing in oak barrels such as the one depicted in Figure 7-1. Oak imparts a distinctive aroma to wine and increases the tannin level improving the wine's ageing potential. Barrel-aged wines also benefit from the minute, gradual, controlled oxidation that occurs in barrels—and not in glass containers or stainless steel vats. Because wood is a porous material, both oxidation and evaportion occur between and through the wood staves. Even old (but well-kept) barrels concentrate the wine through this minute oxidation/evaporation, lending the finished wine a perfume, a bouquet never possible in inert, totally hermetically sealed ageing containers. Oak barrels also improve

189

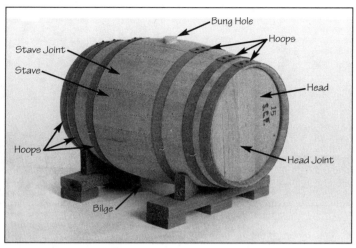

Figure 7-I: An oak barrel

a wine's limpidity and, in the case of red wines, they provide a deeper colour.

Although white oak is the preferred wood for barrels, other types such as chestnut can be used for storing and ageing wine. These are less expensive although not as readily available as oak, and their use is not common in commercial winemaking. This chapter will therefore discuss wine ageing using oak barrels only.

Before deciding to invest in oak barrels, a budget should be established and whether it is worth investing time and patience to care for the barrels. Oak barrels are expensive and require proper preparation and maintenance that can prove to be a tedious task, especially when encountering barrel spoilage problems. When shopping for barrels, one should inquire about their origin, the type of oak used and whether the barrels have been toasted. These factors will affect price.

Oak barrels are now almost exclusively available with galvanized hoops. Barrels with steel hoops should be avoided as these will rust and spoil the wine if it comes in contact with the hoops. Wine can seep through the stave joints and become contaminated from hoop rust on the exterior surface of the barrel. This problem is avoided with galvanized hoops.

A toasted barrel will further enhance the quality of the wine by imparting a distinctive toasty aroma. Light and medium toasted oak barrels for home winemaking are primarily available in American,

French or Hungarian white oak in various capacities ranging from 3 to 30 U.S. gal or from 10 to 110 L. Generally, French oak barrels will be the most expensive and U.S. oak barrels the least expensive. The lower-capacity barrels are costlier, in terms of cost per unit volume, than higher-capacity barrels although the latter are very bulky for home winemaking. The 57-L (15-gal) barrel provides a good compromise between cost and size.

Oak barrels have a lifetime of approximately 3 to 4 years. Beyond this period, there may not be any appreciable extract left. Such barrels are termed neutral barrels. Records of barrel use should be kept to establish the residual lifetime before they become neutral.

7.1 OAK BARREL STORAGE, MAINTENANCE AND PREPARATION

It is always advisable to buy new or reconditioned oak barrels, and to avoid used ones as their origin is unknown. Barrels of unknown origin will require extensive preparation before use and are very risky. If possible, barrels should be bought when ready to transfer wine to avoid maintenance of empty barrels. Otherwise, maintenance of empty barrels can be problem-free by following the recommended treatments.

A thorough inspection of the barrel interior must be done at home just before filling it with wine. The interior of the barrel can be inspected using a light bulb small enough to pass through the bung hole. By inserting it into the barrel, a visual inspection of the interior will detect any obvious defects. The barrels should also be inspected visually for any obvious external defects that might affect their storing and ageing ability. For example, it should be verified that stave and head joints are not too wide, that the bung hole is properly tapered, and that all hoops are properly fastened.

7.1.1 New barrel storage and maintenance

Empty barrels should be stored in a wine cellar at 13° C (55° F) and at 65% to 75% humidity, away from dampness. To improve humidity retention in a cellar with less-than-desirable-conditions, barrels can be wrapped in cellophane. Quite often, barrel manufacturers ship barrels already wrapped in cellophane. Cellophane should be wrapped around the main body of the barrel, covering the staves only. The top and bottom head sections should not be wrapped to allow the barrel to "breathe" properly. Head sections wrapped in cellophane will trap moisture causing mould to form and spoiling the barrel beyond repair.

Barrels to be stored empty also require proper sulphiting to prevent growth of spoilage organisms that would otherwise make the barrels unusable. Although a sulphite solution can be used, the best method to sulphite a barrel is by burning a piece of sulphur stick. A barrel can be stored empty for an indefinite amount of time if properly preserved by sulphur.

To prepare an empty barrel for storage, the interior should be first thoroughly rinsed with water, drained well and left to dry. A piece

Figure 7-2: Sulphur sticks for oak barrel maintenance

of sulphur stick should then be burnt inside the barrel. Burnt sulphur, or sulphur dioxide (SO_2) gas, replaces the air, fills the barrel, and protects it from spoilage organisms. Sulphur sticks, shown in Figure 7-2, are typically sold in 20-cm lengths. A 2.5-cm by 2.5-cm piece of sulphur stick is sufficient for a 57- or 76-L (l5- or 20-gal) barrel.

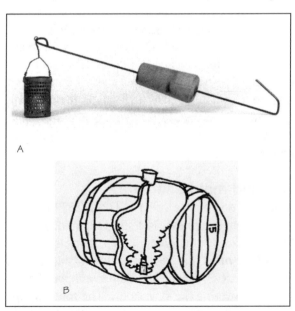

Figure 7-3: Procedure for burning sulphur in an oak barrel

Figure 7-3A illustrates a handy device consisting of a small fireproof container which can be used to burn sulphur inside an oak barrel. A sulphur stick is then lit, deposited in the container and introduced inside the barrel, as shown in Figure 7-3B. Once that has been done, the bung hole should be covered to prevent the SO_2 gas from escaping from the barrel. The stick should be left to burn for several minutes until completely extinguished. When the stick has completely burnt, it can be removed and the bung replaced into the hole again. Silicone rubber, cork or wood bungs can be used to provide an airtight seal.

Every 3 to 4 weeks, the inside of the barrel should be smelled for the presence of SO_2. If detected, the bung can simply be replaced. If no smell is detected, more sulphur should be burnt.

Caution: It is very important to work in a well-ventilated area. SO_2 fumes can burn nasal passages. When sniffing the inside of a barrel for presence of SO_2, it is advisable to take only a small sniff. If burnt sulphur drops inside the barrel, it may cause hydrogen sulphide to form during wine storage, which will cause the wine to spoil. Hydrogen sulphide imparts a rotten-egg smell. Refer to section 12.7 on how to treat the presence of hydrogen sulphide.

7.1.2 New barrel preparation

Although it is possible to transfer wine directly into a new barrel without any treatment, there is always a risk of leakage. It is therefore recommended to swell a new barrel with water. Swelling of the wood staves and heads will form tighter joints minimizing and/or eliminating wine seepage. Seepage most often occurs at the head joints. This will cause wine loss and will also promote spoilage organisms forming on the barrel surface if not properly maintained on a regular basis. A leaky barrel also allows the wine to be exposed to air causing oxidation. If seepage cannot be stopped, the barrel may be unusable and will be very costly to repair. A water-tested leaky barrel can be returned to the barrel supply shop.

Swelling a new barrel in preparation for ageing wine can be performed by two methods: 1) using a hot-water treatment or 2) using an overnight water-soaking treatment. Both methods have the advantage of using no chemicals that would otherwise excessively leach out the oak flavour from the barrel. The second method, however, has the disadvantage of leaching out some oak flavour owing to the longer soak period.

As a first step for either method, all the SO_2 gas should be let out. The barrel should then be rinsed with lukewarm water at least twice ensuring the entire inner surface is cleaned.

The hot-water treatment method, a French technique for swelling a barrel, has the advantage of requiring much less water. Clean water, if properly used, should be the only treatment necessary for a barrel in good condition. Water that contains solids or a high-iron content should be avoided. A small volume of hot water should be poured into the barrel. The recommended approximate volume ratio of hot water to barrel size is 1-to-10. For example, 6 L of hot water should be used for a 57-L barrel.

The barrel should be properly bunged and then sloshed around to coat the entire interior surface. The vapour pressure created by this action will accelerate any seepage through the stave and head joints. The barrel should then be placed upright, and the head area should be filled with hot water. The barrel should be left to stand for 15 minutes before repeating for the other head area. When this treatment is completed, the water should be drained completely and the barrel should be allowed to dry and to cool down. Initially, some water seepage will be noticeable. If it stops, the barrel is ready for use; if not, the barrel may be defective, in which case, the second method for swelling a barrel can be used.

This second method can also be used as the primary method for swelling a barrel. It is specifically recommended for barrels that have been in dry storage for a prolonged time.

The barrel should be filled and topped up with cool water. Initially, the barrel may leak, mostly from the head joints, but leaks will usually plug themselves up after a few hours. The barrel should be placed horizontally and should be left to soak overnight. The soaking period can be extended to a maximum between 24 and 36 hours if leakage persists. If there is still leakage after this soaking period, the barrel is defective and should be returned.

Warning: *The recommended maximum soaking period should NEVER be exceeded. Otherwise, mould can form and can spoil the barrel. There are no remedies to eliminate mould from an oak barrel.*

At the end of the soaking period, when all leakage has stopped, the barrel should be drained by placing it in the bung-down position. No puddling of water should remain in the bilge (the cross-section area of the barrel with the largest diameter). The barrel should be allowed to dry and then filled immediately with wine. If the barrel cannot be filled with wine, it can be stored empty by burning sulphur. It is very important that the barrel be drained and dried completely before burning sulphur. Failure to do so will cause SO_2 to hydrate and form into sulphurous acid. This will adversely affect the taste of wine and may cause spoilage.

The barrel's exterior surface requires no special preparation although it should be inspected regularly for mould. Section 7.5.2 describes how to prevent and to treat mould that has formed on the barrel's exterior surface. Optionally, it can be treated with Mildewcide to inhibit mould and insects. A two-coat treatment of Mildewcide using a paintbrush should be applied and then left to dry to a clear finish.

Warning: Some manufacturers recommend a soda ash treatment for barrel preparation. Soda ash or any chlorine-based chemicals will leach out the oak flavour, and in some cases, impart undesirable flavours to the wood that will react negatively with the wine. Such chemicals should be used strictly in the treatment of oak barrels affected by a spoilage organism. Refer to section 7.5.2.

7.1.3 Used barrel storage and maintenance

Storage and maintenance of empty used barrels are tedious, but necessary tasks. If not properly maintained, used barrels can contaminate and spoil wine. When possible, it is preferable to transfer new wine into a used barrel after having transferred out aged wine. This has the advantage that the barrel requires little or no preparation. For this reason, it is recommended to have a continuous supply of wine to be aged in oak barrels so that these need not be maintained.

If a used barrel is to be stored empty for a prolonged period of time, it must be treated so as not to dry out. Sulphur will also need to be burnt to prevent mould and bacterium growth. The hot-water treatment or the overnight water-soaking treatment can be used to keep the barrel from drying out. This treatment along with burnt sulphur should be repeated every 6 to 8 weeks.

If this procedure proves to be inconvenient, and to reduce the risk of spoilage problems, a sulphur-citric holding solution can be used for barrel storage. A holding solution will promote sterility and keep the barrel smelling sweet. This procedure is not recommended for new barrels or barrels less than one year old. The oak extract will be stripped in the process.

To prepare a holding solution, 1 g of citric acid and 2 g of potassium metabisulphite for each litre of barrel volume should be dissolved in hot water. The barrel should be filled two-thirds with water, and then the holding solution should be added. The barrel should be topped up with water and then bunged for storage. The barrel should be topped up with water or the holding solution every 4 to 6 weeks. This will allow the barrel to be stored indefinitely without the risk of spoilage.

7.1.4 Used barrel preparation

Used barrels require no special preparation, beyond a simple water rinse if desired, when transferring wine out and in immediately. If the barrel has been stored with a holding solution, the barrel should be drained and rinsed thoroughly. A neutralizer for the holding solution is not required since sulphur and citric residues are compatible with wine. The barrel can then be filled with wine.

If the barrel has tartrate buildup, hot water and a fair amount of athletic barrel swirling will help take out some of the tartrate. Soda ash, sold under the brand name Barrel-Kleen, will help speed up the process although it will leach out some of the oak flavour. The barrel should be swirled well to splash the hot water solution all over the barrel's inside, and then, the barrel should be put through several rinses with fresh water.

Warning: The sulphur-citric holding solution will etch a concrete floor. The floor should be hosed with water to prevent this.

7.2 BARREL FERMENTATION

Without a doubt, barrel-fermented wines are more complex and of superior quality over wines fermented in glass, stainless steel, or other types of fermentation vessels. Wines that have been barrel-fermented also absorb the oak qualities in a softer way, as opposed to picking up the harsher principles when merely oak-aged.

Barrel fermentation is used extensively in white wine production, especially for Chardonnay. The fermentation of white grape juice in oak barrels is a traditional Burgundian technique that can yield high-quality wine. However, as it is quite easy to oxidize white wine if it is not constantly topped up, only the most meticulous and experienced home winemakers should attempt this technique. Topping of white-wine oak barrels requires constant care and supervision.

Bâtonnage, or lees stirring, during barrel fermentation should also be performed on a regular basis—weekly for the first couple of months and then monthly—to increase a wine's complexity and richness. To further increase the complexity of barrel-fermented white wines, it is recommended to carry out ML fermentation in barrels. *Bâtonnage* is not recommended during the ML fermentation phase as the additional aeration could cause the ML bacteria to cease. Initial conditions and instructions on carrying out ML fermentation should be as per section 4.6.

When **initiating** fermentation in oak barrels, the temperature should be above 15° C (59° F). It can then be lowered, if desired, to between 10° and 14° C (50° and 57° F) for white wines and between 22° and 28° C (72° and 82° F) for red wines to carry out a cooler fermentation. If fermenting wine is transferred to oak barrels, fermentation can be carried out to completion at the lower temperature.

Refer to sections 4.5.2 and 4.6.1 for more details on conducting the alcoholic and ML fermentations, respectively.

7.3 OAK-BARREL AGEING

Red wine varieties are most suitable for oak ageing although white wine varieties such as Chardonnay and Sauvignon Blanc can be aged in oak barrels, albeit for a much shorter period. White wines should not be left to age in oak barrels for an extended time, otherwise, excessive tannins will be absorbed. The wine will become unbalanced, oxidized, and potentially, undrinkable.

7.3.1 Red wine maturation

In red wine production from grapes, wine is usually transferred to oak barrels after pressing to finish fermentation. It would be impractical to conduct maceration in oak barrels—transferring grapes and pomace in and out would be quite a task. When the level of colour and tannin extraction is obtained from maceration and alcoholic fermentation, the wine is transferred to oak barrels. The wine should then be allowed to ferment to dryness with lees contact.

The amount of oak imparted to a wine during maturation depends on the barrel size and age (new vs. old oak), and the barrel maturation period. A small-volume barrel will impart oak flavour quicker than a larger barrel owing to the higher surface-to-volume ratio in a smaller barrel. Different grape varieties will also have different barrel maturation requirements as some may have more of an oak affinity than other varieties. For example, varieties high in tannin content will require less barrel ageing. Therefore, wines undergoing barrel maturation should be monitored and tasted regularly to avoid imparting too much of oak taste.

For the first several months—this depends on the size and age of the barrel—wine should be smelled and tasted on a weekly basis to determine when the desired level of oak character has been achieved. This may occur very early as new oak imparts its flavour very quickly. The first and second batches in a new barrel will tend to be high in tannin content. The third and fourth batches will produce the higher-quality wine, and wine can be stored for a much longer period as tannins are transferred from the oak to the wine at a much slower rate.

As guidelines for 57-L (15-gal) barrels, the first batch should be aged in a new barrel for 4 to 6 weeks, the second batch for 8 to 10 weeks, the third batch between 2 and 6 months, and the fourth batch between 6 and 12 months. For the first 2 months, the barrel will need to be topped up twice per week due to the rapid rate of absorption and evaporation of the wine. The rate of absorption and the need for topping should be monitored frequently. Wine should be topped up with the same variety, ideally from the same batch.

It is recommended not to oak-age all wine in order to blend aged and non-aged wines and achieve the right level of oak flavour.

It has also been observed that red wines that have been ML fermented in barrels retain more of their colour than their glass or stainless steel counterparts.

Wine stored in oak barrels may be racked depending on the clarity of the wine. Wine will clarify during the oak-ageing process as it acquires tannins. Racking of unfiltered wines at 3-month intervals is a good practice. After each racking, the barrel should be rinsed 2 or 3 times thoroughly with cold water to remove all deposits.

Wine should be stored at cellar temperature, approximately 13° C (55° F), during the ageing process. The relative humidity should be approximately 65%. A cellar's humidity below this level will favour evaporation of wine from the barrel, whereas humidity above this level will favour the growth of spoilage organisms. Barrel bung holes should be sealed with silicone rubber bungs.

Following the oak-ageing period, an additional period of up to 2 or 3 years of bottle ageing is recommended to let the wine evolve and let the tannins soften which will further add complexity. The wine should be tasted at regular intervals during the evolution period to determine when the wine has reached the right balance for one's taste.

7.4 ALTERNATIVES TO BARREL-AGEING FOR IMPARTING OAK AROMAS

There are no proven alternatives to barrel ageing which benefit wines to the extent that oak barrels do. These benefits are a direct result of the barrel's physical properties, namely, the wood's porosity and staves which provide controlled oxidation. However, several inexpensive techniques are available to home winemakers to impart oak aromas. These do not benefit the wine's ageing, and do not enhance the complexity in flavour and aroma as oak barrels do. The most common techniques are the use of oak mor chips and oak extract.

7.4.1 Oak mor chips

The low-cost alternative of imparting oak flavour to wine is by using oak mor chips. They do not add any significant amount of tannins, and as such, cannot be used for ageing wine. Oak chips, therefore, yield an oaky wine ready for early drinking. This method is becoming increasingly popular in the winemaking industry as an alternative to expensive oak barrels. Some wineries are also experimenting with the use of solid oak planks immersed directly into the wine.

Oak mor, shown in Figure 7-4, is available as fine sawdust, small, and large chips as well as plain or toasted. The best-quality French or American oak chips should be used. The recommended usage for white wines is 1-2 g/L for 1 to 2 weeks, and for red wines, 2-4 g/L for 1 to 2 weeks. These quantities can be modified depending on the desired oak

Figure 7-4: Oak mor chips

flavour intensity. French and American oak impart different flavours with different intensities. Therefore, the above quantities should be adjusted accordingly.

Oak chips should be prepared as follows before use. The required amount should be weighed and washed in a sieve with cool tap water until no more dust or colour is being washed out. For an added dimension, the chips may be toasted, while the chips are still moist, under the broiler at about 200° C (392° F) until most are browned but not burnt to a crisp. The chips should be dropped loosely in the wine during the closed-container alcoholic fermentation. They will settle at the bottom in a day or so. The wine should be tasted and sniffed frequently until the desired aroma and flavour reaches a good intensity. Lastly, the wine should be racked carefully away from the chips.

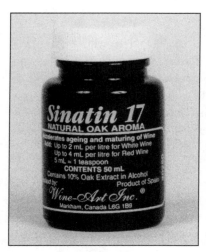

Figure 7-5: Wine-Art Sinatin 17 oak extract

7.4.2 Oak extract

Oak extract is yet another inexpensive alternative to impart an oak flavour to wine. Figure 7-5 shows Wine-Art's Sinatin 17 oak extract available at winemaking shops. Oak extract additive is produced by macerating oak chips in ethanol. The required dosage depends on the concentration of oak flavour extracted from maceration. A 10%-oak extract additive, such as Sinatin 17, should be added at a rate of 2 mL/L of white wine and 4 mL/L of red wine.

Oak extract accelerates wine ageing and is, therefore, not a recommended practice. This method is not accepted within the commercial winemaking industry.

7.5 OAK-BARREL SPOILAGE

Oak barrels, if properly maintained, should not cause any problems. Spoilage problems can happen, however, since wood is a good breeding medium for bacteria and other spoilage organisms, especially in the presence of water or wine. The risk of spoilage problems is also increased as no chemicals are used in treating barrels. Chemicals leach out much of the oak extract in the wood and are therefore only recommended as a last resort in treating spoilage problems.

7.5.1 Types of oak-barrel spoilage problems

There exist four types of spoilage problems that can occur in oak barrels: 1) mould, 2) acetic acid, 3) yeasts and 4) lactic acid bacteria.

Mould is the most frequent type of spoilage problem encountered and is very difficult to eradicate. Mould attacks and transforms the wood on the barrel's interior surface, causing mouse-like or mushroom-like flavours in wine. A barrel affected by mould is no longer usable and should be discarded. Tiny amounts of mould growing inside an empty barrel can, however, be treated using sodium percarbonate.

Mould can also form on the exterior surface of a barrel caused from wine seepage, or water residues, or an overly humid cellar. There is little danger of this mould penetrating from the outside of a barrel but it should be removed and cleaned immediately. When barrels are opened for sampling or topping, some mould spores could enter the barrel; however, these moulds are aerobic and will not grow in a full wine barrel.

The most common area of mould formation on the exterior surface is around the bung hole. The bung area will absorb wine rapidly due to the increased surface area, and will saturate on the exterior promoting the growth of *penicillium* mould.

A periodic cleaning of the bung area and other parts of a barrel's exterior surface contaminated with wine can prevent this problem. The affected area should be scrubbed using a natural- or plastic-bristle brush. A wire brush should never be used for cleaning a barrel. A scrubbing solution can be prepared by dissolving equal parts of sodium metabisulphite and citric acid in water. This solution is acidic and should not come into contact with the galvanized hoops. If this happens, the hoops should be rinsed promptly with water. When scrubbing the bung area, the solution should not be allowed to enter the bung hole or to drip in the wine. To avoid this, the solution should be left to dry before pulling the bung.

Mould can also spread to or grow on cork or wood bungs, penetrate the bung hole and contaminate the wine. Using silicone rubber bungs when storing wine in oak barrels can prevent this risk of spoilage.

A second frequent type of spoilage problem is the formation of acetobacter. These vinegar bacteria, responsible for acetic acid (VA), grow in an aerobic environment and can be prevented by keeping barrels topped up. Acetobacter can be easily detected by smelling the interior of the barrel. Volatile acidity in the early stages will smell like clean vinegar, though faint. A wine would require an undrinkable level of VA to produce a pronounced vinegar odour when the barrel is emptied. Therefore, the acetic acid in an empty barrel more likely comes from wine residues having oxidized. This problem is often the result of insufficient sulphuring when the barrel is stored empty. In later stages, the acetic acid combines with alcohol residues to form ethyl acetate, which smells distinctly like nail-polish remover. This problem is very difficult to eradicate in the cleaning process.

The third type of spoilage problem is yeast formation. Many of the spoilage-causing types of yeast cannot live in an alcohol solution above 10% alc./vol. These are, therefore, not a cause of concern. However, species from the *Brettanomyces* genus can cause a serious problem as it metabolizes extremely low levels of sugar, even wood cellulose sugars in new barrels. In wine, it can produce an attractive complexity at low levels, but as it grows, the wine takes on a "medicine cabinet" smell. This type of spoilage problem can be prevented through careful barrel maintenance.

The last type of spoilage problem is the formation of lactic acid bacteria, specifically, species from *Lactobacillis* and *Pediococcus* genera, giving wine a sour-milk taste. These bacteria form in wines with a very high pH (above 3.7), in wines with very low levels of SO_2, or in wines that have had a problem fermenting to dryness. This spoilage problem is best avoided by prevention, through careful vinification.

7.5.2 Treating oak-barrel spoilage problems

Treating oak-barrel spoilage problems is a multi-step process. First, the barrel should be filled two-thirds with water. An alkaline solution should then be prepared by dissolving either sodium carbonate or sodium percarbonate in water. The solution should be added to the barrel and then topped up. The amounts of chemical to use depend on the severity of the problem and the barrel size. For mild spoilage problems, sodium carbonate or sodium percarbonate should be dissolved at a rate of approximately 1 g/L of water. For more serious problems, the concentration can be increased to 3 g/L of water. This prescription should never be exceeded as these chemicals could attack the wood and dissolve the oak lignins.

The barrel should be left to soak overnight. It should never be left to soak longer than 24 hours as it may develop other spoilage problems. The barrel should then be emptied and rinsed thoroughly. A rinsing with a citric acid solution to neutralize any possible alkaline residues should follow this. Trace residues of sodium carbonate or sodium percarbonate in a barrel are not poisonous, but they will affect the taste of wine if allowed to come into contact with it. To rinse with a citric acid solution, the barrel should first be filled two-thirds with water. A citric acid solution should be prepared by dissolving citric acid powder at a rate of 0.5-1 g/L of water and poured into the barrel. The barrel should then be topped up and left to soak overnight. Lastly, the barrel should be emptied, rinsed thoroughly, drained completely and left to dry. The barrel can be smelled for any off odours to ensure the treatment worked. If the barrel does not smell completely clean, the treatment should be repeated.

This treatment for correcting oak-barrel spoilage problems is a very tedious process without shortcuts. In addition, the oak extracts from a newer barrel will be stripped in the process. Therefore, the best policy will always be prevention.

8
BOTTLING

Bottling is the final process in winemaking where aged wine is bottled either for immediate consumption or for further ageing. A bottle of properly-labeled homemade wine is the winemaker's ultimate reward.

The quality of bottled wine depends greatly on bottling techniques and closures, such as corks. As in all winemaking procedures, wine exposure to air must be minimized and only the best material available should be used, especially if bottle-ageing wine for long periods.

There are various tools available to home winemakers to facilitate and to accelerate the bottling process. Many of these tools are manufactured in and imported from Italy, and as such, they may not be readily available in winemaking shops. These imported tools are usually pricey but the investment may be well justified when bottling more than a few cases of wine at a time.

8.1 BOTTLING APPARATUS

Bottling homemade wine is still very much a manual process. It involves assembling the right quantity and type of bottles, washing and sanitizing each bottle, filling each one with wine, corking, dressing the bottle top with a plastic capsule, and labeling each bottle.

8.1.1 Bottles

Bottles come in a plethora of shapes, tints, sizes and thicknesses. Winemaking aficionados are adamant about bottling Cabernet Sauvignon and Chardonnay in Bordeaux- and Burgundy-style bottles, respectively. The choice of bottle type and shape, however, should be based on the wine type, the ageing period and the physical bottle-storage arrangement.

High-shouldered Bordeaux-style bottles are frequently used for varietals such as Cabernet Sauvignon, Merlot, Zinfandel and Sauvignon Blanc. This style and shape represent the best choice when bottles are to be pyramid-stacked on simple wine racks. Figure 8-IA illustrates the pyramid-stacking arrangement. This stacking method provides very good stability for Bordeaux-style bottles. One disadvantage is the loss of storage space if the wine rack is not built with sides. The bin-stacking arrangement

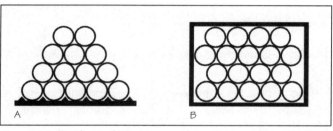

Figure 8-I: Bottle-stacking arrangements: A, pyramid and B, bin

shown in Figure 8-IB can be used to circumvent the pyramid-stacking disadvantage. It can also be used for stacking other types of bottles, which are not as stable as Bordeaux-style bottles. Burgundy, Alsace and Champagne bottle styles do not provide the same level of stability as Bordeaux-style bottles.

Sloping-shouldered Burgundy-style bottles are the standard used for varietals such as Pinot Noir and Chardonnay, while longer sloping-shouldered Alsace-style bottles are usually used for varietals such as Riesling and Gewürztraminer. For sparkling wines, only thick-walled Champagne-style bottles should be used. Standard still-wine bottles should never be used for sparkling wines as they may explode under pressure. Heavily tinted or black port-style bottles should be used to protect long-ageing port wines from sunlight. Figure 8-2 illustrates the various bottle shapes. Various bottle types also have a

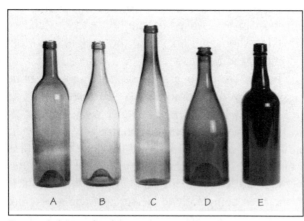

Figure 8-2: Bottle shapes: A, Bordeaux, B, Burgundy, C, Alsace, D, Champagne and E, Port

punt—an indentation in the bottom of the bottle. Many theories have been offered as to the origin and intended use of the punt in wine bottles. The industry claim is that the punt does not serve any function or purpose except in Champagne-style bottles. One purpose of the punt is to deflect the inside pressure away from the bottom of sparkling-wine bottles. By minimizing pressure on this part of the bottle, the risk of bottle explosion is greatly reduced. Another purpose is to allow bottles to be stacked upside down during the bottle fermentation phase. This stacking arrangement provides space savings for sparkling-wine producers. In still-wine bottles, the punt is often used to make bottles look bigger.

White wines should be stored in either green, brown or yellow-tinted glass bottles, or clear un-tinted bottles if the wine is to be drunk early. Red wines should be stored and aged in green- or brown-tinted glass bottles.

The choice of bottle size depends on expected drinking needs. A good mix of half-bottles (375 mL), standard 750-mL bottles, and magnums (1.5 L) will allow for the opening of the right-size bottle for the right occasion. The smaller 250-mL and 500-mL bottles are very practical for serving one or two people, respectively.

Screw cap-type bottles should be avoided as they do not guarantee an airtight seal and may oxidize wine prematurely. Bottles with a cork closure are the only choice for premium wines, particularly when bottle-ageing. The nominal inside diameter of the mouth opening of a standard 750-mL bottle is 18.5 mm. Bottles may be manufactured with different mouth diameters. Therefore, corks should be selected based on this diameter. Section 8.1.4 recommends cork sizes for different diameters. There is now a proliferation of flange-top drip-free bottles that have an extended lip around the bottle opening. The flange-top bottle type is not compatible with existing corkers. To promote a greener environment, no capsule is used on the bottleneck. Standard capsules from winemaking shops will not fit on the neck either. Until a new corker is available, these bottles should be avoided.

Bottles can be bought from winemaking supply shops or can be obtained from a local bring-your-own-bottle (BYOB) restaurant. The restaurant owner will typically be very happy to give away empty bottles. Bottles should be cleaned and sanitized thoroughly, and labels and capsules should be removed. Label removal can take a little time depending on the glue type used by the wineries where the bottles came from. The best method for removing labels is to fill each bottle with very hot water and then completely immerse each under very hot water in a large sink. The bottles should be left underwater for 24 hours. Labels may easily peel off or may need to be scraped off with a sharp knife.

8.1.2 Bottle washing devices

The importance of clean and sanitized bottles cannot be over-emphasized. A number of very effective and easy-to-use tools are available to home winemakers. They comprise the bottle washer, the bottle drainer and rinser/sterilizer (more appropriately called a rinser/sanitizer).

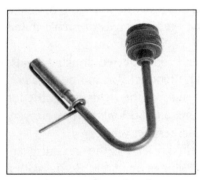

Figure 8-3: Bottle washer for rinsing bottles

The bottle washer is a device used to rinse bottles under high water pressure from a faucet. It has a built-in device to start and stop the flow of water. This device is most effective when water is sprayed instantaneously several times as opposed to spraying continuously. The latter method will cause water to accumulate inside the bottle and restrict the flow of pressurized water on the inner surface. Figure 8-3 illustrates a bottle washer used to rinse bottles. It can also be used to rinse other glass containers such as carboys and demijohns.

Warning: This bottle washer has been reported to cause pipe problems in some cases due to the spontaneous and very strong on/off action which causes excessive strain on the water main. Watch out for strange behaviors in the house water system, for example, if there is no more

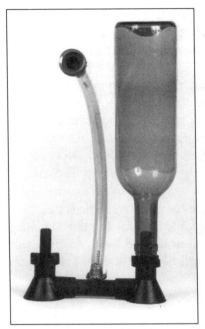

Figure 8-4: The Double Blast
Bottle Washer

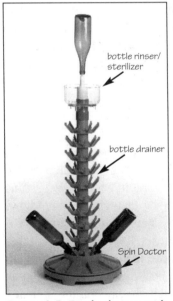

bottle rinser/
sterilizer

bottle drainer

Spin Doctor

Figure 8-5: Bottle drainer with
rinser/sterilizer

*hot water supply throughout the house
after use.*

An alternative device to the bottle washer to circumvent pipe problems is the Double Blast Bottle Washer, shown in Figure 8-4, manufactured by Fermtech Ltd. (Canada). The Double Blast Bottle Washer operates on the same principle, however, it does not cause any pipe problems or damages. It has the added advantage of requiring much less water than traditional bottle washers require and can also rinse two bottles at a time. The Double Blast Bottle Washer can be used to rinse carboys, demijohns as well as siphoning tubes.

Bottles should be rinsed once under hot-water pressure and then allowed to drip onto a bottle drainer (Figure 8-5). For stubborn stains on the inside wall, bottles can be filled with a chlorine-detergent solution and left to stand for 24 hours, and then rinsed under pressure.

The bottle drainer is a device to stack bottles upside down to completely drain any residual liquid. Its modular design can accommodate up to 90 bottles by stacking 9-bottle modules. Although the device can be further expanded, the weight of 90 bottles is the practical limit. Figure 8-5 illustrates a 90-bottle drainer built from 10 stacked modules.

The bottle drainer can also accommodate a pump-action bottle rinser/sterilizer at the top. The bottle rinser/sterilizer is used to rinse and sanitize bottles under pressure with a sulphite solution. Bottles should be rinsed three or four times by exerting pressure on the rinser and then allowed to drip on the drainer. Optionally, a final rinsing may be required with purified

209

water especially if there is excess sulphite remaining in the bottle. Traces of residual sulphite on the inside wall can be used as additional preservative if desired. Figure 8-5 illustrates the bottle rinser/sterilizer mounted on the bottle drainer.

The bottle drainer can be mounted on a spinning device, known as the Spin Doctor, which allows the drainer and bottles to be rotated full revolutions. The Spin Doctor is a practical device simplifying the positioning of bottles on the drainer. Figure 8-5 illustrates the bottle drainer mounted on the Spin Doctor.

8.1.3 Bottling devices

Various practical devices are available for quick and efficient bottling of still wines. These devices are not intended for bottling sparkling wines. Such wines are bottled as still wines and then carbonated or bottle-fermented. Otherwise, there will be a substantial loss of precious carbon dioxide gas.

There are four different methods using different apparatus for bottling still wine: 1) the vacuum-stoppered funnel, 2) the integrated, automatic vacuum-stoppered filler, 3) the stem-and-valve filler, and 4) the high-production filler.

The vacuum-stoppered funnel is a device to fill bottles to a preset level and then stopped automatically. The funnel has a built-in diverter enabling wine to pour down the bottle wall. A regular funnel, on the other hand, allows wine to drop directly down and to splash. This accelerates wine aeration and premature oxidation. The vacuum-stoppered funnel with a diverter circumvents this problem. Figure 8-6 illustrates a vacuum-stoppered funnel for filling bottles.

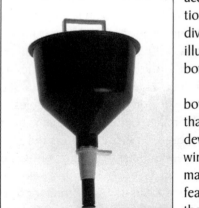

Figure 8-6: A vacuum-stoppered funnel for filling bottles

The automatic vacuum-stoppered bottle filler is a completely integrated device that minimizes aeration and spillage. This device, depicted in Figure 8-7, withdraws wine from a container and fills bottles automatically to a preset level. It offers all the features of the above funnel in addition to further facilitating the bottling operation. It is well worth the small incremental investment.

Figure 8-7: Automatic bottle filler

To operate the automatic bottle filler, the siphoning tube should be inserted in the container (5) and the device should be positioned in the bottle opening (4). The device should be set in the open position (2) and air should then be withdrawn from the overflow tube (I). This tube should be inserted into a bottle during bottling to avoid any overflow. When the bottle is filled to the preset level, the device closes automatically. It should then be transferred to another bottle to be filled. The device simply needs to be reopened to let the wine flow (3) again.

Buon Vino has developed the FILLjet, an electric version of the automatic bottle filler. The FILLjet, shown in Figure 8-8, uses a similar device as the automatic bottle filler but the wine is displaced with the use of a small electrical (positive displacement) pump. Its greatest advantage is that heavy demijohns or other containers no longer need to be placed at a certain height. They can rest right on the floor since the force of gravity is not required to fill bottles. Its operation is quite simple and greatly facilitates bottling.

The intake hose, equipped with an antidreg tip, is placed in the container full of wine. An overflow tube is inserted into an empty standard bottle to collect overflow wine during bottling.

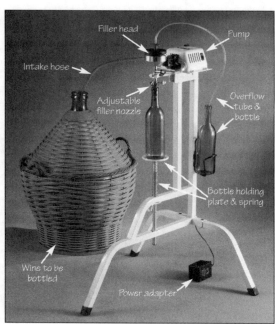

Figure 8-8: The Buon Vino FILLjet bottle filler

211

Figure 8-9: Stem-and-valve bottling device

An empty bottle is then inserted under the filler head with the bottle opening over the filler nozzle. The bottle holding plate and spring exert an upward pressure on the bottle to create a perfect seal with the filler nozzle to ensure proper operation of the filler head. When ready, the pump is turned on and wine will start filling the bottle. Once the bottle is full, the filler head automatically shuts off the pump. The full bottle is removed and the next empty bottle is placed in position. The filling head button is then pressed to restart the filling operation. The switch on the pump need not be turned on/off. It is left in the ON position for the remainder of the filling operation.

The filler nozzle can be adjusted to accept small and large bottles with different mouth diameters, and to control the fill level depending on the length of corks used.

Follow the manufacturer's instructions for operating, flushing, cleaning and maintaining the FILLjet to ensure many years of problem-free bottle filling.

Another very useful and practical bottling device is a tube-like apparatus—also known as the stem-and-valve filler—with a plastic 'foot' valve that operates on pressure. The stem-and-valve filler, shown in Figure 8-9, is attached to a siphon and the flow of wine is started. It is then inserted into a bottle to be filled with wine. Pressure is applied on the foot valve at the bottom of the device to start flow of wine. When the wine level reaches the top of the bottle, pressure is released to stop the

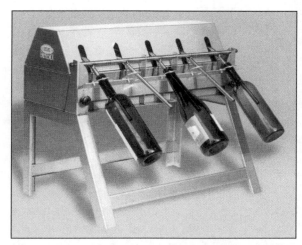

Figure 8-10: High-production floor model bottle filler

flow of wine. The device is removed and the wine level falls down to the required level for corking. This works well for standard 750-mL bottles but it is harder to operate when the bottle has a deep punt.

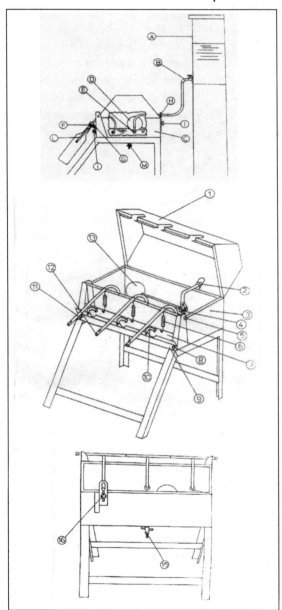

Also, the filler itself displaces a fair amount of wine, and it can be difficult to fill a bottle very full.

For serious home winemaking, a new high-production device is now available. This floor-model device, shown in Figure 8-10, allows for continuous bottle filling. It is available in 3- and 5-spout AISI 304 stainless steel models capable of an hourly production rate of 275 and 390 bottles, respectively. Stainless steel cleaning instructions should be followed as described in section 2.3.4.

This type of filler consists of a wine reservoir that is continuously fed by siphon action from a demijohn or other wine container. A pump can also be used to feed the reservoir when it is not practical to have the wine container at a level higher than the filler. In the pump setup, a T-connector is required to feed the reservoir and to return the overflow wine back into the container. Otherwise, the pumping action will force wine into the tank and

Figure 8-11: Operation and components of the high-production bottle filler

overflow it. A float ball and a rubber valve at the wine inlet tube control the wine level in the reservoir.

Each spout should be primed using a siphoning action. Bottles are inserted under each spout and then lowered to start the flow of wine. When the bottle is filled to the preset level, the flow is stopped automatically and the bottle is then removed. The wine falls down to the desired level ready for corking. As bottles are retrieved once filled, empty bottles are inserted to continue the filling operation. The bottle ullage can be adjusted to the desired preset level by raising or lowering the bottle rest and/or the wine inlet tube. Figure 8-11 illustrates the operation and components of the high-production bottle filler.

When bottling, there should be approximately 2 cm of air space, or ullage, between the wine and the cork to allow for expansion owing to temperature fluctuations. If the ullage is too small, corks can pop out under pressure. If there is too much air space, the ratio of air to wine surface is greatly increased therefore accelerating oxidation.

8.1.4 Corks for still-wine bottles

For bottling still wine, corks of varying quality are available produced from natural or agglomerated cork material extracted from oak trees. Figure 8-12 illustrates a natural and agglomerated corks.

Agglomerated corks are manufactured from natural cork granules of different sizes tightly bound by glue. Cork quality and density uniformity depend on the granule sizes. A good-quality agglomerate cork will be manufactured from granules that are neither too small nor too large to ensure that an optimal density is achieved. The cork material is then compressed to a high density to decrease the cork's porosity. Manufacturing surface defects are patched (colmated) with "plugs" from cork material to provide density and quality consistency. Since agglomerated corks contain glue, they contain less cork material. Therefore, these corks tend to be harder and require greater compression when inserted into bottles. Agglomerated corks are relatively inexpensive and are used mainly for bottling early-drinking wines.

Natural corks are costlier and are mainly used for bottling wines to be aged although

Figure 8-12: Natural and agglomerated corks

Table 8-1
Dimensions for popular cork sizes

Size number	Diameter (mm)
7	20
8	21
8½	22
9	24
10	25

they can also be used for bottling early-drinking wines. These corks are manufactured from natural oak bark without the use of glue. The density is lower than for agglomerated corks, therefore, less compression is required to insert natural corks into bottles. The more supple material also provides a better airtight seal once inserted. Being a natural product, these corks will not be of consistent quality. They may have different degrees of porosity. This should not cause any problems if the corks are not defective. A defective cork is easily detected by visible cracks along its length. Natural corks can be used for bottle ageing for a period of up to 5 years. Recent manufacturing and material improvements now allow production of high-quality corks with a lifetime beyond 5 years. These corks are the most expensive.

Corks are available in two standard lengths: short (38 mm, 1½ in) and long (45 mm, 1¾ in). Commercial wineries often use 54 mm (2 in) corks for their best wines. These very long corks are very difficult to find in home winemaking shops. For wine to be drunk early, a good-quality short or long cork should be used; however, the best-quality long cork should be selected for wine to be aged beyond 2 years.

Corks come in several diameters. Table 8-1 gives the diameter of the most popular cork sizes. A No. 9 cork is the recommended size for regular 750-mL bottles. The other sizes are for smaller or bigger bottles with non-standard mouth diameter (the mouth diameter of a standard 750-mL bottle is 18.5 mm).

Corks are available with or without chamfered edges. Although chamfered-edge corks ease the corking operation, these are not recommended for extended bottle ageing as the total effective length of the corks is reduced by more than 10 percent. Corks without chamfered edges are recommended since there is no reduction in effective length.

Corks should be completely sanitized before corking. Natural corks should be completely immersed in a sulphite solution for a few minutes. Agglomerated corks should not be soaked in water. They

Figure 8-13: Floor model and hand corkers

should be immersed in a sulphite solution for a few minutes only. After sanitization, the corks can be used immediately for bottling. Some manufacturers now provide sanitized, pre-treated and special-ly-coated (with silicone) corks that require no soaking while easing the corking operation. This is a key benefit when bottling a large quantity of wine, e.g., 200 bottles or more. Soaking that many corks can be a cumbersome task. In addition, corks requiring no soaking greatly reduce the probability of introducing spoilage microorganisms. Water from soaking may contain such microorganisms which can get trapped in and around the cork, and contaminate the wine.

Once the bottles are corked, they should stand upright for approximately 5 days to release pressure that might force the cork out or cause the wine to seep. A simple and effective method for removing excess bottle pressure consists of inserting a sanitized piece of string between the bottle opening and cork. Once the cork is inserted, a few seconds should be allowed to release the pressure, and then the string is pulled out. As a last step, a capsule should be secured on the bottle to protect the cork from dust and other elements. Bottles are then ready to be stacked in a cellar.

8.1.5 Corker

There are two main types of corkers for still-wine bottles: the floor-model corker and the hand corker. These are depicted in Figure 8-13.

The floor-model corker is the most convenient and practical for corking a large quantity of standard- and magnum-size bottles. The hand corker can be used for corking bottle sizes that the floor-model corker cannot. To use a floor corker for small quantities of half-bottles, a block of wood roughly the size of a brick can be inserted on the platform, and then the bottle can be placed on the wood for the bottling operation. One should be careful, though, as this is not a secure way to bottle a large quantity of half-bottles.

The floor-model corker has an adjustable corking rod to set the depth of the cork in the bottle. The rod should be adjusted so that the cork is level with the bottle opening once inserted. The corker is conveniently designed with an auto-locking mechanism to hold the bottle firmly in position and to facilitate insertion of the cork.

All parts of the corker that will come into contact with corks should be sanitized to avoid any contamination.

When inserting the cork, the corker lever should be held down for several seconds to allow excess pressure to escape the bottle and to prevent corks from popping out.

8.1.6 Capsules

Capsules are used to retard mould formation on corks by protecting them from excess humidity, and to give bottles a cleaner look. Capsules are available in such colours as red, burgundy red, white, yellow, gold, green and black.

Shrink-wrap capsules are the most practical type that, when fitted over the mouth of bottles, can be shrunk with boiling water, steam or hot air. These capsules can be used on both regular still- and port-wine bottles corked with regular and stopper-type corks, respectively.

To shrink a capsule using the boiling water method, the bottle with capsule is inverted and is immersed in boiling water. The capsule need only be held momentarily until it starts shrinking. This method is practical for small production only as it not convenient to keep water boiling for an extended period of time. It does, however, shrink the capsule evenly.

To shrink a capsule using the steam method, the bottle with capsule should be held for several seconds over hot steam from a continuous-boil kettle—the type without auto-shutoff. The bottle should be rotated as the capsule shrinks to ensure even shrinkage. This takes a little practice. Figure 8-14 illustrates this method of shrinking a capsule. It is convenient for small to medium productions but is not practical for larger productions, unless the humidity level in one's house needs to be increased significantly.

Caution: Steam is very hot and can scald fingers in a couple of seconds. Fingers should be kept away from the steam.

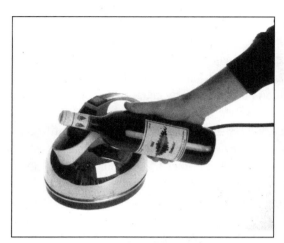

Figure 8-14: Shrink-wrapping a capsule

A new tool that greatly eases the capsule-shrink operation is now available for high production winemaking. The capsule-shrinker, shown in Figure 8-15, is a device resembling a hair blow dryer, which consists of a heating element and a small blower. When the heating element is ready for use, the capsule-shrinker is placed over the bottleneck and capsule to be shrunk. This operation takes a second or two—it should not be held for longer.

8.1.7 Labels

Labels provide the finishing touch on a wine bottle and are used to convey information on the bottle's content, as well as to display the winemaker's pride. Labels should indicate the wine style, including varietal(s), alcohol content and date of production or bottling. Pre-printed labels with this information are available from local winemaking supply shops.

Pre-printed labels have the advantage of having water-soluble glue on the backing making them very easy to remove. Gummed labels can be removed by immersing the bottle under very hot running water. The label will quickly peel off. The only disadvantage with water-soluble glue-backed labels is that they peel when immersed in a bucket of

Figure 8-15: High heat, high production capsule shrinker

cold water and ice when chilling wine. The alternative is to use water-resistant glue; however, peeling labels will be time-consuming. These will need to be scraped off with a sharp knife.

Labels can also be customized and personalized with the use of a personal computer and a good-quality printer. Labels can be produced and printed in batches on gummed paper available from a good print shop.

The easiest method to apply labels on bottles is by using a water-soaked sponge. The label backing should be entirely moistened and then applied to the bottle.

Note: Labels printed on an ink-jet printer are not recommended as cellar humidity or water from an ice bucket (when chilling wine) will cause the ink to run off. Alternatively, colour photocopies of ink-jet printed labels can be used to solve this problem.

8.2 CELLAR AGEING

What is the optimal time for drinking and enjoying a good bottle of homemade wine? How long should a wine be aged? These questions can spark controversial discussions, as there is no single correct answer. Each wine will have a different maturity lifecycle and will therefore evolve differently. Wines first go through an ageing period to allow flavours and aromas to develop and evolve into the varietals' characteristics. Wines then reach maturity as flavours and aromas plateau out. Over time, these will start declining and wines should be drunk as soon as possible to avoid disappointment. The winemaker's challenge is to strike a balance in the various phases of a wine's evolution. Decisions on ageing methods should depend on the style and type of wine desired. The ageing period should not be too quick for age-worthy wines; otherwise, they will plateau out quickly and will have to be drunk early. Conversely, the ageing period should not be slowed down to a point where the wine is not allowed to evolve.

The duration that wines spend in each phase of the lifecycle depends on many factors. These include grape variety, provenance of the fruit (cool vs. hot-climate region), vinification and winemaking methods, ageing media (glass or stainless steel vs. oak), and storage and ageing environmental characteristics. Assessing all these factors is obviously a complex task and requires extensive experience in winemaking, wine tasting and evaluation. Home winemakers often neglect the last factor, i.e. storage and ageing environmental characteristics, which greatly influences a wine's ageing process.

For proper storage and ageing of wine, the ideal cellar should provide the following environmental characteristics:

a) a constant temperature between 10° and 13° C (50° and 55° F),
b) a constant relative humidity between 55% and 75%,
c) freedom from any smell that might penetrate the cork and into the wine bottle,
d) freedom from any vibration that affects the stability of the wine, and
e) total darkness.

Of these characteristics, temperature is the one most difficult to control. Gradual temperature fluctuations should not cause concern, especially if not ageing the wine. Wide spontaneous fluctuations, such as going from 20° C (68° F) down to 12° C (54° F) within a few hours, should be avoided. However, even a fairly large seasonal swing in temperature, if it is very gradual (over a few months) will not prematurely age the wine. Spontaneous fluctuations will hamper the wine's ability to evolve and to mature into a complex wine, and will accelerate its ageing. If living in a cold-climate area, a portable space heater can be used to maintain the temperature at a desired level and preventing it from dropping below 10° C (50° F). A space heater can be wired to a thermostat for automatic temperature control. It should be noted that a space heater will reduce the humidity level and therefore this will need to be compensated with a humidifier. If living in a hot-climate area, it is highly recommended to invest in a wine-cooling unit that controls both temperature and humidity. Room air conditioning units for use in a cellar are not recommended. These units were not designed to operate continuously, especially at high humidity levels. In addition, air conditioning units operate by removing moisture in the air thereby reducing the much-needed humidity in the cellar.

Humidity is required to prevent corks from drying out and letting air inside the bottle causing the wine to spoil. Although humidity fluctuations are not as critical, it is recommended to maintain a minimum relative humidity level of 55%. If oak barrels will be used to age wine, the relative humidity should be increased to between 55% and 65%. A room humidifier does a good job of maintaining the humidity at a desired level. A hygrometer will prove quite useful in measuring and monitoring the cellar humidity level.

The above pointers work well for small and well-insulated cellars up to 20 cubic meters (740 cubic ft) in volume. For larger-volume cellars, a wine cellar specialist should be consulted to advise on the right equipment required to control cellar temperature and humidity.

MAKING SPARKLING WINE

9

Sparkling wine, or bubbly, is the wine par excellence to raise a toast or to celebrate a special occasion. The magic of sparkling wine, such as Champagne, always brings a festive mood to any occasion. This is why this type of wine has gained popularity; however, it should not be limited to celebrations. It will make an excellent aperitif, especially with hors d'oeuvres, or with a seafood entrée, or enjoyed with dessert if the wine is sweet.

Sparkling wine is usually labeled as either vintage or non-vintage. A vintage sparkling wine is produced strictly from blended or unblended wines from a single vintage. Non-vintage (the term multivintage is also often used) wines is produced using the same process except that wines from different vintages are used in the final blended wine.

Sparkling wine is produced from still wine (referred to as the base wine or *cuvée* in Champagne) by conducting a second alcoholic fermentation (to produce the carbon dioxide gas) by one of two methods, or a variation of these.

The best-known method in the production of premium sparkling wine is to conduct the second alcoholic fermentation in the bottle.

223

Known as *prise de mousse* in French, this bottle-fermentation technique is key in the traditional *méthode champenoise* process for Champagne production. It is also used in the production of premium California and Italian sparkling wines as well as Spanish cava.

In this method, the sparkling wine is kept in the same bottle throughout the second fermentation, during the extended period of ageing on the lees (a process known as autoysis and is what gives Champagne its distinctive aromas and flavours), and at bottling. The yeast deposit (lees) from the long and cool fermentation is collected in a special cap by inverting the bottle. The bottle is inverted from a horizontal to a vertical position in systematic and progressive fashion—a process known as riddling, or *remuage* in French. The neck of the bottle is then frozen to remove the cap and frozen deposit without disturbing the clarity of the wine. This bottle-clarification process is known as disgorgement. Lastly, *a dosage* (a small volume of cuvée to which a little sugar is added) is added to each bottle to sweeten the wine to obtain a desired style. In Champagne, the practice of dosage is required to balance the high acidity of the base wine resulting from grapes grown in a very cool climate. Cool-climate grapes do not achieve full maturity and, therefore, the sugar level is low and acidity is high.

Sparkling wine can only be labeled Champagne if it is produced in France's northeastern region of Champagne according to the méthode champenoise. This process is labour-intensive and requires much experience to achieve successful results. Both the size and the amount of bubbles measure the quality of a sparkling wine. Many tiny rapid-forming and long-lasting bubbles characterize the best-quality sparkling wines. Sections 9.1 to 9.3 describe sparkling wine production using variations of the méthode champenoise.

The second method consists in conducting a bulk second fermentation in a stainless steel pressure-resistant tank. This method, known as the *cuve close* (tank fermentation) or Charmat process, bypasses the need for bottle fermentation, riddling and disgorgement. The sparkling wine is refrigerated in preparation for bottling. Pressurized bottling is used so as not to lose any precious carbon dioxide gas. The only disadvantage with the Charmat process is that the second fermentation produces sediment at the bottom of the tank. Sediment needs to be separated by racking which will cause a slight loss of gas. The Charmat process for sparkling wine production is a less costly method

Figure 9-1: Ten-week sparkling wine kit

compared to the méthode champenoise, and is commonly used in commercial winemaking. Asti Spumante, the famous low-alcohol (approximately 8% alc./vol.) sweet sparkling wine from Piedmont (Italy) is produced using a variation of the tank fermentation process.

For home winemaking, there are two simple and inexpensive alternatives to produce early-drinking sparkling wines: using a sparkling wine kit or by carbonation.

Ten-week sparkling wine kits, such as the one shown in Figure 9-1, contain the concentrate, all necessary ingredients (bentonite, sugar, yeast, etc.), stoppers, wire hoods, capsules and labels. These kits use a variation of the méthode champenoise; they still ferment in the bottle but the sediment is not disgorged. The final wine requires careful pouring from the bottle when serving so as not to disturb the sediment at the bottom.

Carbonation is the process used in soft-drink production where a beverage is injected with carbon dioxide gas. This method produces very good sparkling wines with much less effort and risk—a few large bubbles that fade quickly compared to premium sparkling wines characterize carbonated sparkling wines. Section 9.4 describes the method for producing sparkling wines by carbonation.

Sparkling wines are produced mainly as white or rosé although there have been many unsuccessful attempts to commercialize sparkling red wines. As with still wines, sparkling wines are also classified according to the amount of residual sugar. Countries have different designations and requirements relative to residual sugar content. For example, Brut (medium dry, *demi-sec*) and Extra Brut (dry, *sec*) sparkling wines may have a maximum allowable residual sugar content of 15 g/L and 6 g/L, respectively, as well as a less complex taste profile

225

because the step where the wine spends time in bottle on yeast (less yeast contact and autolysis) has been removed. For some producers, the Brut is their driest cuvée, with little or no dosage, while others also offer a sparkling wine called Brut Extra, Brut Ultra or Brut Nature, denoting no dosage or residual sugar at all.

Warning: Sparkling wine production requires the handling of high-pressure containers and bottles. Safety precautions should be followed to avoid accidents. Protective eyewear should be worn at all times.

9.1 PREPARATION

A well-balanced still base wine (cuvée) with an alcoholic content between 10.0% and 11.0% alc./vol. should be used to make a good sparkling wine. The cuvée should not exceed 11.0% alc./vol. as bottle fermentation will produce additional alcohol, approximately 1.2% to 1.5% alc./vol. A good-quality sparkling wine should not exceed 12.5% alc./vol. The sparkling wine produced in the method described in this section will be sweetened, therefore, the cuvée should have a TA high in the recommended range (refer to Table 3-3 on page 83).

Table 1-1 and Table 1-2 on pages 34 to 37, respectively, list some recommended grape varieties suitable for sparkling wine. In making Champagne, the cuvée is typically a dry-style white wine blend from Chardonnay, Pinot Meunier and Pinot Noir. *Blanc de Blancs* Champagne is produced from Chardonnay only while *Blanc de Noirs* is made using non-macerated white juice from red grapes such as Pinot Meunier or Pinot Noir. Other non-Champagne grape varieties, for example, Chenin Blanc, Muscat or Riesling, can also be used for making excellent sparkling wines.

The cuvée should be cellar-aged for at least 6 months, and should be clarified and cold stabilized to avoid tartrate precipitation during the time when the sparkling wine is placed in cold storage. It should have a free SO_2 level of 15 mg/L or less to ensure successful bottle fermentation. ML fermentation should also be completed and stabilized before making sparkling wine.

Warning: The cuvée should not be preserved with a high level of sulphite or be stabilized with potassium sorbate, or clarified with isinglass, as these will prevent the wine from sparkling.

A small dosage volume should be prepared by siphoning between 2 and 4 percent of the cuvée into a glass container and adding an equal volume of sweetener-conditioner. The container should be properly sealed to protect the wine from oxidation, and placed in cold storage at a temperature between 4° and 8° C (39° and 46° F).

9.2 BOTTLE FERMENTATION

The cuvée should be allowed to reach a temperature between 18° and 21° C (65° and 70° F) to facilitate sugar dissolution and to favour yeast fermentation. Twenty to 25 g of fermentable sugar—dextrose or sucrose—should be added per litre of wine and dissolved thoroughly. This will produce an additional 1.2% to 1.5% alc./vol. in the finished sparkling wine. To ensure a successful fermentation, twice the recommended maximum of yeast nutrients should be added to the cuvée, i.e., 2×20 g/hL = 40 g/hL.

Note: The prescribed maximum amount of sugar should not be exceeded to produce more bubbles. Exceeding the maximum will produce excessive pressure build-up in the bottle that could cause it to explode.

The yeast inoculum can be prepared by first using an alcohol-tolerant cold temperature-resistant *S. cerevisiae* wine yeast or, preferably, a *S. bayanus* sparkling wine yeast such as the Lalvin® EC-1118® or RED STAR® Premier Cuvée strains. It is recommended to double the prescribed inoculum volume to favour a good fermentation. The inoculum should then be added to the cuvée and stirred gently.

During bottle fermentation, sediment will deposit on the bottle walls and will need to be shaken, by riddling, for later removal when disgorging. To ease this operation, a riddling aid, such as tannin, should be added to the cuvée at the rate of 20 g/hL. The tannin should be dissolved in a small amount of wine and then added to the remainder of the cuvée. Bentonite can also be used as a riddling aid.

At this point, there are two options to prepare for bottle fermentation. If all fermentation environmental conditions are and will remain ideal, the cuvée can be siphoned into individual bottles. Otherwise, the cuvée can be started in bulk. In the latter case, a fermentation lock with a sulphite solution should be attached to the container. The cuvée should remain at the recommended temperature until yeast activity starts.

9.2.1 Conducting bottle fermentation

A sufficient number of sanitized and water-rinsed sparkling-wine bottles should be prepared for the cuvée.

When the cuvée starts fermenting (when done in bulk), it should be gently stirred to set the yeast in suspension to ensure good bottle fermentation. The cuvée should not be allowed to ferment beyond its starting point in the large vessel, as carbon dioxide gas will be lost. When fermentation begins, the cuvée can be siphoned into the bottles.

A special plastic bottle-fermentation stopper, shown in Figure 9-2, should be used and then secured with a wirehood. Known as a vintrap, the special bottle-fermentation stopper is similar to a regular sparkling-wine bottle stopper, but it has an elongated container to collect sediment from bottle fermentation as the bottle is inverted. The wirehood should be held in place by twisting the wire 5½ revolutions using the tool shown in Figure 9-3.

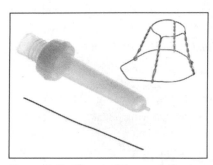

Figure 9-2: The vintrap — a plastic bottle-fermentation cap

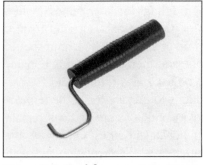

Figure 9-3: Tool for securing wirehood on sparkling-wine bottles

In commercial sparkling wine production using the méthode champenoise, the technique of lees collection is accomplished using crown caps—similar to the ones used to stopper beer bottles—equipped with a *bidule*. The bidule is a special holder designed to receive the settling lees and facilitate disgorgement. Two types of crown cap/bidules are available: integrated and separate. In the integrated type, shown in Figure 9-4A, the bidule is part of the crown cap. A plastic liner under the cap provides a perfect seal. In the separate type, shown in Figure 9-4B, the small plastic container (bidule) is inserted into the bottle opening and the crown cap is placed over it. A cork liner under the cap provides a perfect seal for this type of bidule. The only drawback of the separate bidule is

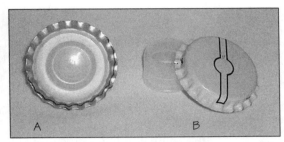

Figure 9-4: Bidules: A, Integrated with crown cap, B, Separate from crown cap

that occasionally it remains stuck in the bottle, even under the high pressure of the sparkling wine, when the sediment is frozen during disgorgement. The crown cap for both types is fastened to the bottle opening using a home winemaking crown capper, such as the one shown in Figure 9-5. Crown caps are pressure-resistant and will maintain all carbon dioxide gas produced during bottle fermentation.

Note: Bidules come in different sizes to fit either US or European bottles. Europeans bottles have a slightly wider opening and require 29 mm bidules (sold under the Scelnox brand name). Crown cappers are usually equipped with different size attachments for capping US and European bottles.

Note: The techniques of crown-capping and disgorging sparkling wine bottles require extensive experience and are not recommended for novice winemakers. Crown-capped bottles will need disgorging, which involves decrowning sparkling wine bottles under very high pressure. Only experienced winemakers should attempt this operation. Refer to section 9.3 for more details and for instructions on how to prepare fake "sparkling" wine for the purpose of practicing disgorging.

Figure 9-5: A crown capper

All bottles should then be transferred to a wine cellar for a cool, long and slow bottle fermentation at a temperature of approximately 13° C (55° F). The cellar temperature should not be lower than the yeast's optimum fermentation temperature range recommended by the manufacturer. The bottles can be stored horizontally on wine racks for 12 to 18 months depending on the desired extent of lees contact. For the first 4 to 8 weeks, each bottle should be shaken gently 2 or 3 times per week to stir the yeast to favour a good fermentation, and then returned to a horizontal position. At the end of the fermentation and lees ageing period, each bottle should be inverted to allow all sediment to deposit in the vintrap or bidule.

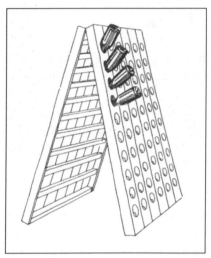

Figure 9-6: A riddling rack

Once fully inverted, bottles should remain in the inverted position until all sediment has been deposited in the vintrap or bidule and the sparkling wine is clear. There should be no trace of cloudiness. The elongated portion of the vintrap should be folded above the sediment level. A short metal wire (refer to Figure 9-2) is used to secure the fold to prevent the sediment from dropping back in the wine. The use of this short wire is optional if the sediment in the stopper will be frozen before removal. It does, however, serve as an additional safeguard against sediment dropping back in the wine.

Riddling

Alternatively, a riddling rack, known as a *pupitre* in French and shown in Figure 9-6, can be used to tilt each bottle progressively until fully inverted. Riddling serves two purposes that go hand-in-hand. First, as sediment deposits along the long side of the bottle, a greater surface area is created to maximize the benefits of lees contact. Secondly, to prepare the bottles for disgorgement, the lees are disturbed in such a way as to collect them in the vintrap or bidule, and therefore clarifying the sparkling wine.

Figure 9-7 illustrates a typical standard riddling program used in the méthode champenoise. In this program, each bottle is rotated sharply according to Figure 9-7 over a 21-day period to dislodge the sediment. During the rotation of each bottle, these should also be progressively tilted upwards to move each bottle from a horizontal position to an almost vertical position by the time the program is

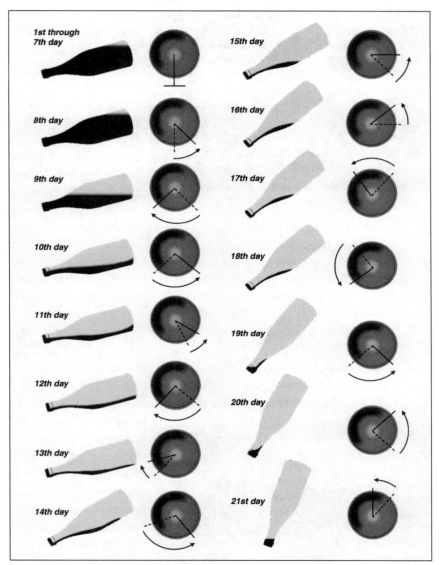

Figure 9-7: Standard riddling program

completed. In Figure 9-7, the shaded portion of the bottle represents the sediment, and illustrates how it travels to the vintrap or bidule during riddling. The punt (bottom) portion of the bottle also illustrates the start and end positions of the bottle when riddled, using a

231

Figure 9-8: A *remueur* riddling Champagne bottles

dotted and solid line, respectively. The punt of each bottle should be marked with a short, white line using enamel paint where the T-line is indicated on the first bottle (1st through 7th day) in Figure 9-7. This greatly simplifies keeping track of bottle positions throughout the riddling period.

Figure 9-8 depicts a *remueur* manually riddling thousands of bottles per day. In modern sparkling winemaking, manual riddling is being replaced by the use of automated riddling machines known as gyropalettes.

When riddling is completed, the sediment in each bottle will be collected in the vintrap or bidule, ready for disgorgement. Figure 9-9 shows how sediment is collected in bidules following riddling.

Riddling has the advantage of disturbing the sediment minimally while depositing them in the vintrap or bidule (by gravity), therefore maintaining clarity of the wine. The disadvantage is that this process requires more work to tilt each bottle, but it's fun! The alternative is to separate the sediment from the wine by racking or decanting each bottle. This is still a tedious procedure yielding less-than-satisfactory results as there will always be some sediment getting into the finished wine.

At the end of the 21st day, the riddled bottles can be placed in carton wine cases for several weeks or months for further ageing. The crown-capped ends should be at the bottom, i.e. bottles should remain in the inverted position.

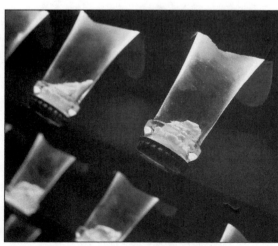

Figure 9-9: Sediment collected in bidules

9.3 DISGORGEMENT, DOSAGE AND BOTTLING

Before proceeding with disgorgement, ensure that bottle fermentation is complete. It will complete within a couple of months if carried out in a cool cellar at 12° C (54° F). After the long ageing sojourn, fermentation will certainly be over and one can disgorge without any worries. If fermentation is not allowed to complete, it can restart after corking resulting in more bottle sediment and an unstable wine.

Caution: As the bottles are under pressure, they should be handled with care with safety gloves during the following bottling operations. A protective face guard should also be worn during disgorgement.

Disgorgement (vintrap)
The riddled bottles of sparkling wine should be transferred, in the inverted position, to a deep freezer at a temperature between –7° and –4° C (20° and 25° F). When ice crystals start to form—this can take up to 3 hours—one bottle at a time should be retrieved, and the wire-hood and vintrap removed to disgorge the sediment. As the sediment has frozen inside the vintrap, it can be removed without leaving any deposit in the wine. Almost no gas will escape since, at this near-freezing temperature, most of the precious carbon dioxide will remain dissolved in the wine.

Figure 9-10: Disgorging the sediment

Disgorgement (bidule)
Disgorging sparkling wine bottles with bidules is a tricky proposition, which requires a lot of practice. See Figure 9-10. This is not for novice winemakers.

When disgorging, the crown cap, bidule and frozen sediment will fly off. To prevent any injury and to avoid making a mess, a large container should be used to collect the flying debris. Champenois disgorgers often use an old oak barrel, in the upright position, having a large cutout in the center approximately 0.5 m x 0.5 m (18 in x 18 in) in size.

Disgorgement is performed using a disgorging key, also known as a decrowner—a tool that operates on the same principle as the old soda or beer bottle openers. The only difference is that the key pulls the crown cap using a downward instead of an upward motion. Conventional bottle openers will not do the job; they will not work since the upward motion will interfere with flying debris. Figure 9-IIA shows a disgorging key.

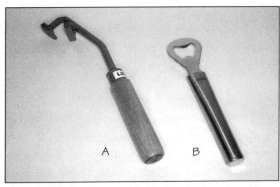

Figure 9-II: Disgorging keys: A, Conventional key, B, Bottle opener

Special bottle openers, such as the one shown in Figure 9-IIB, that operate with either an upward or downward motion can also be used. For disgorging, these bottle openers must be used with a downward motion to remove the crown cap.

A large and shallow container, which can hold up to ten or more bottles in the inverted position in a brine solution, will be required. The solution will be used to freeze approximately 2.5 to 3.0 cm (I to 1¼ in) of the neck portion of the bottle, or just above the sediment level. The wine should not be frozen too high above the sediment level, which would otherwise make disgorgement more difficult.

The number of bottles and size of the container will depend on how quickly one can disgorge. It is suggested to start out with a few bottles and to adjust accordingly based on skill. The rate of disgorgement will also depend on how quickly the solution can freeze the neck of the bottles. The method described below will freeze the sediment in five to ten minutes.

The brine solution can be prepared using ice, or snow if you live in a cold region, and plain coarse salt. The ice should be crushed finely and placed in a thin layer, just enough to be slightly higher than the sediment level, in the container. Working in a cool cellar will allow more time before the ice starts melting. The salt should be spread evenly over the ice. Approximately a quarter to a third of the ice volume will be required.

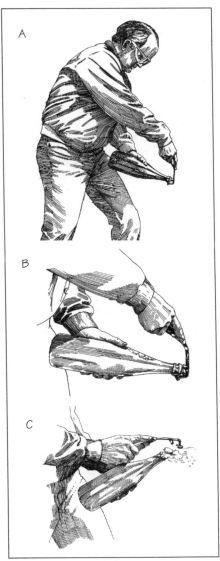

Figure 9-12: Disgorgement

The plain-salt brine solution is adequate for freezing the bottlenecks quickly; however, it can be accelerated by substituting plain salt with hydrated calcium chloride, available from a supplier of chemicals. Hydrated calcium chloride lowers the freezing point of water considerably more than plain salt—approximately -55° C (-67° F) versus -20° C (-4° F), respectively.

Prior to transferring bottles to the container, the bottles should be chilled in a refrigerator to minimize the loss of precious carbon dioxide gas during disgorgement. Otherwise, a higher bottle temperature will cause the high-pressured wine to gush out uncontrollably.

Warning: *Do not attempt to disgorge* à la volée *(on the fly)—without freezing the sediment. This is very difficult and will result in much wine loss unless you become an expert disgorger.*

Refer to Figure 9-12 for the sequence of disgorgement steps explained below.

One bottle at a time, the brine solution is rinsed from the neck of the bottle by dipping it in a small bucket of water. The bottle is held horizontally using a firm grip (Figure 9-12A), with the punt resting against the leg. Using the other hand, the disgorging key is placed in position over the crown cap, and while pulling the cap with a downward motion (Figure 9-12B), the bottle is rotated upwards to a 45-degree angle while completely removing the cap (Figure 9-12C). When timed correctly, the crown cap is removed as the air bubble in the bottle reaches the neck portion, and will cause the wine to gush

235

out and the sediment to fly out. There will be some wine loss, which will need to be replaced at dosage time. Remember to point the bottle and flying ice plug into a container to avoid any accident or mess.

If too much wine is lost, the bottle can be held by the neck so that the thumb can reach over and block the mouth once the crown cap is removed. The thumb should be removed very slowly to release pressure—a hissing sound will be heard. With a lot of practice and dexterity, this operation can be performed without too much pressure loss and with less than 20 mL of wine loss. This will be replaced with the liqueur de dosage prior to corking.

Dosage and bottling

A small amount of dosage should now be added to each bottle to obtain the desired sweetness level (and to balance it with the acidity) in the finished sparkling wine. Each bottle should be topped up again with good-quality still wine so that a 2-cm (¾-in) ullage is left between the wine and the stopper.

Optionally, a small amount of sulphite (50 mg/L) can be added at this stage for extra protection along with some metatartaric acid (10 g/hL) in case the wine was not previously cold stabilized. Dilute sulphite and metatartaric acid solutions can be used, and are added at a rate of 0.5 mL and 0.8 mL per bottle, respectively, using a small syringe.

The bottles are now ready to be corked. The closure of choice is the traditional sparkling wine corks, shown in Figure 9-13A, better recognized as the mushroom-shaped cork shown in Figure 9-13B. The cork must be secured with a wirehood, shown in Figure 9-13C, using the wirehooding tool shown in Figure 9-3.

Sparkling wine corks are very difficult to insert because of their high density and large diameter (30 mm, 1 5/16 in). A floor corker specifically designed for inserting this type of cork should be used. Corks can be inserted dry or can be briefly soaked in a sulphite solution. The non-tapered end of the cork should be inserted first, and only partially so that the

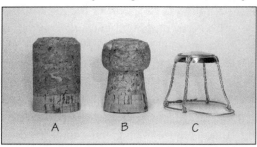

Figure 9-13: A, Sparkling wine cork, B, Cork after bottle is opened, C, Wirehood

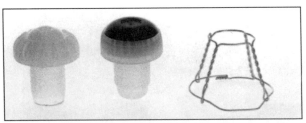

Figure 9-14: Plastic stoppers and wirehood for sparkling-wine bottles

wirehood can be properly secured under the lip of the bottle. This is very important to avoid corks popping out of bottles.

Alternatively bottles can be re-capped with plastic mushroom-shaped stoppers, purposely designed for sparkling-wine bottles, and secured with a wirehood.

Two types of stoppers, shown in Figure 9-14, are available depending on the type of bottles used. European sparkling-wine bottles have a slightly larger opening and require the black-top stopper type shown in Figure 9-14. The proper stopper should be used so bottles remain properly sealed.

Plastic stoppers should be sanitized in a sulphite solution. These are inserted by hand by applying a downward pressure until the stopper comes to rest on the bottle opening. They are then secured in place with a wirehood using a wirehooding tool.

All bottles should be transferred to a wine cellar, and then each bottle should be shaken gently to thoroughly mix the dosage with the wine. Bottles can be stored horizontally, or left upright. The sparkling wine will further benefit from 6 months of cellar ageing.

Foil capsules are also available to dress sparkling-wine bottles. These are available in such colours as white, black, pink and gold. These are simply inserted over the stopper and bottleneck, and fitted by squeezing the wrapper in place.

Making fake "sparkling" wine for practicing disgorgement
Méthode champenoise is very diffcult. To practice the technique, a fake sparkling wine can be concocted by fermenting a sweet solution. Five mL (1 tsp) of fermentable sugar—dextrose or sucrose—should be dissolved in 500 mL of water with 15 mL (1 tbsp) of lemon juice, and then a *S. bayanus* yeast strain such as Lalvin's EC-1118 is added. Each bottle should be topped with water to 750 mL and sealed with a crown cap. As many bottles as needed to practice can be prepared.

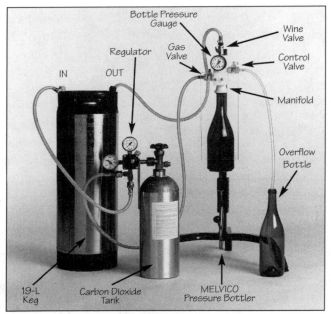

Figure 9-15: Sparkling wine production by carbonation using a MELVICO pressure bottler

9.4 CARBONATION METHOD

Making sparkling wines by carbonation is a relatively simple procedure if one is properly equipped and experienced. Many wine supply shops offer wine carbonation as a service. Figure 9-15 illustrates the setup for producing sparkling wine using the carbonation method.

The method[13] described here uses a MELVICO pressure bottler. The cuvée should be sweetened as desired before gassing it. Once the wine has been injected with carbon dioxide gas, it is recommended to seal the bottles with a plastic stopper as quickly as possible. Since the carbonation procedure does not alter the flavours or aromas of the wine (as in the case of bottle fermentation), there is no point in adding the dosage before bottling.

The carbonation method requires a stainless steel pressure-resistant container or keg, purposely designed for carbonating drinks, a carbon dioxide tank, and a MELVICO pressure bottler equipped with a pressure gauge. The keg should be rated for a pressure of 890 kPa

[13]This method is based on instructions provided with the MELVICO pressure bottler, and it is used here with the permission of MELVICO INC.

(130 psi). A 19-L keg is the most readily available size. It is equipped with an IN plug for gassing and an OUT plug to draw out wine and into a bottle. The OUT plug is connected to a feed tube that extends to the bottom of the keg. The carbon dioxide tank is equipped with a regulator to monitor and control bottle pressure. Equal volumes of wine and carbon dioxide will be required. Sparkling-wine bottles should be used as they will be subjected to high pressure.

The MELVICO pressure bottler consists of a bottle stand apparatus with a 3-valve assembly (the newer model has a 4-valve assembly—the control valve consists of 2 separate valves) and pressure gauge mounted on a manifold. The left-hand valve, referred to as the gas valve, is connected to the carbon dioxide tank and regulates its flow. Similarly, the upper valve, referred to as the wine valve, is connected to the OUT plug on the keg. This valve regulates the flow of wine into the bottle. The right-hand valve, referred to as the control valve, regulates the bottle pressure. An overflow tube from the control valve should be placed in a bottle to collect any wine that may overflow during bottling. Lastly, the carbon dioxide tank should also be connected to the IN plug on the keg. The 3-valve manifold assembly is also equipped with a rubber seal to provide an airtight seal during bottling.

To clean the keg and MELVICO pressure bottler apparatus, the keg should first be rinsed with water and then half-filled with a sulphite solution. The components shown in Figure 9-15 should then be assembled as indicated. The control valve should be opened completely. With a bottle properly set under the manifold, the wine valve should be opened to let the sulphite solution flow through the overflow tube. The solution should be collected in a large container. Lastly, the keg should be rinsed with water and the cleaning operation repeated with the keg half-filled with water.

To carbonate wine, one should start with a dry or sweet, cold stabilized wine at a desired alcohol level—this will not be altered with this method—and a total acidity balanced with the residual sugar content. With this method, the wine can be fined and preserved with isinglass and sulphite, respectively, as the wine will not undergo another fermentation.

The wine should be poured into the keg and placed in a freezer until it reaches a temperature of approximately of 0° C (32° F). The wine should not be allowed to freeze. When ready to carbonate the wine, the components shown in Figure 9-15 should be assembled as indicated, except for the wine valve tube to the OUT plug on the keg. All valves, including the main control knob on the gas tank, should be in the CLOSED position.

The keg should then be inverted and the main control knob on the gas tank valve should be opened. The gas tank pressure should be adjusted between 275 kPa (40 psi) and 345 kPa (50 psi). Care should be taken not to exceed the recommended maximum pressure; otherwise, bottles may explode. The keg should be shaken until the hissing sound from the gas can no longer be heard and then returned to the upright position. This procedure will saturate the wine with carbon dioxide gas, and should take approximately 8 to 10 minutes for a 19-L keg. The wine valve tube can then be connected to the OUT plug on the keg, and the overflow tube (2 tubes in the newer model) from the control valve should be inserted in the overflow bottle.

A sparkling wine bottle—specifically designed to withstand pressure—should be placed on the stand and be properly seated against the manifold seal. The bottle should be airtight. The gas valve should then be opened to let pressure build up inside the bottle. The wine valve should then be opened and the gas valve closed. Wine will not flow until the control valve is opened since the pressure in the bottle and the keg are equal. The control valve should then be opened **slowly** to lower the pressure inside the bottle and to allow wine into the bottle. If the control valve is opened too much or too quickly, foam will build up in the bottle. The bottle should be filled to allow a gap of approximately 2 cm when the plastic bottle stopper is inserted. The wine valve should then be turned to the CLOSED position and the pressure dropped to 70 kPa (10 psi). On the newer MELVICO bottler model, the second control valve can be opened at this point to let the pressure drop to zero, and then re-closed. Effervescence in the bottle should be allowed to stabilize before removing it from the pressure bottler apparatus.

After the control valve is adjusted correctly with the first bottle, it will require no further adjustment for the duration of the bottling operation, as long as same-size bottles are used.

The bottle should be removed, stoppered immediately, and secured with a wirehood. This is repeated for the complete batch of wine.

Carbonated sparkling wines should be drunk soon after bottling. Ageing the wine any further will not improve it.

10
MAKING PORT WINE

Port is a type of age-worthy fortified wine, originating in Portugal, or more precisely from the city of Oporto in the Douro Valley. Port, or *Porto* as it is known in Portugal, is made from either red or white grapes (although red is by far the most popular) and is fairly sweet with a high (typically 20% alc./vol.) alcohol content. Port wine is made by adding alcohol to fermenting must therefore stopping fermentation and yielding a high residual sugar content. Red port wines have gained a wide market appeal and are therefore very high in demand compared to white port wines. This chapter discusses red port wines.

There are many different port-wine styles depending on the maturation and ageing methods and duration selected. These methods will alter the chemical structure of the wine thereby requiring different fining and/or filtration techniques. Different styles of port wine can also be obtained by blending different varietals, from the same or different vintages. The most popular port-wine styles are ruby, tawny, vintage and Late-Bottled Vintage (LBV).

Ruby port is a very young wine, most often a blend of a number of varietals from one or more vintages, which can be matured for a short duration in oak barrels or aged in bottles. Being a young wine, ruby port will have a very fruity aroma and a deep ruby colour. Ruby port is filtered before bottling to minimize sediment and therefore does not require decanting. It is a style suitable for quick commercialization and for early drinking.

Tawny port is vinified much like a ruby port; however, it is matured for a much longer time in oak barrels, typically between five and seven years. Tawny port wine will therefore have a predominantly oak character and will not be as fruity as a ruby port. The extended maturation period will also cause the wine to become lighter, due to the fining action of the tannins from oak barrels, and will acquire a tawny-brown colour. Due to the long sojourn in wood, and the controlled interaction with oxygen, the wine's organoleptic qualities have also become more complex.

Vintage port is unquestionably the choice of port wine aficionados due its high quality. This port style is produced from a blend of the best grapes in a single vintage. Vintage port is only "declared" (produced) in years yielding the best-quality grapes. Port wine which is not "declared" (i.e., it does not meet vintage port requirements) is declassified. It will then be vinified differently according to the desired style. Vintage port requires a short two-year maturation period followed by a very long bottle-ageing period of 10, 20, 30 or more years. The wine is not filtered before bottling and will therefore be very deep in colour and will produce a heavy sediment requiring decanting. As it ages, the colour will become lighter.

Late-Bottled Vintage (LBV) port is a port-style wine from a single vintage bottled after four to six years following the harvest. LBV port is produced from grapes in a vintage not worthy of being "declared". This wine style may be filtered and therefore will not require decanting. LBV port, unlike vintage port, is meant for early consumption once available on the market.

This chapter describes a specific recipe on how to produce a tawny port-style wine from red-juice concentrate. Fermentation is carried out to dryness with the residual sugar content obtained by adding a portion of the syrupy concentrate to the wine at the end of fermentation. The desired amount of alcohol is then added for fortification. The added alcohol also prevents refermentation as yeast is inhibited at a high alcohol content. The oak maturation process is replaced by the addition of oak extract.

The recipe has been adapted from Wine-Art's Port Wine recipe[14] to include alcohol fortification and uses 5 L of concentrate. This will pro-

[14]Used with permission of Wine-Art Inc.

duce 19 L of "base" port wine. A volume of alcohol (brandy) will also be added depending on the desired final alcohol level. Any grape variety concentrate can be used although it is recommended to use a good-quality port-wine concentrate. Organoleptic qualities of the wine will be more typical of a port wine produced using traditional methods.

10.1 MUST PREPARATION

I L of the concentrate should be poured into a sanitized bottle and sealed airtight. This should be stored in a freezer for later use.

The remaining 4 L of concentrate should be added to a sanitized 23 L open fermentor, such as a plastic pail. 5 L of hot water should then be added to the concentrate and stirred thoroughly. The following ingredients should then be added to the concentrate:

- ⊷ 500 g of glucose solids
- ⊷ 2.2 kg of corn sugar
- ⊷ 10 mL (2 tsp) of yeast nutrients
- ⊷ 15 mL (3 tsp) of grape tannins

The must should be stirred thoroughly to completely dissolve all solids. Lastly, the following ingredients should be added to the must:

- ⊷ 140 g of dried elderberries
- ⊷ 57 g of banana flakes or 1.4 kg of fresh bananas

Note: The elderberries should be tied up in a nylon bag for easier removal later.

Lastly, 10 L of cold water should be added to bring the must to a total volume of 19 L. The actual volume will be higher because of dissolved solids; however, after rackings and filtration, there will be a loss of volume. The final yield will be approximately 19 L.

Sugar concentration and total acidity should be measured. The sugar concentration should be approximately 26.5 B° (1.110) and the starting TA should be approximately 4.6 g/L.

10.2 CONDUCTING ALCOHOLIC FERMENTATION

The must should be inoculated with two packages of Lalvin® EC-1118® or KIV-1116® yeast strains, or two packages of RED STAR® Premier Cuvée or Pasteur Red™ yeast strains. These strains are recommended because of their high-alcohol tolerance.

The fermentor should be covered with a protective plastic sheet or lid. Alcoholic fermentation should be carried out for one week, or until the sugar concentration has dropped to 7.5 B° (1.030) or less, at a temperature between 17° and 20° C (63° and 68° F). During fermentation, the must should be stirred once daily.

In the following chaptalization steps, it is important to let fermentation progress actively before adding more sugar. By chaptalizing progressively, the yeast is allowed to transform the sugar into alcohol without causing a stuck fermentation.

1 L of the fermenting must should be withdrawn and poured into a clean stainless steel saucepan. The must should be heated slowly while adding and dissolving 3 cups (approximately 750 mL) of corn sugar. When the corn sugar is completely dissolved, the heated must should be let to cool just a little so as not to shock the resident yeast population in the fermentor. It should then be re-added to the fermenting must in the fermentor. The must should be stirred thoroughly and covered properly.

Fermentation should be carried out for 3 more days. The must should be stirred once daily. Using the method above, another 3 cups (approximately 750 mL) of corn sugar should be added and stirred into the must.

Fermentation should be carried out for 3 more days. The must should be stirred once daily. Again using the method above, 5 cups (approximately 1250 mL) of corn sugar should be added and stirred into the must. At this point, the elderberries should be removed before replacing the lid on the fermentor.

Fermentation should be allowed to continue for 3 more days **without** stirring. After this time, the must should be racked into a clean and sanitized glass fermentor. The wine should be allowed to splash at the bottom of the fermentor. The fermentor should be topped up and then secured with a bung and fermentation lock. Fermentation should be allowed to progress, at a temperature of approximately 18° C (64° F), until all yeast activity ceases. This should last approximately 4 weeks.

When fermentation activity has ceased, the wine should be racked into a sanitized glass container. The 1 L reserved concentrate should be allowed to thaw completely and then should be added to the wine. The following ingredients should then be added to the wine and stirred in thoroughly:

↬ 120 mL (8 tbsp) of glycerol
↬ 50 mL (10 tsp) of Sinatin 17 liquid oak extract
↬ 10 mL (2 tsp) of potassium sorbate
↬ 2.5 mL (½ tsp) sulphite powder

The fermentor should be sealed with a fermentation lock and the wine should be aged for 6 months. Following the ageing period, the wine may be coarse-filtered using No. 2 pads. Optionally, the wine may be racked without filtering. Before alcohol fortification, the wine should be sulphited, if required, to achieve a maximum free SO_2 level of 50 mg/L.

10.3 ALCOHOL FORTIFICATION

The resulting wine will have an alcohol content of approximately 17% or 18% alc./vol. The desired final alcohol content should be between 18% and 20% alc./vol. for a port wine. This is achieved by adding the required volume of brandy, typically with an alcohol content of 40% alc./vol. Brandy will add body to the final wine and will also further clarify the wine. It is therefore recommended to age the wine for an additional 2 to 4 months before bottling.

The required volume of brandy for a desired alcohol content can be calculated according to the blending formula presented in section 6.1. Assuming a 40% alc./vol. brandy is used and that an alcohol content of 20% alc./vol. is desired, the required volume of brandy (denoted by E) for 19 L of 17%-alc./vol. port wine is calculated as follows:

$$\frac{(17 \times 19) + (40 \times E)}{(19 + E)} = 20\% \text{ alc.vol}$$

$$E = 2.85 \text{ L}$$

Figure 10-1: Cork closure with plastic stopper for fortified-wine bottles

Therefore, 2.85 L of 40% alc./vol. brandy is required to bring 19 L of a 17% alc./vol. port wine to 20%.

Following the ageing period, the port wine may be bottled in port-style bottles and corked using stopper-type corks, shown in Figure 10-1.

Port and other fortified-wine bottles can be corked by using a regular cork; however, the tradi-

245

tional closure for these types of bottles is a cork with a plastic stopper, commonly referred to as a stopper-type cork. Aficionados insist on using this type of closure for fortified-wine bottles to keep with tradition.

These corks, available in 19-mm (¾-in) lengths, have the same properties as the regular corks and are sanitized in the same fashion. The only major difference is that fortified-wine corks are inserted in the bottle by hand instead of using a corker. These corks tend to pop out easily once inserted given their short length. The string trick (to release pressure) is very practical when using stopper-type corks driven by hand.

11
MAKING ICEWINE

Note: *The Ontario (Canada) winemaking industry is governed by rules and regulations set by the Vintners Quality Alliance (VQA). These are part of an appellation system—similar to the Appellation d'Origine Contrôlée (AOC) system in France—designed to regulate viticultural, winemaking and marketing practices. British Columbia (Canada) has also adopted VQA rules and regulations. These explicitly state that commercial Icewine can only be labeled as such if grapes are naturally frozen on the vines, and not artificially frozen (cryoextraction), and cannot be chaptalized. Grapes (only specific Ontario- and British Columbia-grown grapes are allowed) can only be harvested with a minimum sugar level of 32 B° and at a minimum temperature of -7° C.*

Icewine, also known as Eiswein of German fame, is a high-acidity sweet dessert wine produced from frozen grapes. Grapes are allowed to freeze on the vines (see Figure 11-1) and are then harvested at night at subfreezing temperatures, typically below -7° C (19° F). These conditions allow the water content in the dehydrated grape berries to freeze and therefore concentrate sugars, acids and flavour compounds. Whole-cluster grapes are pressed outdoors immediately

Figure II-I: Frozen Vidal grapes on vines

following harvesting, still at subfreezing temperatures, to extract the sugar-rich syrup and to discard the frozen water content. Fermenting the syrup yields a very sweet wine with good acidity, intense flavours and immense complexity. The high price of Icewine is due to high production costs associated with manual harvesting in subfreezing temperatures, but more important, due to the low yield of the grapes. Since more than 70 percent of grape juice is actually water, a significant juice volume is lost when pressing frozen grapes.

When weather conditions do not allow for the freezing of grapes on the vines or if the grapes cannot attain optimal sugar and acidity levels, grapes are allowed to freeze artificially in temperature-controlled containers before vinification. This controversial process, called cryoextraction, is commonly practiced nowadays by reputable wineries in sweet wine production although certain countries, such as Canada and Germany, do not allow such wines to be labeled Icewine or Eiswein. Excellent Icewine-style wine can be produced at home by cryoextraction of grape juice or from concentrate. Icewine concentrate kits are now available which greatly simplify the production process. This chapter discusses Icewine-style wine production using the cryoextraction method using fresh grape juice.

Riesling and Gewürztraminer are recommended *V. vinifera* grape varieties for making Icewine although the Vidal variety (a hybrid of *V. vinifera* and *V. labrusca* species) is widely used in Ontario Icewines. The winemaking process for producing Icewine-style wine at home consists of freezing the grape juice so the sugar-rich syrup can be extracted while leaving the water content behind. The syrup is then fermented in gradually-increasing quantities so the yeast can start fermentation and survive in the sugar-rich environment. Fermentation is stopped by deep cooling when the desired residual sugar content and alcohol level are achieved, typically in the range 15-20 B° and 10-12% alc./vol., respectively. Lastly, the wine is stabilized by sterile filtration to remove any active yeast still present after fermentation is stopped, and then aged a minimum of 6 months.

11.1 MUST PREPARATION

This specific process uses 23 L of fresh Riesling, Gewürztraminer or Palomino grape juice to produce approximately 9 L (24 half-bottles) of finished Icewine-style wine. The volume, alcohol content and residual sugar content of the wine will depend on the volume of syrup extracted. The juice should be transferred to 2 separate 20-L pails to allow for expansion of water as it freezes. The juice in each pail should be stirred thoroughly and then placed into a deep freezer for approximately 1 week to allow the water content to freeze completely—the syrup will not freeze.

Once the water has frozen, the pails should be retrieved from the freezer and hung by the handle, in the cellar at a cool temperature, so the bottom of each pail is above floor level. Empty pails should be placed under them to collect the syrup to be extracted. The syrup is extracted by drilling 3 2-cm holes on the bottom of each pail—the syrup will start flowing out. The syrup should be extracted until the desired sugar concentration is obtained. This will take several hours. The sugar concentration should be constantly monitored, as ice will soon start melting therefore diluting the syrup. The syrup should have an initial sugar concentration between 38 B° (1.153) and 42 B° (1.167). The preferred method for measuring the sugar concentration is by using a high-range refractometer. If a high-range refractometer is not available, the sugar concentration can be measured by using a hydrometer. A test sample of the syrup is diluted in water at a rate of 50 percent until a reading between 19 B° (1.077) and 21 B° (1.085) is obtained.

Total acidity should also be measured and should be at least 9.0 g/L. It should be adjusted, if necessary, so that acidity and residual sugar content in the finished wine will be well balanced.

11.2 CONDUCTING ALCOHOLIC FERMENTATION

As the syrup is very rich in sugar content, the fermentation should be carried out progressively in increasing amounts of syrup.

First, 500 mL (approximately 2 cups) of syrup should be transferred to a 4-L glass container and the remainder should be reserved in cool (not cold) storage so it does not start fermenting on its own. A *S. bayanus* yeast strain, Lalvin® EC-1118® or RED STAR® Premier Cuvée, should be prepared and added to the 500 mL of syrup. Alternatively, a Lalvin® 71B-1122® or a RED STAR® Côte des Blancs strain can be used as these are more temperature-sensitive therefore making the stopping of fermentation by cooling easier to accomplish. Yeast nutrients should be added at the maximum rate of 20 g/hL and stirred well. A fermentation lock with a sulphite solution should be attached.

Fermentation should start within 24 hours. When a good foam forms, 500 mL (approximately 2 cups) of the reserved syrup should be added and the fermentation lock re-attached. Within 12 to 24 hours, a good foam will form again. Again, 1 L of the reserved syrup should be added and the fermentation lock re-attached. This process should be repeated again by adding 2 L of syrup, then 4 L and finally the remainder of the syrup. This progressive addition of syrup to the fermenting must will ensure a successful fermentation. The must should be fermented for 2 to 5 days until the sugar concentration reaches between 18.5 B° (1.075) and 22 B° (1.090). A reading should be taken on a daily basis, as the fermentation becomes vigourous very rapidly.

11.3 STOPPING ALCOHOLIC FERMENTATION

When the fermenting must has reached a sugar concentration slightly above the desired sugar concentration, 100 mg/L of sulphite should be added, without racking, to halt fermentation. The container should then be placed in cold storage at a temperature between 2° and 8° C (36° and 46° F) for approximately 1 week. Fermentation cannot be halted spontaneously, therefore, there will be a further reduction in sugar content. Duration of fermentation following the sulphite addition depends largely on the cold storage temperature.

The wine should then be racked and coarse filtered using No. 1 pads. The container should be placed once again in cold storage for approximately 2 weeks.

After this period, the wine should be racked, medium filtered using No. 2 pads, and sulphited an additional 50 mg/L. The container should be placed in cold storage for 2 more weeks.

Although optional, it is recommended at this point to flash-pasteurize the wine to ensure that any yeast still present is annihilated.

Sulphiting and cold storage may not have completely annihilated all yeast cells. The wine may still contain a significant amount of inactive yeast cells which may cause fermentation to restart if cellar conditions become favourable for renewed yeast activity. In home winemaking, flash-pasteurization cannot be performed practically with large volumes of wine. For small volumes of 10 L or less, wine can be flash-pasteurized by heating the wine for 3 to 4 minutes at approximately 60° C (140° F) or for a few seconds at 100° C (212° F). These durations should not be exceeded so as to avoid the risk of imparting a "cooked" flavour to the wine.

The wine should be allowed to cool down to room temperature before racking and medium filtering using No. 2 pads. The wine should then be placed in cold storage for 2 more weeks.

One last racking should be performed before fine filtering the wine using No. 5 pads. This step can be repeated after 2 weeks of cold storage if the presence of yeast is still suspected.

Lastly, the wine should be aged up to 6 months, and sulphite should be added, if necessary, to achieve a free SO_2 level of 50 mg/L before bottling.

This cooling, sulphiting and filtering regimen will produce a wine which will last over 5 years easily. The disadvantage is that the colour is lighter. The number of filtering operations can be reduced down to one or two using No. 2 and/or No. 3 pads to produce a wine with a more intense colour and which will be drunk within 12 to 18 months.

12
WINEMAKING AND VINIFICATION PROBLEMS

Premium wine production at home can be a relatively easy task, free of any problems if great care is exercised during the various winemaking and vinification phases. Problems, however, can sometimes occur and winemakers have to be able to recover from them to protect their investment. A good knowledge of how to circumvent such problems will prove very useful in those rare occasions. The following are the most common problems encountered in home winemaking:

1. Stuck alcoholic fermentation: this condition, undesirable in the production of dry wines, occurs when yeast activity has ceased and it can no longer convert sugar into alcohol.
2. Stuck ML fermentation: this condition occurs when ML bacteria are no longer able to convert malic acid into lactic acid.
3. Sulphur smell: this condition of unpleasant wine smell is a result of over-processing with sulphite.
4. Autolysis: this condition of unpleasant wine smell is a result of the wine being in contact with its lees for too long.
5. Cloudiness: this condition of poor clarity in wines is due to particles being still in suspension and is a result of improper clarification, either fining or filtration.

6. Tartrate crystals: this condition is only a minor aesthetic fault and is a result of wine having been subjected to cold temperatures for an extended period of time.

7. Rotten-egg smell: this unpleasant smell condition is caused by the presence of hydrogen sulphide resulting from winemaking or vinification problems.

8. Acetic spoilage and mycoderma: these conditions of advanced oxidation are a direct result of a wine being exposed to air for an extended period of time.

9. Carbon dioxide: this condition of perceptible or excessive carbon dioxide gas present in a finished still wine is a result of an incomplete fermentation, either alcoholic or malolactic.

10. Sugar level: the more common condition of a wine being too sweet, when undesired, is due to an incomplete alcoholic fermentation resulting from a stuck fermentation or too high of an initial sugar level.

11. Total acidity and pH level: these conditions, usually manifested as a wine being too tart or too flat, are due to improper acidity or pH levels and are a result of any of a number of winemaking or vinification problems. The fault may also be a result of a poor balance with the wine's sugar level.

12. Bitterness: this condition is most often a result of too much tannin in a wine.

13. Colour: this condition of poor colour is most often a result of oxidation in white wines and insufficient maceration in red wines, and/or excessive clarification.

14. Alcohol level: this condition of too little or too much alcohol in a finished wine is a function of the total sugar content during fermentation.

15. Geranium smell: this off-odour is the result of a reaction between sorbic acid, found in potassium sorbate, and lactic bacteria used for ML fermentation.

Winemaking and vinification problems associated with oak barrels are described in Chapter 7.

12.1 STUCK ALCOHOLIC FERMENTATION

A good alcoholic fermentation requires a favourable environment for yeast to become active. Otherwise, fermentation may fail to start or may stop before completion. These conditions are known as stuck alcoholic fermentation or stuck fermentation. Stuck fermentation is not uncommon in commercial winemaking and is a common occurrence in home winemaking. In most cases, fermentation can be successfully restarted without affecting the wine's quality.

If yeast activity seems to have ceased and fermentation is stuck, the probable causes must be identified and assessed. The probable causes include:

a) Fermentation temperature is too low or too high,

b) Sugar concentration is too high,

c) Alcohol content is too high,

d) Lack of oxygen is preventing yeast from starting fermentation,

e) Free SO_2 content is too high,

f) Substantial amount of mould present in the grapes, or

g) Yeast content is insufficient to complete fermentation.

The recommended temperature ranges for white- and red-wine vinifications should be observed. If the fermentation temperature is outside the recommended range, the temperature can be increased or decreased as required. The must should be stirred vigorously, and fermentation should then restart within 24 hours.

Excessively high sugar concentration in musts may inhibit yeast activity. If the sugar concentration is too high, the recommended method to restart fermentation is to conduct a progressive fermentation by incrementing the must volume. A small must volume should be inoculated with a Lalvin® EC-1118® or Red Star® Premier Cuvée yeast strain. When yeast activity has started and fermentation is vigourous, the must volume can be doubled. Fermentation will slow down for a short time but will become vigourous once again. The must volume can be doubled repeatedly in this manner until the whole batch is fermenting. If fermentation seems to become vigourous shortly after each volume addition of must, the entire volume may be combined at approximately the halfway point. This method has the drawback of producing a sweet high-alcohol-content wine depending on the sugar concentration in the must. The alternative is to dilute the must to the desired sugar concentration level and restart fermentation.

When adding sugar to must to increase the alcohol content, over-chaptalization should be avoided to prevent stuck fermentation. Chaptalization should be conducted progressively for a successful fermentation.

High alcohol content in musts will inhibit yeast activity. If the alcohol content has exceeded the recommended level for the selected yeast type, an alcohol-tolerant yeast strain such as the Lalvin® EC-1118® or Red Star® Premier Cuvée should be used. A 5-percent volume of must can be inoculated to restart fermentation. When the must is fermenting vigourously, it can be added to the remaining must. This should restart fermentation of the whole batch.

Oxygen (air) affects wine quality. However, yeast needs a small amount of oxygen to start fermentation. Aerating the must by racking or stirring vigourously may add the required oxygen to restart fermentation. This is also recommended to reduce the amount of free SO_2 present to start or restart fermentation. Excessively high free SO_2 content will inhibit yeast activity.

The presence of a substantial amount of mould in the grapes can create a lack of nutrients for the yeast. Yeast nutrients should be added at the maximum recommended rate to feed the yeast when using mouldy grapes. Although an increased sulphite level can help, the best way to prevent this problem is to do a severe triage (pre-selection) discarding any mouldy bunches.

If the above procedures fail to start or restart fermentation, the next alternative is to add fresh yeast recommended for stuck fermentation such as Lalvin® KIV-1116® or EC-1118®, or Red Star® Pasteur Champagne or Pasteur Red™ strains. Alternatively, fermenting must can be used as inoculum. A volume between 3 and 5 percent of the must to be inoculated should be used. As in the cases of high sugar concentration and alcohol content, fermentation should be restarted in a small quantity and then added to the whole batch when the fermentation becomes vigourous. Aeration by stirring or pumping over will stimulate fermentation, which should restart within 24 to 48 hours.

All the above procedures will benefit by an addition of yeast nutrients. It is also recommended to rack the wine if bentonite was added before the start of fermentation. Bentonite will cause the yeast to sediment and therefore hamper fermentation. By racking the wine, the bentonite can be separated and discarded.

If fermentation ceases during the maceration period—when making wine from grapes—the juice should first be racked and separated from the pomace, and then transferred to a closed container. The cause of stuck fermentation should then be assessed and corrected according to the above remedies.

To prevent stuck fermentation, the must should be fermented under the recommended conditions, and the recommended yeast for the desired wine type and style should be used. Refer to section 4.5 for more details on how to conduct alcoholic fermentation.

12.2 Stuck ML fermentation

As with alcoholic fermentation, ML fermentation also requires favourable environmental conditions to complete successfully. Adverse conditions will cause a stuck ML fermentation. Unlike alcoholic fermentation, however, these adverse conditions are more difficult to monitor and control if one is not properly equipped. The added danger of creating favourable ML conditions is that these also favour growth of spoilage organisms. Extra precautions are therefore required.

Paper chromatography should always be used to monitor ML fermentation progress to ensure that malic acid is being converted into lactic acid. The presence or lack of carbon dioxide bubbles is not sufficiently reliable to make a positive determination.

If ML fermentation did not start or is stuck, the probable causes must be identified and assessed. The probable causes include:

a) Free SO_2 content is too high,

b) pH is too low,

c) Fermentation temperature is too low or too high,

d) ML bacteria have insufficient nutrients,

e) Oxygen (air) has annihilated ML bacteria, or

f) Alcohol content is too high.

ML bacteria are very sensitive to free SO_2. A high concentration of free SO_2 will inhibit ML fermentation. The maximum level depends on the type of ML bacterium selected. The maximum is typically 15 mg/L although some strains will tolerate only up to 5 mg/L. The manufacturer's recommendations should be closely followed. To reduce the free SO_2 concentration, the wine can be stored in a cool cellar to let the free SO_2 dissipate. This may take a long time, especially at very high free SO_2 levels. Alternatively, the wine can be racked successively and vigourously to accelerate dissipation. Section 12.3 describes another method using a dilute hydrogen peroxide solution although only experienced winemakers knowledgeable with chemicals and handling procedures should use this.

ML bacteria can also become annihilated in low pH wines. The typical minimum pH value is 3.2 although different ML bacterium strains will have slightly different requirements. A wine's pH can be increased by lowering acidity by one of several methods described in sections 3.2.2 and 3.3.2.

Temperature should be maintained within the recommended range to favour a successful ML fermentation, and increased or decreased accordingly.

As with yeasts, ML bacteria require nutrients. It is therefore recommended to carry out ML fermentation with a good volume of fine lees which will serve as nutrients. If ML fermentation is stuck even in the presence of fine lees, these can be stirred gently into suspension. Stirring vigourously will accelerate oxidation of ML bacteria and potentially rendering these ineffective. Yeast nutrients may also be added if the fine lees do not provide sufficient nutrients.

Most ML bacteria used in home winemaking are from anaerobic species and should therefore be protected from oxygen. Fermentation vessels should be properly sealed with a fermentation lock, and oxidation-promoting operations (e.g., racking and stirring) should be avoided. The manufacturer's recommendations should be followed.

Table wines usually have an alcohol content of up to 13.5% or 14.0% alc./vol. ML bacteria can tolerate this alcohol level although certain strains may have special requirements. For fortified wines or wines with very high alcohol contents, ML fermentation should be carried out at the same time as the alcoholic fermentation. Therefore, ML fermentation will complete before the alcohol content becomes too high. This may require extending the alcoholic fermentation period by slowing down the rate of fermentation. This can be accomplished by lowering the temperature to the minimum level.

Concentrated and sterilized juices are not ML-compatible since ML bacteria have been eradicated during the concentration or sterilization procedures. These musts have also been tartrate-stabilized during their production and thus contain a very high proportion of malic acid, which would be converted to lactic acid. The wine would have very little acid, and a pH above 3.8 making it very susceptible to bacterial in-fections. Therefore, ML fermentation should not be attempted in these types of musts.

Musts from grapes or fresh juice may already contain ML bacteria for ML fermentation to start on its own accord if all other conditions are favourable. It is still recommended to add ML culture for these types of musts to avoid complications.

In addition to these recommended solutions, all will benefit from the addition of fresh ML culture, and, for more difficult conditions, the ML inoculum can be first conditioned using commercial apple juice. A yeast favouring ML fermentation (see Table 4-8 on page 133) is also recommended for the alcoholic fermentation phase.

12.3 SULPHUR SMELL

A sulphur smell is a result of over-processing with sulphite. Sulphur smell can be detected at free SO_2 levels beyond 50 mg/L and can become overpowering if it exceeds this level considerably. It can be easily detected by its distinctive pungent burnt-match smell.

If a sulphur smell is detected in the fermentor, the wine should be aerated by successive vigourous rackings. If detected in the bottle, the wine should be aerated by decanting and/or by letting the bottle stand open upright for approximately 2 hours.

Commercial wineries use a dilute solution of hydrogen peroxide as an effective agent in reducing free SO_2 content. To reduce the free SO_2 content by 10 mg/L, the recommended concentration is 50 g/hL of wine using a 1%-hydrogen peroxide solution. The use of hydrogen peroxide requires chemistry laboratory experience and is therefore only recommended for experienced home winemakers. Excessive addition of hydrogen peroxide can negatively affect the quality of wine. Reference 7 [Margalit] in Appendix E details analytical and laboratory procedures to reduce free SO_2 content.

To prevent sulphur smell, the recommended sulphite dosage guidelines should be followed strictly for the various winemaking and vinification steps. Refer to section 3.4 for more details on free SO_2 analysis and control.

12.4 AUTOLYSIS

Wine or fermenting must, which still has yeast present, can acquire a bad taste if allowed to be in contact with the lees for an extended time, generally, beyond 18 months. This is particularly true for gross lees.

259

This interaction between yeast and lees is known as autolysis. It can be easily detected by its yeasty smell and/or taste.

There is no known cure for autolysis; however, racking the must or wine from its lees according to the recommended schedule can prevent it.

12.5 CLOUDINESS

Cloudiness in a wine may result from improper racking, where sediment is disturbed and allowed to go into suspension, from improper clarification, or from excessive aeration, particularly in high-iron content wine (a condition known as ferric casse). Cloudiness may reappear in perfectly clear and brilliant-colour wines during ageing. This will happen in wines which have not been properly stabilized.

To reduce and/or eliminate cloudiness, the sediment should be left to settle to the bottom of the container and then the wine should be racked very carefully. The wine can be clarified by fining followed by another racking. The recommended quantity of fining agent should be administered, and the fining procedure should be strictly followed. If cloudiness persists, the wine can be filtered. Refer to chapter 5 for more details on fining and filtration operations.

Ascorbic acid can also be added before bottling to prevent oxidation or ferric casse in wines that will be subjected to excessive aeration. Refer to section 4.7.1 for more details.

The wine should also be tested for the presence of pectin (see test in section 5.2.7) that could cause bottled wine to become cloudy. Excessive pectin can be reduced by the addition of pectic enzymes. To prevent cloudiness due to pectin, pectic enzymes can be added at the time of grape crushing.

12.6 TARTRATE CRYSTALS

When wine is subjected to cold temperatures, tartaric acid crystallizes and precipitates as tartrate crystals. Tartrate crystals affect the appearance of a wine but do not affect its taste. They are easily separated from wine by racking.

To prevent tartrate crystals from forming in the bottle, the wine should be cold stabilized and racked to separate the crystals. Alternatively, metatartaric acid can be added to the finished wine. Cold stabilization and metatartaric acid addition will alter a wine's total acidity and pH which may require correction.

Refer to section 4.7.2 for more details on cold stabilization and metatartaric acid addition.

12.7 Rotten-egg smell (hydrogen sulphide, H₂S)

A rotten-egg smell in wines is caused by the presence of hydrogen sulphide, and may be cured depending on its intensity.

The presence of hydrogen sulphide can be due to several factors. Vinification from grapes that have been over-treated with sulphur-based vineyard mildew and fungus inhibitors is a common cause. Red wines are more prone to hydrogen sulphide problems as the juice is allowed to macerate with the grape skins therefore soaking the inhibitors in the must. In white wines, the settling of particles before yeast inoculation and alcoholic fermentation allows for the separation of the juice from sulphur-contaminated particles. Similarly, prolonged ageing of wine in the presence of sulphur deposits—arising from burnt sulphur during barrel maintenance—in oak barrels will cause hydrogen sulphide to form. Another source of this problem may result from any pressed red wine left on the gross lees for too long a period, whether in glass containers, stainless steel tanks or oak barrels. Sulphite additions to the must in excess of the recommended quantities will also cause a potential problem. A lesser common cause is nitrogen deficiency in juice from grapes which have not properly matured. Lastly, cultured yeasts used to inoculate must will always produce hydrogen sulphide, albeit in very small quantities. If detected early, these faults can be corrected easily.

In all cases, hydrogen sulphide can be reduced by racking the wine while aerating abundantly against the wall of the container. This has the drawback of accelerating oxidation and has to be assessed against the severity of the hydrogen sulphide problem. Alternatively, or in addition, the wine should be sulphited at a rate of 100 mg/L and then filtered to strip it of elemental sulphur. This procedure should be repeated after 3 months depending on the severity of the problem. If the problem is due to nitrogen deficiency, yeast nutrients (diammonium phosphate) can be added to the must to replenish the nitrogen content.

Commercial wineries treat hydrogen sulphide problems with minuscule amounts (4 drops/hL) of a dilute 1% copper-sulfate solution, not readily available to home winemakers. The addition should be performed once fermentation is complete.

If hydrogen sulphide is not treated early, it will react in the wine to form first into mercaptans followed by disulphides. Mercaptans and disulphides are foul-smelling compounds that cause wine to spoil. The presence of either compound is practically irreversible in home wine-making. Extensive chemistry knowledge and experience, and access to analytical laboratory equipment and chemicals are required. Therefore, the best cure for hydrogen sulphide is prevention. Reference 7 [Margalit] in Appendix E can be consulted for a thorough description of hydrogen sulphide treatments with copper sulfate.

12.8 ACETIC SPOILAGE AND MYCODERMA

Oxidation is the result of acetaldehyde forming in must or wine which has been overly exposed to air. Prolonged exposure to air will cause excessive oxidation and will produce acetobacter causing acetic spoil-age. Depending on the duration of air exposure, the problem can man-ifest itself as a strong acetic acid smell, or in the worst case, a white film forms on the wine's surface. The latter condition is referred to as mycoderma. These point to a serious problem in the winemaking equip-ment, to its improper use, or to poor topping practice, and often, a too high pH or too low acidity problem.

A common cause of acetic spoilage is a poor seal from bungs. To prevent oxidation and acetic spoilage, the bungs should form an air-tight seal. Also, fermentation locks should be properly filled with a sulphite solution, and containers should be topped up properly or pro-tected under a layer of non-toxic inert gases. Fermentation should also be conducted at the recommended temperature and the exposure of wine to air should be minimized during winemaking operations such as racking.

At too high pH or too low acidity, SO_2 is much less effective. Therefore, such wines are that much more prone to oxidation, acetic spoilage and mycoderma. A bigger dose of sulphite will be required to produce the same effect. Refer to section 3.4 for a rule-of-thumb cal-culation of additional sulphite required.

In general, proper and timely sulphiting and stabilization should prevent any oxidation problem.

Wine affected by advanced acetic spoilage cannot be cured. If it is slightly affected, there is still a chance to cure the wine. In this case, the wine should be filtered through double cheesecloth to remove all particles of the white film. The wine should be sulphited to a level of l00 mg/L and bottled immediately. It should be drunk as soon as possible.

Total acidity should be monitored when curing oxidation or acetic spoilage, and corrected if necessary.

12.9 CARBON DIOXIDE

A fizzy wine signifies that carbon dioxide is still present and that perhaps, alcoholic and/or malolactic fermentations are not completely over. As a first step, the wine should be left to complete fermenting and then stabilized for an extended time until there is no more carbon dioxide present. This is preferred for premium wine production. Otherwise, for early drinking wines, excess carbon dioxide can be reduced and eliminated by a vigourous racking and/or by stirring the finished wine vigourously 2 or 3 times per day for 3 days. This method has the disadvantage of accelerating oxidation. The wine should then be properly stabilized prior to bottling.

If carbon dioxide is detected in bottled wine, all the wine from the same batch should be poured in a large vessel. Bottles may explode if allowed to store wine with residual carbon dioxide. For incomplete alcoholic fermentation, the wine can then be fermented to dryness by the addition of yeast. One should proceed cautiously by following instructions on stuck fermentation. Alternatively, for a sweet dessert wine, the wine can be stabilized with a treatment of sulphite and potassium sorbate. The residual carbon dioxide can be eliminated by vigourous stirrings before re-bottling the wine. For incomplete ML fermentation, the wine can be ML fermented or properly stabilized against this fermentation before bottling.

12.10 SUGAR LEVEL

If a wine's unusually high sugar content is acceptable and is well balanced with the acidity, potassium sorbate can be added to stabilize the wine and turn it into a good dessert wine.

On the other hand, a cloyingly sweet wine may not be drinkable, even as a dessert wine, and is probably the result of stopped or stuck fermentation. The wine can be re-fermented to convert as much sugar as possible into alcohol or it can be blended with a dry wine to reduce the sugar level.

If a wine is too dry (the residual sugar content is too low), it can be easily corrected by adding a sweetener-conditioner or by blending the dry wine with a sweeter wine.

Refer to section 3.1 for more details on sugar analysis and control.

12.11 TOTAL ACIDITY AND pH LEVEL

Low TA and high pH, or high TA and low pH in wine may be due to the grape variety used or due to a poor vintage, or may be the result of a chemical imbalance during vinification. Refer to sections 3.2 and 3.3 for more details on acid and pH correction procedures, respectively.

The more complex problems of either high TA/high pH or low TA/low pH pose a much greater challenge to home winemakers. Commercial wineries make use of special chemicals and processes not readily available to home winemakers. Acid-reducing or pH-augmenting solutions cannot be used, as these will correct one parameter at the expense of the other. The best solution is to blend wines that improve both TA and pH levels. For example, a high TA/high pH wine can be corrected by blending it with a wine of normal TA and pH or low TA/low pH. The drawback of this method is that it requires stocking TA- and pH-unbalanced wines. Such wines cannot be stored for an extended time as they are prone to bacterial infection or other spoilage problems.

Before blending, it is recommended first to determine the root cause of the problem with the high TA/high pH or low TA/low pH wine. If the root cause points to a serious wine fault, the wine should not be blended with a healthy wine. This could spoil a perfectly good batch of wine. If the root cause points to a chemical imbalance from grape components, for example, it is safe to blend the wine.

When the pH level in a high-pH, high-TA wine must be reduced, phosphoric acid can be added although it will affect both the taste and texture of the wine. Refer to section 3.3.2.

A common reason for a seemingly low TA is the use of a sodium hydroxide (NaOH) titrate solution that has lost its strength, i.e. its Normality is no longer 0.1N or 0.2N, when measuring the TA. There may be nothing wrong with the actual TA except for a false measurement that must be compensated for the weaker titrate solution. Refer to section 3.2.1 for a description of how to determine the actual strength of a sodium hydroxide solution and how to correct the measured TA.

12.12 BITTERNESS

A wine that seems overly bitter may be the result of a number of factors. The most common being high astringency caused by a high tannin level. Tannins will soften over time, therefore, reducing astringency when ageing wine.

The tannin level can be reduced by several means in the various winemaking and vinification processes. At the time of grape crushing and pressing, reducing or eliminating stems and stalks will reduce astringency in the final wine. Also, free-run and press-run juices should be fermented separately and then blended until the desired tannin level is achieved.

If oak-barrel ageing, the ageing period should be reduced as oak will add tannins to the wine. Alternatively, for red wines, fining with egg whites or gelatin will soften the astringency.

Astringency and tannin level can also be corrected through blending of softer wines. On the other hand, if the tannin level is too low, grape tannin can be added or the wine may be aged in oak.

The alcohol content should also be compared to the tannin level. Highly tannic wines require a minimum alcohol level to be properly balanced. These wine types require an alcohol level between 12.5% and 14.0% alc./vol. If a highly tannic wine has a low alcohol content, a high-alcohol-content tannic wine should be used for blending.

12.13 COLOUR

In white wines, poor colour problems are often a result of oxidation. To improve colour affected by slight oxidation, a casein treatment using the maximum dosage of 100 g/hL is recommended.

In red wines, the typical problem is either a colour that is too light or too dark. The recommended method to lighten or darken the colour of a red wine is through blending. The drawback of this method is that it requires stocking different wines. Large volumes are also required to achieve significant colour changes. To add more colour to light-coloured red wines, the most effective method is to use natural (dehydrated) grape skin powder; it does not affect the taste of wine. The powder should be added to red wine, before fining or filtering, at a rate of 5 g/hL by first dissolving it in a little volume of wine. This addition can be repeated until the desired colour is obtained. The use of unorthodox colour-enhancing methods, such as food-colouring addition, is not effective and is not recommended.

Colour is best controlled throughout all winemaking stages to achieve desired results. At grape crushing and pressing, the reduction or elimination of stems and stalks will produce a lighter colour. For red wines, the recommended maceration period should be observed to achieve the desired colour level. This period can be adjusted according to preference. The colour can also be lightened by additional clarification, such as filtration. And in general, wine will always lighten from the start of fermentation to a finished wine.

Lastly, all wines should always be protected from air exposure to prevent oxidation and colour problems.

12.14 ALCOHOL LEVEL

A wine's alcohol level is determined by the amount of sugar in the must that is allowed to ferment. If the alcohol level is too low and it has been determined that stuck fermentation is the cause, fermentation should be restarted. Otherwise, if fermentation is complete, the finished wine should be blended with a higher-alcohol-level wine. If the alcohol level of the finished wine is too high, it should be blended with a lower-alcohol-level wine.

Before the alcoholic fermentation, if the sugar level is too low for the desired alcohol level, the must should be chaptalized to the desired level.

12.15 GERANIUM SMELL

A geranium off-odour in wines is the result of a reaction between sorbic acid, found in potassium sorbate, and lactic bacteria. This reaction yields hexadienol, otherwise known as geraniol, which produces the strong and disagreeable odour of rotting geraniums—a highly undesirable outcome that cannot be fixed. Potassium sorbate is an ingredient used to stabilize wines by inhibiting the growth of yeast and mould. Wines that have undergone ML fermentation may still have lactic bacteria present unless adequately inhibited with sulphite.

This problem, for which there is no cure, is best avoided by eliminating the use of potassium sorbate, especially in totally dry wines, unless it is required to stabilize a sweet wine. In the latter case, it is best if the wine is not subjected to ML fermentation. This is accomplished most effectively by properly sulphiting the wine.

Refer to sections 4.6 and 4.7.1 for more information.

13
THE PASSION OF
HOME WINEMAKING

Per-capita wine consumption in North America has been on a steady annual increase as more and more people embrace the claimed health benefits of moderate and regular wine drinking—this being defined as one glass of wine per day, ideally with a meal. The now-famous *60 Minutes* televised report on the French Paradox, initially aired in November 1991, and recent medical research have been key factors in shaping this trend. The report and medical data conclude that the French, despite their high-fat diet, have a lower heart-related mortality rate because of their wine-drinking habits. Red wines are specifically cited as most beneficial in lowering heart-related diseases since they are rich in protective "chemicals" known as antioxidants. The US commercial winemaking industry used this data to lobby the federal government and the BATF (Bureau of Alcohol, Tobacco and Firearms) in changing wine label regulations. Recently, regulations have been amended to allow wineries to include a message directing consumers to the benefits of moderate wine drinking.

A greater number of consumers are therefore now making wine their beverage of choice to accompany dinner or as a social drink. Wine appreciation is gaining popularity as consumers become more knowledgeable about wine and its benefits. Personally, in addition to wine being an integral part of our family dinners, I have come to appreciate wine not only for its benefits but also because of why these benefits exist and because of my fascination with wine production technology. I owe this fascination to my keen interest in pure and applied sciences and my academic and professional background in engineering. A solid understanding of wine science and production technology has made me appreciate to a much greater extent the subtleties of wine, e.g., assessing how a wine has been oak-aged, if malolactic fermentation was used, the extent of maceration in red wines, etc. As a home winemaker aspiring to make the best wines possible, this knowledge is fundamental in order to be able to modify and adapt the different processes to achieve desired results.

This point was illustrated in a recent vertical tasting[15] of Château Mouton-Rothschild wines spanning eight decades of winemaking and thirty-two vintages ranging from 1929 to 1996, including the highly-rated 1961, 1982 and 1986 vintages. In such an extensive tasting, the effects of vintage variations (e.g., sunshine, rain, growing period, seasonal temperatures, etc.), production technology (e.g., type of oak barrels), and winemaking philosophy become more obvious and one can better appreciate the wine's qualities. For example, the use of oak is more prominent in the château's wines produced under the directorship of the Baroness Philippine de Rothschild (since 1988) as opposed to her father's (Baron Philippe de Rothschild) more refined use of oak. I suspect that the Baroness opted for a more pronounced oak character to satisfy the taste of American palates as the US became an important market for the château.

This fascination, the pride of sharing the fruits of one's labour, and the lure of wine competitions can turn one's interest in winemaking into a passion or even an obsession, as is my case. There seems to be no frontier in quality, and any excuse becomes justifiable for lavish investments in time and/or money. And this is true of such top-rated wineries as Château Pétrus, Château d'Yquem, Domaine de la Romanée-Conti, Sassicaia, and Opus One (a Baron Philippe de Rothschild-Robert Mondavi joint venture winery), just to name a few. No effort or money is spared, and their wines, consequently, are sold at exorbitant prices. Such wineries still harvest manually without the

---

[15]A vertical tasting is an organized and systematic tasting of many vintages from the same winery. A tasting involving a single vintage from many wineries is referred to as a horizontal tasting.

aid of mechanical apparatus. New World wineries in the US, Chile and even Canada (in the production of Icewine) are now adopting similar processes and investing a lot of money to produce their Reserve (usually their best, almost always their most expensive) wines.

Besides all this, I had some major work to do with my father's wine to achieve an acceptable level of quality for drinking. After all, this would allow him to display his pride and to provide for lively discussions while playing cards or *bocce*.

As a youngster and son of an Italian family, I was summoned to the manual crusher to help my father make his wine. I still remember those painful blisters from crushing twenty-five or thirty cases of grapes. Unfortunately, winemaking knowledge amongst Italian families was limited to crushing, fermentation, one or two rackings followed by bottling four to six months later. To a large extent, this process has not changed much with these "hard-line" winemakers except that they seem to have reduced the use of stems during maceration of red musts, eliminated open-vat maceration for white musts, and adopted some form of clarification before bottling.

My extensive knowledge and experience in home winemaking seem to have provided me with an honorary degree in my father's eyes. He follows my instructions to the letter, and he displays his pride amongst his friends. Now, if only I can could change his beliefs about the effects of racking wine during a full moon! I have not found any documented reference in winemaking literature on the effects of a full moon. I was once told that the atmospheric pressure increases during a full moon which, in turn, affects the quality of the wine if racked in open air.

And this book will provide you too with the know-how to produce high-quality wines that will impress the most astute wine connoisseurs. You will develop experience through trying out the many procedures and variations presented. Experiment. Try new combinations or procedures that you have never attempted before and adopt what works best for you. Undoubtedly, you will make mistakes, as I have. But from mistakes, you will learn. And as you learn, you will want to discover more and more, and soon, the passion will turn into an obsession. A confession from an obsessed home winemaker!

APPENDIXES

A   Conversion factors between Metric and U.S. systems

B   Sugar concentration and alcohol level conversions

C   Winemaking log chart

D   Winemaking chemicals, ingredients and concentrations

E   Bibliography

Appendix A—Conversion factors between Metric and U.S. systems

The following table provides a list of abbreviations for units of measure used in this book.

Unit of Measure	Abbreviation
Brix degrees	B°
centimeter	cm
cup(s)	cup(s)
degrees Celsius	°C
degrees Fahrenheit	°F
fluid ounce	fl oz
foot (feet)	ft
gallon	gal
gram	g
hectolitre	hL
inch	in
kilogram	kg
kiloPascal	kPa
litre	L
meter	m
milligram	mg
millilitre	mL
millimeter	mm
ounce	oz
parts per million	ppm
pound(s)	lb(s)
pounds per square inch	psi
Specific Gravity	SG
tablespoon	tbsp
teaspoon	tsp

All equivalents are approximate due to rounding.

Length
1 cm = 10 mm = 0.39 in
1 in = 2.54 cm
1 m = 39.37 in = 3.28 ft
1 ft = 0.30 m

Mass and Weight
1 g = 0.035 oz
1 kg = 2.2 lbs
1 lb = 16 oz = 454 g
1 oz = 28.35 g

Volume
1 L = 0.26 U.S. gal = 0.22 Imp gal
1 U.S. gal = 128 U.S. fl oz = 0.83 Imp gal = 3.79 L
1 Imp gal = 160 Imp fl oz = 1.2 U.S. gal = 4.55 L
1 mL = 0.034 U.S. fl oz = 0.035 Imp fl oz
1 U.S. fl oz = 29.57 mL
1 Imp fl oz = 28.41 mL
1 tsp = 5 mL
1 tbsp = 3 tsp = 15 mL
1 cup = 8 U.S. fl oz = 237 mL

Concentration and Density
1 ppm = 1 mg/L (based on a density of 1 g per mL)
1000 ppm = 0.01 lb/gal (based on a density of 1¼ oz per U.S. fl oz)

Temperature
$°F = 9/5 \times (°C) + 32$
$°C = 5/9 \times [(°F) - 32]$

Pressure
1 kPa = 0.145 psi
1 psi = 6.89 kPa
1 bar = 100 kPa

Appendix B—Sugar concentration and alcohol level conversions

The following table[16] will prove useful when required to convert between Brix degrees, Specific Gravity, potential alcohol level, and amount of sugar in a given volume. Other references may provide the amount of sugar to be added to a given volume. These two very different measurements should not be confused. For example, 250 g of sugar in 1 L of must represents a total volume of 1 L, whereas 250 g of sugar added to 1 L will give a total volume of approximately 1.2 L. In addition, these measurements are approximate given the hydrometer's limitations and inaccuracy, specifically in the presence of other solubles and/or alcohol. The margin of error on the measured alcohol content will be less than 0.5% alc./vol., which is quite acceptable.

The following measurements are valid at a temperature of 15.5° C (60° F).

---

[16]Adapted from DeFalco's for Brewers & Winemakers (Ottawa) instructions on "WHAT IS A HYDROMETER?".

SG	Brix	Approximate potential % alc./vol.	Approximate grams of sugar in one litre	Approximate amount of sugar in one gallon	
				lb	oz
0.990	0.0	0.0	0		0
0.995	0.0	0.0	0		0
1.000	0.0	0.0	0		0
1.005	0.0	0.5	7		1
1.010	2.4	0.9	15		2
1.015	4.0	1.6	30		4
1.020	5.0	2.3	52		7
1.025	6.5	3.0	67		9
1.030	7.5	3.7	90		12
1.035	9.0	4.4	112		15
1.040	10.0	5.1	127	1	1
1.045	11.5	5.8	142	1	3
1.050	12.5	6.5	157	1	5
1.055	14.0	7.2	172	1	7
1.060	15.0	7.8	187	1	9
1.065	16.5	8.6	202	1	11
1.070	17.5	9.2	217	1	13
1.075	18.5	9.9	232	1	15
1.080	20.0	10.6	254	2	2
1.085	21.0	11.3	269	2	4
1.090	22.0	12.0	284	2	6
1.095	23.0	12.7	299	2	8
1.100	24.0	13.4	314	2	10
1.105	25.0	14.1	329	2	12
1.110	26.5	14.9	344	2	14
1.115	27.5	15.6	359	3	0
1.120	28.5	16.3	374	3	2
1.125	29.5	17.0	389	3	4
1.130	30.5	17.7	404	3	6
1.135	32.0	18.4	419	3	8

Appendix C—Winemaking log chart

Keeping records of all vinification and winemaking measurements and operations is essential in the production of premium quality wines. By quantitatively following the evolution of wine and its many components, critical elements—temperature, sugar concentration, alcohol content, total acidity (TA), pH, and free SO_2—can be adjusted to maintain the required balance favouring successful winemaking. This data will also prove useful for future reference when wanting to duplicate specific results or when needing to identify the root-cause of a winemaking problem.

Measurements should be recorded as per the recommended frequency for each element. Frequency will be a function of the winemaking phase.

In addition to the above elements, the type of operation, and ingredients and quantities added should also be recorded. Type of operation will include procedures such as: crushing, destemming, maceration, pressing, alcoholic fermentation, malolactic fermentation, racking, fining, filtration, microbial and cold stabilization, blending, oak-ageing, and bottling.

Notice: The winemaking log chart on the opposite page can be photocopied with enlargement to fit an 8½ by 11 inch page or otherwise reproduced for the purpose of maintaining winemaking records. Alternatively, a full-page template of this log chart can be downloaded from the following web site: http://www.vehiculepress.com.

Batch ID No. _____

Vintage _____

Date Started _____

Grape Variety _____

Quantity _____

Price _____

Juice _____ Volume

Free-run _____

Press-run _____

Date	Type of Operation	Ingredient Added	Quantity Added	Temp. (°C)	Brix (B°)	Potential % alc./vol.	TA (g/L)	pH	Free SO$_2$ (mg/L)	Remarks & Observations

APPENDIX D — Winemaking chemicals, ingredients and concentrations

Chemical / Ingredient	Usage	Recommended concentration	Comments
Acid blend (tartaric, malic, citric) 3:2:1	Increase total acidity	1 g/L	Increase TA by 1 g/L
Ascorbic acid	Anti-oxidant	2-3 g/hL	Only to be used with sulphite
Bentonite	Fining white and red wines / Fining sparkling wines	25-100 g/hL / 25-50 g/hL	Dissolve in water
Bio-Clean	Clean equipment	15 mL (1 tbsp) per 4 L of warm water	
Bio-San	Sanitize equipment	15 mL (1 tbsp) per 4 L of hot water	
Casein	Fining white wines and improve colour in white wines	50-100 g/hL	Dissolve in water
Chlorinated cleaner (pink powder)	Clean and sanitize equipment	5 mL (1 tsp) per 4 L of water	Should not be used on plastic equipment or oak barrels
Citric acid	Increase effectiveness of sulphite solution for sanitizing equipment	45 mL (3 tbsp) per 4 L of water	Dissolve in warm water
Copper sulphate	Reduce hydrogen sulphide	4 drops/hL using a 1% solution	
Dextrose or sucrose	Increase potential alcohol level	17 g/L	Increase potential alcohol level by 1.0%
Egg whites	Fining red wines	5-10 g/hL	Combine with a salted water solution
Gelatin	Fining red wines	1-5 g/hL (increase up to 25 g/hL for high-pectin wines)	Dissolve in water
Grape tannins	Increase tannin content	10-30 g/hL (increase to 50 g/hL when fining high-pectin wines with gelatin)	Dissolve in warm water
Hydrogen peroxide	Reduce free SO_2 content	50 g/hL (using a 1% solution)	Reduce free SO_2 content by 10 mg/L
Isinglass	Fining white wines	Liquid: 1 mL/L Powder: 1-3 g/hL	Liquid: dilute in wine Powder: dissolve in water
Kieselsol	Fining white and red wines	25-50 mL/hL	
Metatartaric acid	Prevent precipitation of tartrate crystals	Up to 10g/hL	Dissolve in water

Winemaking chemicals, ingredients and concentrations—*continued*

Oak chips	Add oak aroma to wines	Whites: 1-2 g/L Reds: 2-4 g/L	
Oak extract (10% solution)	Add oak aroma to wines	Whites: 2 mL/L Reds: 4 mL/L	Dissolve in water
Pectic enzymes	Fining wines	Whites: 1-2 g/hL Reds: 2-4 g/hL	
Phosphoric acid	Reduce pH in high-TA wines	1 or 2 drops of 30% solution/L	
Potassium bicarbonate	Reduce total acidity	1-2 g/L	Reduce TA by 1 g/L
Potassium metabisulphite	A. Crushing of grapes B. Must preparation (concentrated, sterilized, and fresh juices) C. Stabilization D. Bottling	A. 50 mg/L B. 50 mg/L C. 50 mg/L D. 50 mg/L	A. Decrease to 5-10 mg/L of must for MLF. Dissolve in warm water B, C, and D. Dissolve in warm water
Potassium sorbate	Prevent re-fermentation of bottled wines	10-20 g/hL	Do not use in ML-fermented wines
Sodium carbonate (soda ash)	Clean plastic equipment	8-12 g/L of water	Dissolve in hot water
Sodium percarbonate	Treat oak barrel spoilage problems	1-3 g/L of water	Dissolve in hot water
Sodium metabisulphite	Sanitize equipment	45 mL (3 tbsp) per 4 L of water	Dissolve in warm water
Sparkolloid®	Fining white and red wines	10-40 g/hL	Dissolve in water
Sweetener-conditioner	Sweeten a finished wine	12-25 mL/L of wine	Prevent renewed fermentation
Tannisol	Preserve/stabilize wine	1-3 tablets per hL	
Tartaric acid	Increase total acidity or reduce pH	1-2 g/L	Increase TA by 1 g/L or reduce pH by 0.1 unit
Yeast (active dried)	Alcoholic fermentation	5 g for 4.5 to 23 L of must	
Yeast nutrients (diammonium phosphate)	Enhance fermentation capability of yeast	10-20 g/hL	Dissolve in warm water

Appendix E—Bibliography

I. American Wine Society, The. THE COMPLETE HANDBOOK OF WINE-MAKING. Ann Arbor: G.W. Kent, Inc. 1993.

This handbook is a collection of technical articles from renowned authorities from the wine trade and academia as well as from avid home winemakers. This reference textbook will prove most useful to advanced winemakers as the contents tend to be too technical for beginners. It assumes that readers have a good knowledge of winemaking techniques and processes. Wine analysis is discussed in details although discussions on the use of different types of wine yeasts and clarification agents and filtration techniques are cursory. A chapter on sparkling wine production presents the true méthode champenoise procedure for practical home winemaking use. In addition to winemaking, this book describes the elements (visual, olfactory, and gustatory) of wine tasting and how to organize and conduct wine tastings.

2. Barrel Builders, Inc. BARREL MAINTENANCE AND REPAIR MANUAL. St. Helena: Barrel Builders, Inc. 1995.

This concise, 33-page manual is an excellent reference on how to prepare, treat and maintain both used and new oak barrels. This manual was written by experienced coopers who have been serving the California wine industry for over 20 years. Therefore, their advice on barrel maintenance has stood the test of time. Although the section on barrel repairs is beyond the woodworking abilities of most winemakers, it does provide interesting reading.

3. Boulton, R.B., V.L. Singleton, L.F. Bisson, and R.E. Kunkee. PRINCIPLES AND PRACTICES OF WINEMAKING. New York: Chapman & Hall (International Thomson Publishing). 1996.

Anyone considering a professional career in œnology should read this textbook, authored by viticulture and œnology professors from the University of California at Davis. It provides highly technical and in-depth discussions of modern winemaking practices and equipment. The book is structured for use as a teaching aid and is geared to professional winemaking. It assumes a solid technical background in pure and applied sciences, namely, chemistry, biochemistry and microbiology. Advanced home winemakers wanting to further their technical knowledge of winemaking will find this book indispensable.

4. Fugelsang, Kenneth C. WINE MICROBIOLOGY. New York: Chapman & Hall (International Thomson Publishing). 1997.

This technical textbook on wine microbiology complements PRINCIPLES AND PRACTICES OF WINEMAKING. Also geared to professional winemaking, this book provides in-depth descriptions of various bacteria, yeasts and moulds, and their role in winemaking. This textbook is very technical and requires a good knowledge of microbiology. The author is a Winemaster and Professor of Enology in the Department of Enology, Food Science, and Nutrition at California State University, Fresno.

5. Jackisch, Philip. MODERN WINEMAKING. Ithaca: Cornell University Press. 1985.

This complete handbook is an excellent reference for serious winemakers. It offers one of the most complete lists of winemaking problems, and how to prevent and correct these problems. The author, a research chemist, shares his wealth of winemaking knowledge from his years of experience as winemaker, wine consultant, wine competition judge, and teacher. Readers should have a good technical background. Those interested in submitting their homemade wines into wine competitions will find a short but useful section on competition rules and judging procedures.

6. Johnson, Hugh and James Halliday. THE VINTNER'S ART: HOW GREAT WINES ARE MADE. New York: Simon and Schuster, 1992.

Hugh Johnson is a world-renowned and authoritative wine writer. James Halliday is a wine writer and also the owner and winemaker of a small Australian winery. Together, they have authored an excellent book geared to those interested in acquiring a general knowledge of wine production without all the intricate technical details. The book is logically sequenced in three sections describing wine production from vineyard to winery to bottle. First, the effects of terroir, climate, grape variety, harvesting techniques and other viticultural factors on wine quality are described. Second, production processes for different types and styles of wine—from light-bodied white wines to full-bodied red wines and fortified wines—are outlined and explained in very simple language. Third, the chemistry and analysis of wine are briefly, but effectively, treated. Stunning photographs and superb illustrations enhance the visual dimension of this fascinating book.

7. Margalit, Phd., Yair. WINERY TECHNOLOGY & OPERATIONS: A HAND-BOOK FOR SMALL WINERIES. San Francisco: The Wine Appreciation Guild. 1990.

This handbook should belong in every serious home winemaker's library. Although quite technical in nature—the author has an academic background in chemistry and physical chemistry in addition to his experience in small-winery winemaking—the book is very concise and offers practical advice on all winemaking procedures. It is a truly practical handbook. For example, procedures for basic analysis of must and wine are detailed. Unfortunately, the lack of a detailed index makes searching of specific topics somewhat difficult.

8. Olney, Richard. ROMANÉE-CONTI: THE WORLD'S MOST FABLED WINE. New York: Rizzoli International Publications, Inc. 1995.

Richard Olney is a food writer with a seemingly keen interest in top-rate wineries and their highly acclaimed legendary wines. This book recounts the fascinating history and winemaking practices of Le Domaine de La Romanée-Conti (DRC), unquestionably the most famous Burgundian winery located in the Côte d'Or. It describes the winemaking philosophy and practices in the production of such premium DRC wines as La Tâche, Grands Echézeaux, Richebourg, and, of course, Romanée-Conti. Home winemakers can now get an appreciation of how these great Burgundian wines are made and the extent to which such wineries will go to achieve the highest quality standards possible.

9. Olney, Richard. YQUEM. Suisse: Flammarion. 1985.

Richard Olney recounts the fascinating history and winemaking practices of Château d'Yquem, the producer of the legendary *Premier Grand Cru Classé* Sauternes wine. Written with the same purpose and style as his book on Le Domaine de La Romanée-Conti, YQUEM, however, is supplemented with superb glossy photographs such as the 32 vintage bottles ranging from 1858 to 1944.

10. Ough, C.S. and M.A. Amerine. METHODS FOR ANALYSIS OF MUSTS AND WINES. New York: John Wiley & Sons, Inc. 1988.

Ough and Amerine have been two of the most influential œnologists in American winemaking. Researchers, professors and writers, they have laid much of the initial groundwork in California in the post-Prohibition era to revive the winemaking industry. This book is strictly geared for those pursuing a career in professional winemaking, or more specifically, in wine analysis. The contents are highly technical and require extensive knowledge in various branches of chemistry. It does, however, provide very detailed descriptions of analytical procedures which are otherwise very difficult to find in other textbooks.

11. Peynaud, Emile. KNOWING AND MAKING WINE. Spencer, Alan F., tr. New York: John Wiley & Sons, Inc. 1984.

Emile Peynaud has been unquestionably the leading authoritative research œnologist and teacher of modern winemaking. In spite of its very technical content, this scholarly book is still indispensable and should be part of any winemaker's library. It is one of the most complete practical textbooks on winemaking. The many lists of advantages and disadvantages of various equipment, winemaking and vinification procedures will prove very helpful when deciding which to use.

12. Peynaud, Emile. THE TASTE OF WINE: THE ART AND SCIENCE OF WINE APPRECIATION. Schuster, Michael, tr. London: Macdonald & Co. (Publishers) Ltd. 1987.

Making wine is half the fun! The other half is tasting wine. And once again, Emile Peynaud has done a scholarly job of describing the science and practice of wine tasting. Specifically, it describes how to assess the visual, olfactory and gustatory aspects of wine, and outlines tasting techniques. Assessing and describing a wine requires a very rich and descriptive vocabulary. Emile Peynaud provides a comprehensive vocabulary with accurate definitions used in wine tasting. One's ability to accurately describe a wine depends on mastery of this vocabulary.

13. Ribéreau-Gayon, P., Dubourdieu, D., Donèche, B., and A. Lonvaud. HANDBOOK OF ENOLOGY: VOLUME 1 - THE MICROBIOLOGY OF WINE AND VINIFICATIONS. Branco, Jeffrey M., tr. Chichester: John Wiley & Sons Ltd. 2000.

Pascal Ribéreau-Gayon, director of the Institut d'Œnologie de Bordeaux and son of Jean Ribéreau-Gayon, the "father of modern œnology" and Emile Peynaud's mentor, has teamed up with other Bordeaux scholars to produce this authoritative textbook on the microbiology of wine. This book is intended for those having a chemistry background and wanting to pursue a career in commercial winemaking, research in œnology, or wine analysis. This first volume focuses on the role of yeasts, bacteria and sulphur dioxide in red and white wine vinifications.

14. Ribéreau-Gayon, P., Glories, Y., Maujean, A., and D. Dubourdieu. HANDBOOK OF ENOLOGY: VOLUME 2 - THE CHEMISTRY OF WINE, STABILIZATION AND TREATMENTS. Aquitrad Traduction, tr. Chichester: John Wiley & Sons Ltd. 2000.

In this second volume, Pascal Ribéreau-Gayon and his co-authors focus on the chemistry of wines—alcohols, carbohydrates, phenolic compounds, aromas, etc.—as a prelude to detailed discussions on stabilization procedures and treatments of wine including fining, filtration, and ageing. In spite of the highly technical nature of this text, as well as Volume I, the authors provide valuable practical advice, recommended additive concentrations and limits imposed by the European Community, and much more.

15. Robinson, Jancis, ed. THE OXFORD COMPANION TO WINE. Oxford: Oxford University Press. 1994.

Jancis Robinson, a Master of Wine, writer and leading authority in œnology, is the editor of this beautiful masterpiece. This heavy 6-cm (2½-in) encyclopedia-style book contains over 3000 entries from *abboccato to Zweigelt*. Over 80 Master of Wines, writers, researchers, professors, œnologists, wine consultants and others have contributed to this work. Each entry is concise and yet thorough and informative. There are not many entries that are not listed. This reference textbook also includes superb photographs, illustrations, and maps of wine-producing regions. A must-have in every library.

16. Robinson, Jancis. VINES, GRAPES & WINES. New York: Mitchell Beazley Publishers. 1986.

Ever wondered what Auxerrois or Valdepeñas are? Or what are the differences between the various Muscat grape varieties? These grape variety entries and over 800 more can be found in this reference book with detailed descriptions of origin, characteristics, and the type of wines they produce. Illustrations of grape bunches are useful in learning about grape physiology. A very useful comprehensive list of synonyms for each grape variety is also provided. If a grape variety cannot be found in this textbook, it probably does not exist! Although there is considerable overlap with Robinson's OXFORD COMPANION TO WINE, this book still offers a lot more details.

IMAGE CREDITS

The author and publisher wish to thank the following organizations and individuals for their kind permission to reproduce the images and other material in this book. Copyright owners are identified in bold.

American Wine Society, Figure I-2. Reproduced from American Wine Society, THE COMPLETE HANDBOOK OF WINEMAKING. Ann Arbor: G.W. Kent, Inc. 1993. For further information on The American Wine Society, please contact (716) 225-7613.

American Wine Society, Figures 9-6, 9-12. Reproduced from Manual #16, "Sparkling Wine" by Jim Gifford. AWS, 3006 Latta Road, Rochester, NY 14612. Illustrations by William Benson.

Buon Vino Manufacturing Inc., Figures 8-7, 8-8.

Charles Plant, Table 3-7. Adapted from Plant, Charles. "The Use of Sulphur Dioxide (SO_2) in Winemaking." *VAWA - Using Sulphur Dioxide To Protect Wine*, http://www.bcwine.com/vawa/using-so2.htm/. 1997.

CHEMetrics, Inc., Figure 3-11.

Comité Interprofessionnel du Vin de Champagne (CIVC) Photothèque, Figures 9-8 (Photo ROHRSCHEID Collection CIVC), 9-10.

DeFalco's for Brewers & Winemakers (Ottawa), Table in Appendix B.

Enotecnica di Pillan R.L.I. snc, Figures 5-4B, 5-9, 5-10, 8-10, 8-11.

Fisher Scientific Company L.L.C., Figure 3-2B.

Ghidi divisione INOX, Figure 2-7A.

Fratelli Marchisio & C. S.p.A., Figure 2-8.

Kevin Argue, Mick Rock/Cephas Picture Library, Figure 11-1.

Lallemand, Inc., Figures 4-3, 4-6B, Tables 4-2, 4-3, 4-4.

Logsdons' Wyeast Laboratories, Figure 4-5.

Mick Rock/Image Network Inc., Figure 9-9.

Ohaus Corporation, Figure 2-18.

Piazza & Associates/LMI Lithographers Ltd., Figure 2-5.

RED STAR® Yeast & Products Division of Universal Foods Corporation, Tables 4-5, 4-6, 4-7.

Spectre, Figures 4-1, 9-7. Reproduced from Jens Priewe, WINE: FROM GRAPE TO GLASS. New York: Abbeville Press. 1999. Used with permission of Verlag Zabert Sandmann. GmbH, Munich.

Vinquiry, Inc., Figure 4-6A.

Photographers:

Paul Labelle Photographe Inc., Figures 2-1 to 2-4, 2-6, 2-9, 2-11 to 2-17, 3-1, 3-2A, 3-7, 3-9, 5-1, 5-4A, 5-6, 5-8, 7-1, 8-2, 8-3, 8-5, 8-6, 8-12, 8-13, 8-14, 9-2, 9-3, 9-14, 9-15, 10-1.

Daniel Pambianchi, Figures 2-10A/B, 3-5, 3-6, 3-8, 3-10, 4-2A/B, 4-4 (used with permission of RED STAR® Yeast & Products Division of Universal Foods Corporation), 4-7, 4-10, 5-2, 5-3, 5-5, 5-7, 5-12, 7-2, 7-3A, 7-4, 7-5, 8-4, 8-9, 8-15, 9-1, 9-4, 9-5, 9-11, 9-13.

Illustrators:

Stéphane Roch, Figures 1-1, 1-3 to 1-9, 2-7B, 3-4, 5-11, 7-3B.

Daniel Pambianchi, Figures 3-2C, 3-3, 4-8, 4-9, 8-1.

INDEX

Page numbers in **bold** type indicate important references.